The Book of

YEATS'S POEMS

Portrait of W. B. Yeats, by Augustus John, courtesy of the Art Gallery and Museum, Glasgow.

The Book of

YEATS'S POEMS

Hazard Adams

The Florida State University Press
Tallahassee

Second paperback printing, 1991

Library of Congress Cataloging in Publication Data

Adams, Hazard, 1926–
    The book of Yeats's poems / Hazard Adams.
        p. cm.
    Includes index.
    ISBN 0-8130-0944-8.   ISBN 0-8130-0951-0 (pbk.)
    1. Yeats, W. B. (William Butler), 1865–1939—Criticism and inter-
pretation.   I. Title.
PR5907.A33   1989
821'.8—dc20   89-34576

Printed in the United States of America on acid-free paper

The Florida State University Press is a member of University Presses
of Florida, the scholarly publishing agency of the State University
System of Florida. Books are selected for publication by faculty edito-
rial committees at each of Florida's nine public universities: Florida
A&M University (Tallahassee), Florida Atlantic University (Boca Ra-
ton), Florida International University (Miami), Florida State University (Tallahassee), University of Central Florida (Orlando), University
of Florida (Gainesville), University of North Florida (Jacksonville),
University of South Florida (Tampa), University of West Florida
(Pensacola).

Orders for books published by all member presses should be addressed to University Presses of Florida, 15 NW 15th Street, Gainesville, FL 32603.

For Diana

Also by Hazard Adams

Nonfiction

The Academic Tribes

Fiction

The Horses of Instruction
The Truth about Dragons: An Anti-Romance

Criticism

Blake and Yeats: The Contrary Vision
William Blake: A Reading of the Shorter Poems
The Contexts of Poetry
The Interests of Criticism
Lady Gregory
Philosophy of the Literary Symbolic
Joyce Cary's Trilogies: Pursuit of the Particular Real
Antithetical Essays in Literary Criticism and Liberal Education

Edited by Hazard Adams

Poems by Robert Simeon Adams
Poetry: An Introductory Anthology
Fiction as Process (with Carl Hartman)
William Blake: Jerusalem, Selected Poetry and Prose
Critical Theory since Plato
Critical Theory since 1965 (with Leroy Searle)

Contents

Preface

Among the poets of the so-called modernist period, Yeats has enjoyed a more sustained critical admiration than any other. He has not suffered a decline in critical popularity as Eliot has, and he was recognized as important during his career long before Pound, Stevens, or Williams in theirs. Of course, Yeats was never really a "high" modernist; he was of an earlier generation and by his own accurate account a belated, that is to say, modern, romantic. Poetic fashion tends to reject the grandfather and revive the great-grandfather, and there have been efforts to reject Yeats as grandfather, especially recently in Ireland. But he continues to have vigorous defenders; few have challenged R. P. Blackmur's assertion not long after Yeats's death that he had the greatest lyric gift since Shakespeare. Almost everyone has acknowledged in Yeats's work a fascinating sustained development. Even the so-called *Last Poems*, at first viewed as uneven and not equal to *The Winding Stair and Other Poems*, have more recently enjoyed critical adulation. Everyone has acknowledged Yeats's great dramatic and rhetorical powers. Indeed, for many poets who have written since his death, his voice has been so imposing that to write as he did has seemed sometimes both the only choice and an impossibility. A generation of Irish poets found him to be their major problem. Even an American poet, Theodore Roethke, had a midlife struggle with his influence.

In Ireland recently, a new generation of writers has thought it high time to escape what has long been in certain ways a repressive force. It is not as a poetic craftsman that Yeats has come under attack. Rather, it is his ideology that these writers have criticized—or at least his ideology as these writers have seen it, for it is best to leave room for those who may say that the anxiety of influence has been at work here through the device of misprision. There is little question that Yeats appears or has been made to appear vulnerable on several counts—his later political positions, his attitudes toward women, his view of history, especially Irish history, and the rhetoric in which these views were sometimes expressed.

Of these matters, it is the view of Irish history successfully promul-
gated by Yeats that a new generation has most strongly attacked. The attack implies a certain respect, for these critics are, above all, political critics and put second and subservient everything that they do not see as
political in essence. Yeats's political success they admire—and resist, some
absolutely, and some with the caveat that his views are simply no longer
relevant to today's political issues and are, indeed, subversive of a grasp of
contemporary Irish political reality. For the most part, this attack on Yeats
has been for these critics a way of clearing the ground, and it attests to the
poet's great influence. But when he is quoted or his statements are referred
to, it is almost always his prose writings, his letters, or his notebooks that
are brought forward in evidence. Rarely is it his poems, with some notable
exceptions like "Three Marching Songs." (Even here an earlier version is
sometimes invoked as being indicative of his views.) Yeats is, nevertheless,
viewed as a political poet, partly because in this view everything is politics
and partly because Yeats was himself political.

Yet I believe that his poems, taken as I have taken them in this book,
tell a somewhat different story from that constitutable as his politically
active life. It is my intention to constitute that story on the basis of a particular conception of Yeats's poetry. I do not claim it to be the most spa-
cious or inclusive conception, but I do think that any assessment of Yeats's
career as a poet must take it into account in any attempt to arrive at a
critical judgment of his work and, to some extent, of his life. I consider
Yeats's poems as constituting a book with a fictive story of a fictive poet, its
main character, to be inferred from it. I therefore give special attention to
the movement from poem to poem and to the spaces between poems,
where the story must be constituted.

I invoke historical and personal materials external to the poems when
the poems invite me to do so (and, of course, they often do). As Yeats's
Book proceeds, the fiction becomes more and more an autobiographical
one, to be read in the context of historical events and referring to people
not specifically named but readily identifiable. This, in my view, in no
way diminishes the *Book*'s fictive nature—fictive in the sense of being
shaped in a certain way. An autobiographical fiction is more like a historical novel than a chronicle of fact. We know, of course, from the title page
that these poems are by W. B. Yeats, though it is rather late in the *Book*
that the poet actually names himself in a poem. I separate W. B. Yeats from
the fictive poet he has created even as I know that eventually they come
together. But only in a sense, for the coming together remains a fictive one.
It does, however, justify historical identifications such as that of the subject of "A Bronze Head" with Maud Gonne. That the poet does not actually name her in that poem dramatizes a certain complicated reticence that

is part of the story he tells. In taking this approach, I find that the *Book* of Yeats's poems is primarily a book about a poet's passions and that the political passions are secondary to the sexual and aesthetic ones and are usually dictated by them.

An important point bears on the way I treat the fictive poet in this book: Yeats inherited many of his views of art from the romantic and Victorian poets that he seems to have known, in some cases, by heart. These views were in the main expressivist; that is, they assumed that all great poetry was the inner made outer, the self or personality expressed. Yet in practice some of these poets deliberately interposed between themselves and their poetic expressions a fictive voice, even as they pretended it was themselves. Thus there was often a dramatic practice and an expressivist theory. (Nowhere can this be seen better than in Byron's *Don Juan.*) In my view, Yeats practiced poetic drama in his *Book* of poems, creating a fictive poet who tries to speak from the heart on expressivist principles but gradually learns to be overtly dramatic himself. One of the things the *Book* seems to assume (and perhaps all books have to assume) is that self-expression in the old romantic sense is impossible and is always either inadequately or adequately masked by a role; that self, itself, is always a fictive construction. Direct self-expression is a fiction. Yeats, however, is writing a fiction in which the fiction of self-expression is, as Aristotle put it, a likely impossibility. But it is nevertheless, in its naive romantic form, something of an illusion after all, because it turns out in the story of this *Book* to be only an inadequate mask. The story Yeats tells, then, is of the search not only to find adequate masks but to cast off inadequate ones.

Though I mention or allude to every poem that Yeats included in his *Book*, my aim has not been to provide detailed exegeses. Rather, I have attempted to constitute the mimetic-narrative outline of Yeats's *Book*, considered as a story. I believe that more detailed readings of specific poems or more general studies of Yeats's work must take into account their belonging to this story, though I recognize that the story itself belongs to larger, more inclusive books that tell larger, more inclusive stories—Yeats's whole canon, for example, and so on to encompass that canon in cultural "texts." I limit myself to the more modest aim of telling the story of the *Book* as I have constituted it; I do not apologize for making interpretation into my own storytelling. I hope that I have done so with enough respect for Yeats's *Book* as a *techne*, an artistic work. This is one reason that I have included in brackets remarks that in one way or another can be interpreted as dealing with matters "outside" of the text I have constituted.

Quotations from Yeats in the text are based on *The Poems of W. B. Yeats: A New Edition*, edited by Richard J. Finneran (New York: Macmillan, 1983). Citations following quotations indicate first the poem number, then the page, of this edition; this is followed by poem number and page of *The Variorum Edition of the Poems of W. B. Yeats*, edited by Peter Allt and Russell K. Alspach (New York: Macmillan, 1957). My story is best read along with one of these texts.

Acknowledgments

This book began twelve years ago with an essay bearing the same title in the now defunct *Cornell Review* 1, no. 1 (Spring 1977); some of that essay appears in revised form in chapter 1. I wish to thank the UMI Press for permission to reprint from an essay that appeared in *Yeats: An Annual of Textual and Critical Studies* (1985) and the *ADE Bulletin* for permission to reprint from an essay that appeared in its Fall 1987 issue. Parts of this book have been offered as papers at the Yeats Summer School (Sligo, 1986), the meeting of the American Conference for Irish Studies, Western Division (Santa Barbara, 1976), the meeting of the Modern Language Association (New York, 1986), and the meeting of the American Conference for Irish Studies (Dublin, 1987).

My debts in my study of Yeats go back a long way to the time when I was writing my first book, *Blake and Yeats: The Contrary Vision* (1955), and enjoyed the hospitality of Mrs. Yeats, who permitted me to work in her house with some of her husband's manuscripts and their library. I have accumulated many more debts since then. Some are quite personal; some are to people whose work I have profitably read but whom I have never met. Many of these people are, alas, no longer with us. To name all of them would take too long. I do wish, however, to express my deep appreciation to the students who have read Yeats with me, many of whose ideas have, no doubt, found their way into the discussions that follow.

I owe a special debt of gratitude to Richard J. Finneran, who read the whole manuscript and has enabled me to avoid a number of errors. I am all the more grateful because I know that he disagrees fundamentally with me about my placement and, therefore, treatment of Yeats's "narrative and dramatic" poems. In a last effort to show me the light, he sent to me a copy of the final chapter of his *Editing Yeats's Poems: A Reconsideration*, which will come out after this book has gone to press but before it actually appears. I have taken into account his argument, which warrants careful reading by all who are interested in the textual problem. I have been instructed by it and agree with most of it, though I have not accepted it entirely or rather, perhaps, try to get around it.

I wish also to thank the British Library, the National Library of Ireland, and the library of the University of Washington, in each of which I have worked, and Faith Hines, who carefully prepared the typescript.

Finally, I wish to express my deepest appreciation to my wife, Diana, to whom this book is dedicated and who, from my earliest study of Yeats forty years ago, has been the main help in preparing to write this book.

1

Critical Constitution of the Book

Theoretical and Textual Issues

It is acknowledged that with the advent of poststructuralist deconstruction and now the quarrels that have followed from it, the theory of criticism has reached one of its many moments of crisis. I believe that the criticism of Yeats, for reasons internal as well as external, has also reached a crisis, though certainly more quietly. Yeats criticism very rapidly created and continues to create a massive bibliography of concordances, textual scholarship, biography, editions, and interpretations, including comparative or what would now be called intertextual studies. We have had books comparing Yeats to Blake, Castiglione, Keats, Nietzsche, and Shelley. We have had studies of Yeats and the visual arts, philosophy, politics, folklore, neoplatonism, and the occult. We have had numerous readings of the most anthologized poems, and several critics have taken on the complete body of Yeats's work. *A Vision* has been employed to illuminate both the poems and the plays, and the other prose works have been used to illuminate all three. The history of Yeats's many revisions has also been and continues to be explored.

In general, Yeats's poetry, which is my subject here, has been approached critically in two different ways. In the mode of the New Criticism, his poems or sequences of poems have been treated as discrete units. This has not worked and will not ever work very well with Yeats, whose writings tend to build up patterns of imagery and motifs and insistently connect themselves to each other. The criticism of Yeats has always quoted Yeats a great deal, even when it has chosen to dwell on single poems. Somewhere else in his work—in *A Vision*, in the letters, in the *Autobiography*, or in the essays—Yeats has usually said something that seems to throw more light on the poem than the critic can alone.

The biographical and historical approach has appeared to be more successful, though in important ways delusively so. Within a decade of Yeats's death in 1939, three biographies were published. Though all three are now somewhat outdated, they (especially Richard Ellmann's) have performed a valuable critical service, for Yeats seems to have been a poet of his own life in an extraordinarily intimate way. Studies that have taken this for granted have managed to go farthest with Yeats; but they have all run up against the difference between Yeats's life and his work. This is a difference that Yeats himself was not loath to emphasize, in spite of the sense in which he was a personal poet. It is also a difference that is fundamental to any critical theorizing, though not an absolute disjunction, as my later remarks will show.

After all the valuable work that has accumulated, there has been a slowing down of conventional interpretive activity. It has been replaced by attention to scholarly minutiae of the cottage-industry variety and to the revisionary political criticism now current in Ireland and strongly tied to current events there. We need a new opening outward in which we may continue to offer Yeats's work most fully to ourselves. My book is an effort to change the situation with respect to Yeats's poetry. It accepts the role of mediator, which is in this case storyteller, and makes no further claims for itself.

I propose to constitute, on theoretical and bibliographical grounds (with the help of many who have recently studied this problem), what I call the *Book* of Yeats's poems. Now, Yeats's *Collected Poems* has been a well-known book, visible for many years in bookshops and college classrooms. Surely, I hear you say, nothing could be more obvious than the fact that we have before us a single book with all the weight of the author's intention behind it, with respect to not only what he intended to include but also what he intended the poems to mean. But it is not that simple a matter, viewed in the light of recent scholarship that has accumulated around the problem of Yeats's text. In this chapter, therefore, I take up not only theoretical issues but also issues involving establishment of Yeats's text.

First, some theoretical ones. The most extreme and recently fashionable of theories—that which developed out of phenomenology, structuralism, and Nietzsche in the writings of Jacques Derrida—has declared the radical detachment of writing from its "origin" in an author's intention or in any "center," presumably recapturable by interpretation as we have usually thought of it. Such a theory calls in question the ground of procedures that have been used so often to interpret Yeats. It has also recently been the fashion to view skeptically the notion that writing is profitably divisible into types or even perhaps into discrete formal units. The legitimacy of the idea of genre or even of literature itself has come into question. Derrida rejects the notion of a book with a specifiable content and substitutes the term "text" for what he would talk about. A text is not ever finally specifiable, "a finished corpus of writing, some content enclosed in a book or its margins, but a differential network, a fabric of traces referring endlessly to something other than itself."[1]

Not only is a book, with its beginning, middle, and end, an impossible concept; it is intolerable, because it appears fixed and is thus tyrannical in its apparent insistence on laying down the law of its meaning, which, it implies, stands behind it, as its true word. Derrida, whom one might regard as the Berkeley of the age of language (in the midst of which, following the age of epistemology, we live today),[2] has written in a well-known passage:

> *There is nothing outside the text* ["Il n'y a pas de hors-text" is the original French, and I prefer "There is no outside-the-text"]. And that is neither because Jean-Jacques' life [he is discussing Rousseau's text], or the existence of Mama or Therese themselves, is not of prime interest to us, nor because we have access to their so-called "real" existence only in the text and we have neither any means of altering this, nor any right to neglect this limitation. All reasons of this type would already be sufficient, to be sure, but there are more radical reasons. . . . [In] what one calls the real life of "flesh and bone," beyond and behind what one believes can be circumscribed as Rousseau's text, there has never been anything but writing; there have never been anything but supplements, substitutive significations which could only come forth in a chain of differential relations, the "real" supervening, and being added only while taking on meaning from a trace and from an invocation of the supplement, etc. And thus to infinity. . . .[3]

But one could, like Dr. Johnson, kick a stone, or perhaps in this case a referent, and declare that we might as well agree that there *was* a flesh-and-blood Yeats who stood outside any language constituting him, whether Hone's, Jeffares's, Ellmann's, or Yeats's. It was he who, involved with language, wrote the text of the poems, even though we must, as I shall argue, constitute that text, both bibliographically and critically. For the reason that Derrida admits is sufficient but that does not engage his interest, this historical Yeats must be distinguished from what I call the "authority" of

1. Jacques Derrida, "Living On: Border Lines," in *Deconstruction and Criticism*, ed. H. Bloom et al. (New York: Continuum Press, 1979), pp. 83–84.

2. In this connection see my introduction to *Critical Theory since 1965*, ed. Hazard Adams and Leroy Searle (Tallahassee: Florida State University Press, 1986), pp. 1–22.

3. Jacques Derrida, *Of Grammatology*, trans. Gayatri C. Spivack (Baltimore: Johns Hopkins University Press, 1976), pp. 158–59.

the text as we constitute it from what Yeats left to us. This authority we can still regard as a *human* authority, though not quite the historical Yeats's, for we know of no writers of texts other than human beings.[4] It is necessary to assume that we have before us the performance of a human being. Biographers construct their Yeatses from a far larger range of materials, and they know that often they cannot trust the poetry as materials, at least in any very simple way: There are senses in which or levels on which the poetry may be false or at least misleading about the life, and vice versa.

On the other hand, critics of the poetry cannot always trust the constituted life, not because of some egregious error by the biographer, but because they must always trust the poetry as a true expression of and in the text's authority. Because we trust that Yeats himself did write the poetry, we regard the poetry as both a text and an act, but a literary act which must be seen as the product of an authority located intrinsically *as* the text's being, uncontrolled by a power outside it regarded as its source of meaning. For our purposes, as I have indicated, there must always be a distinction between the historically constituted Yeats and this authority. We know, of course, that our actual statements about the text will never succeed in creating the authority as a presence in *our* language; nor ought that to be our intent. We constitute it as the text by creating a discourse about it. If more is asked of a critic, the critic will inevitably fail. A critic is better judged on distance traveled than on how nearly he or she has come to a point of so-called determinate meaning that all sides admit to be ultimately unlocatable.

So, with respect to the old question of intention, the answer can still be given that we find an intention that should interest us as critics solely in the authority of the text (constituted as best we can with constant awareness of the irony of our situation), not in the historical Yeats or even in the flesh-and-blood Yeats (were he reading his poems directly to us), and for a reason Charles Altieri has put well:

> [We] tend with literary texts to acknowledge authors' intentions,
> yet still to give them a different force than the author desired.
> For example, many contemporary poets like Allen Ginsberg seek
> to break through the idea of persona and present their work as

4. The idea of historical author as "antiauthor" I first offered in connection with a Blakean notion of Antichrist in "Blake and the Muse," *Bucknell Review* 15, no. 2 (May 1967): 112–19; it is developed in a chapter on Blake in my *Philosophy of the Literary Symbolic* (Tallahassee: Florida State University Press, 1983), esp. p. 108. The notion of "authority" I first offered in *Joyce Cary's Trilogies: Pursuit of the Particular Real* (Tallahassee: Florida State University Press, 1983), pp. 247–49; it is further developed to include antiauthority in my "Critical Constitution of the Literary Text: The Example of *Ulysses*," *New Literary History* 17, no. 3 (Spring 1986): 595–616.

the author's direct personal speech addressing an audience. Yet we read such poems less as personal speech than as performance to be understood and assessed in terms of the intellectual, moral, and emotional qualities they exhibit in what we take as a dramatic situation. We immediately generalize the situation: the poem becomes not simply a man speaking to others, but an image of how one can respond to a situation that is typical of an age, a general human problem, and a particular style of thinking and feeling.[5]

Yeats speaking his poems to us would be merely making a performance of what Altieri calls "performance" and I call "authority." There is in Yeats's writings a well-known theory of the mask, grounded on the masks of classic and Noh drama, in which the mask, or one's performance, is made the achievement of one's true self, the self's "authority" in my language. We can see this theory developed as part of the story implicit in the *Book* of Yeats's poems. It can be taken here, for my purposes, as a commentary on the relation of the author of a book to the book. Yeats's own theory supports Altieri against Ginsberg. The author is always masked by what Altieri calls "performance" and I call "authority," even if he comes before us in flesh and blood to try to personalize his work with a performance of a performance. As to whether Yeats was right that his real self is that mask of performance or authority, we cannot know, though we do know that the performance releases cultural possibilities, as Altieri says, and thus has a special sort of power. Ernst Cassirer said that such performances belonged to the symbolic form of art, one of the forms by which we define ourselves as human beings.

But how can we say that *these* performances, these forms that we constitute as possessing this intrinsic authority, are *literature*? Cannot all texts be viewed as performances? Yes, but with a clear sense in many cases that violence has been done to their human intention, and with a diminishment of our sense of relevance, which is to say that we do not with all texts naturally constitute the authority of the text as the source of intention. Rather, we insist on the text's functioning in a different fashion, with an intention that can actually be stated by us without violence to that intention and with relatively little diminishment of the text. Such texts, as I have argued elsewhere, we constitute as fictively projecting an *other* as *other*, as projecting or hypostatizing a meaning as a reference *other than*, or *behind* or *previous* to the text.[6] A historical text, we hold, projects as other

5. Charles Altieri, *Act and Quality* (Amherst: University of Massachusetts Press, 1981), p. 189.
6. See my *Philosophy of the Literary Symbolic*, pp. 325ff.

to itself *how it was* in a certain other time and place. It would be nonsense, or perhaps literature, if we were convinced that this projection was inappropriate because no such other ever existed independent of the text. What is of primary importance, then, is to constitute the *Book*, apart from the historical Yeats or what he would have probably called in any case his "husk," with all the suggestion of death and hollowness that the word implies in *A Vision*.

The main thing that we have traditionally assumed about a book is that it has a form or shape. The terms are metaphorical, of course. The reality of a book, unless we are talking about something like the Book of Kells or the Lindisfarne Gospel, is ideal, not consubstantial with a physical object. In modern times, even William Blake's engraved *Jerusalem* with its five surviving "original copies" transcends each, and no one I know of has proposed that *Jerusalem* consisted of the copper plates and is now lost. Even such a book, then, we constitute critically out of one ideality into another of metaphorical spatiality and temporality.

This constitution is for me the text's *existence*. The term was first employed by Eliseo Vivas, but I use it in a quite different way and with different epistemological implications. He wrote of the meaning of a text as having *sub*sistence, *in*sistence, and *ex*istence, the last of which is roughly the "use" to which the text is put in society.[7] (I refer to the metaphorical shape I constitute the text in and as.) The text has also an *in*sistence, an ideality; but I can do no more with it *as such* than to declare for it as itself— any more than Kant could only declare for things in themselves, for he regarded them as unknowable. I believe the text to be there on the outside, so to speak, and I believe I experience it, but I cannot talk *about* this *in*sistence without bringing it into an *ex*istence denoted by my discourse constituting it, which is all of my experiencing it that I can *know*. But I know that this discourse really constitutes only my means of a pointing *to*, that any *ex*istence it might claim to have made, it must also deny. In this act, my discourse declares itself as nonliterary. (Vivas, a self-avowed "value realist," declared that meanings and values *sub*sist in some inchoate way in the culture, awaiting *in*sistence, by art. I do not understand how we can know this, and I would want in any case to escape some of its possibly reactionary implications.)

There is another issue here, as well. No doubt authors have had germs of ideas for their texts in the manner of Henry James or Joyce Cary,[8] and these are of great interest and often some help to critics. But *sub*sistence in

7. Eliseo Vivas, "The Object of the Poem," in *Creation and Discovery* (Chicago: Henry Regnery, 1955), pp. 199–222.

8. See my *Joyce Cary's Trilogies*, pp. 15–35.

this sense, which is not quite Vivas's, has no critically necessary connection to a text; and I make a claim not for the *sub*sistence of values (as permanent as I think some values ought to be), only for the continual building and rebuilding of values from the human arts and sciences.

Now to discuss a text at all, to make it *exist*, is to require it to become in some sense a book. That is the very thing that Derrida (though his notion of "book" is quite special and broad—I shall come to this) would dissolve (though never quite totally dissolve) into the great undifferentiated flux he calls *écriture*, breaking down the metaphorical boundaries we would erect for it.[9] Derrida would deconstruct the very unity posited tacitly in his original intuition of the text, if we assume that intuitions are synthetic; always have the form of expression (to use Croce's term); and, because they are linguistic, are tropological in shape, shape being itself, of course, a metaphor.

When those boundaries are torn down, what remains? Ultimately, nothing, if the job were completely done (it can't be completely done); or, to put it another way, only the infinite differential chain of language. For, although the tropological differential structure is deemed (according to this way of thinking) intolerable, it is also true that there is nothing *but* metaphor, "alive" or "dead," with which either to speak or to write. Therefore the major deconstructor of the *intolerable that must be endured*, Paul de Man, complains (with a certain satisfaction) of the delusiveness of words. For the deconstructionist the book comes to stand for all of this. For de Man there can be no books whose authors are not self-deluded about what they say. There can be no books not delusory to the unwary. The best that can be accomplished is an awareness of such blindness: the deconstructionist version of truth as a joyful despair.

These theoretical insights are, in their place, of great interest; but they remain for me theoretical and not practical. To have recognized and demonstrated what I have called the intolerable about any one text is to have declared it for all texts. There seems little point in filling the libraries with books on books on books, all pointing this out about their predecessors. We would have not only an infinite regress capable of turning the mills of academe forever but also an unsatisfactory circularity—a declaration that the rules of the game are the rules of a problem to be overcome, even though the problem can never be overcome. The demand that we should question is certainly important and needs the sort of insistent repetition that Derrida, de Man, and others have given it. Unresolvable contradictions are, of course, nothing new. Kant argued that reason always comes to them in the end.

9. For Derrida on the book, see *Of Grammatology*, esp. p. 18.

Deconstruction would go well beyond contradiction. Whether that means that it is necessary to make language (as in de Man) the culprit and seducer—the Satan of a new antitheology—is not in my opinion certain. Nor is it certain that the substitution of critical unreason or free play as a mode evading (while not evading) contradiction and even dissolution is acceptable to anyone who wishes ultimately to engage culture with a text. Language is what we have. If it cannot deliver ultimate theological truths, it is at least the form of the making of our culture, as of course Derrida and de Man well know. Some of its fictions are better to live by than others, but all are fairly open to question. If ultimate truth cannot be written, then other, more modest means of judgment are necessary. In this situation constitution would seem to be the necessary task, constitution with the full knowledge that we are on our own and that there is no eternal model to which we have unfailing access, but that there can be fictions that we may profitably assert as if true.[10]

Deconstruction has warned us that to employ the term "book" in a critical constitution is an undertaking that must be explained, and the term must be qualified. "Book" as a term can mislead us into imagining its *ex*istence to be consubstantial with its *in*sistence. This may be quite all right for the simplistically purposive telephone directory and many other books, but it is not right for what we regard as literary or artistic texts. Therefore, there is a temptation for clarity's sake to call Yeats's *Book* an antibook. It is also true that in the light and language of Derrida's critique of what he calls the book, Yeats's *Book* should be called an antibook, but for another reason, which is that for Derrida there really are no books. All books are antibooks because none is referable to a center of determinate meaning, which is what a book would have if, for Derrida, it were possible to have it. It is only a fixing interpretation, if that were really possible, that constitutes a book.

In my view, we can grasp the intention of the telephone book to be a book in the conventional sense of providing information about a world behind it, so to speak, and we distinguish it from such a book as Yeats's poems. Still, I hold on to the term "book" for Yeats's work because its opposition to the telephone directory or the newspaper (the opposition Mallarmé employed in a famous essay) involves it with those things *by* opposition, and there is no reason short of abdication of the power that the term "book" has in culture to give up the word to opponents. Yeats's *Book*

---

10. This last phrase sounds as if it were Hans Vaihinger's in *The Philosophy of "As If,"* but Vaihinger had little or no interest in artistic fictions, whereas I see them as forms of human intellectual activity that are materials for use. For my discussion of fictions, including Vaihinger's views, see *Philosophy of the Literary Symbolic*, pp, 177–99.

is therefore a book for all that, because opposites require each other in a condition of equality: dying each other's life, living each other's death.

But it is an *antithetical*, poetic book. As such, it opposes itself to the notion of any book that lays down the law of its own interpretation by pointing to something beyond or outside itself, whether the historical Yeats's life or some external reality or miraculous word that it imitates or embodies as a truth from elsewhere. It is also a book in that, in order to read it, we have to constitute it provisionally as some kind of unity, though not a reduced unity. This involves recognizing its integrity in some way. My way is to make considerable use of the logic of inference about the spaces between Yeats's poems, considered as full of activity going on off-stage, between the acts, yet part of the play. Each poem is part of a total drama that we can constitute as a story. It is a fictive story about a poet from young manhood to death, who attempts to deal with himself, with people, with thought, and with time and to create a body of poetry. Some poems are dramatic, spoken moments in this story; some are composed poems or sequences of poems in which fictive characters (doubly fictive because invented in a fiction created by a fictive character) are created in order to solve problems or dramatize them or evade them.

The statements that the poems make are tentative, for they are part of the dramatic development. They are statements that the fictive, speaking, main character often later elaborates, comments on, recalls, refutes, questions, qualifies, or steps back from. Eventually the main character reveals that his name is Yeats, and we realize that this is a historical or autobiographical fiction, and we can infer the historical identity of persons not mentioned by name; but it is a fiction nonetheless. The constant movement of passion and thought is the reason that Yeats's poems cannot easily be discussed out of their place in the *Book*, with its blank spaces, and also that Yeats is so difficult to anthologize without great loss.

In constituting this dramatic narrative of shifting attitudes, which takes the form of a search for creative understanding, I close Yeats's *Book* in one sense—I find a complicated narrative of personal development—but I keep his *Book* open in another sense. I do not claim that the book is a "perfect totality," in the sense in which Derrida claims a "logocentric" view of discourse does—that is, that all of it points to a "transcendental signified" which can be fully recovered by interpretation. Rather, I see Yeats's *Book* as ultimately antinomial, as Yeats thought all our knowledge was, indeed as he thought all reality was. Now, of course, one could claim that the antinomy *is* a transcendental signified, but this seems to me a casuistry making any descriptive adjective carry the burden of noun-ness.

I do claim to begin with the critical fiction of a unity that *cannot ever* be critically recovered, that does not lie behind the text, but is the text itself, something like what the symbol (only a symbol) of the sphere in *A Vision* ironically represents. In a sense, then, I agree with Derrida while disagreeing with him, for I can accept his remark that "what is held within the demarcated closure may continue indefinitely," if he means by this that interpretation can never end.[11] But I also hold that there is such a thing as a fictive referent and that some interpretations are better than others. Such interpretations develop, as mine does, by means of an oscillation back and forth (or in and out) between a construal of "authority" and an apprehension of the parts, with arrival at either pole of the opposition generating a return to modify and extend the other, as in Yeats's own figure of the contrary but interlocking gyres.

Yeats himself began his career believing in the possibility of a *sacred* book, in the Derridean sense of a "logocentric" text that offers the truth of what I have elsewhere called "romantic allegory." [12] But he moved away from this belief or hope as his career progressed, though he continued occasionally to speak of it. In the later stages, his idea seems to have been to construct an antithetical book of the sort I have alluded to, but not a Derridean free play, instead a Blakean contrary to the kind of discourse (for example, scientific, historical, or biographical) that posits the prior existence of a truth to which it refers. (This latter kind of book I shall call "primary." I shall employ the same term to designate a mode of interpretation that forces "sacredness" or fixity on a text.) Instead, his emphasis was on making a fiction.

I see Yeats working toward the making of possibilities of interpretation, but by no means an infinite range of them, since even an antithetical book limits what can be read in it. The terms "antithetical" and "primary" I borrow, of course, from Yeats himself, and I use them in senses similar to Yeats's. I believe I am offering a Yeatsian reading of Yeats, and at the same time I believe my reading establishes some principles that cannot be safely ignored by any reading. I regard critical constitution of the text as somewhere between "creation" and "discovery." (These are Vivas's terms, applied by him to literary texts, but I displace them from Yeats's text to my critical text.) By "discovery" I mean establishment of a general awareness that Yeats's book has certain boundaries. By "creation" I mean a constitutive critical act which, while inevitably closing the text (through discovery, in part) to false readings, declares not for a true one in the Derridean "logocentric" sense but for a constitution that opens the text to apprehension of an order that can never be represented but needs nevertheless to be given a mediating voice.

11. Jacques Derrida, *Positions*, trans. A. Bass (Chicago: University of Chicago Press, 1981), p. 13.
12. See my *Philosophy of the Literary Symbolic*, pp. 12–13.

All efforts to change situations are in the debt of predecessors. I certainly do not claim that my notion and treatment of the Yeatsian book are entirely new. Some readers no doubt have been thinking of an essay of over twenty-five years ago by Hugh Kenner, which laid out—in part—the principles on which I shall proceed. In his "Sacred Book of the Arts," one of the best critical essays written on Yeats, he pointed out with particular respect to *The Tower* and *The Wild Swans at Coole* (the volumes, not the poems) that a Yeats poem is best read with attention to the poems that precede and follow it in the text, that Yeats's arrangement of his poems is "deliberate rather than casual or merely chronological," that *The Tower* as a book has a progression, and that the unit of Yeats's work to study is the volume, "at least from *Responsibilities* (1914) to *A Full Moon in March* (1935)."[13] He observes, as I have, that neither of the mid-twentieth-century notions of poetry works well with Yeats: "—the old one, that poems reflect lives and announce doctrines, the new one, that poems are self-contained or else imperfect—are rendered helpless by Yeats's most radical, most casual, and most characteristic maneuver. He was an architect, not a decorator; he didn't accumulate poems, he wrote books" (p. 13).

I am in agreement with this view, as far as it goes; but it does not go as far as I intend to. Kenner does not develop a notion of the sort of book Yeats finally did make, and his notion would have been different from mine, I think, had he done so. He does not go as far because he does not firmly conclude that *all* of Yeats's volumes are constructed or, in the cases of the earlier volumes, reconstructed, as is *The Tower*; and he does not conclude that these separate volumes make up chapters of a single book. Further, he does not claim that this single book has a narrative-dramatic shape more fundamental than the imagistic and mythological coherence that he finds Yeats himself advocating and that many previous critics, including myself, have claimed to find in his work. My claim is that the created referent contained in the Yeatsian *Book* is fundamentally one of a fictive or feigned life. Finally, I believe that Yeats's *Book*, though he spoke often of the desirability of the "sacred book" Kenner mentions, is properly described as an "antithetical" and "secular" one, as all literary books finally must be.[14]

Other critics, of course, have seen pattern in Yeats's poems, but the pattern has almost always been that of a tightening net of imagistic inter-relations or what has sometimes been called "spatial form," from the early

13. Hugh Kenner's "Sacred Book of the Arts," originally published in *Irish Writing*, appeared in his *Gnomen* and is reprinted in *Yeats*, ed. John Unterecker (Englewood Cliffs, N.J.: Prentice-Hall, 1963), pp. 10–22. It also appears, very slightly revised, in *Critical Essays on W. B. Yeats*, ed. Richard J. Finneran (Boston: G. K. Hall, 1986), pp. 9–20.

14. I first offered this idea in "The 'Book' of Yeats's Poems," *Cornell Review* 1, no. 1 (Spring 1977): 119–28, from which I have taken parts of the argument that follows.

work of A. N. Jeffares to the treatment of *Collected Poems* by John Unter-ecker in his *Reader's Guide to William Butler Yeats.* This pattern has generally been regarded as imposed by Yeats on an autobiographical framework. Unterecker teeters on the edge where Kenner took flight, but he returns to the safety of biography and imagistic patterns, with no theory of the anti-thetical book that will allow him to constitute it as a fiction.

But before considering the question of the book at greater length, I come to the second matter: the question of Yeats's text, or the problem of its scholarly constitution. It is at this point, I am glad to say, that critical interpretation and bibliographical study are easily demonstrated to be interrelated. Clearly the order of Yeats's poems becomes of paramount im-portance, and it is clear also that the order, as Yeats came to conceive of it, was *not* autobiographically chronological but narrative-dramatic and fic-tional. Here it becomes necessary to take note of a dispute about the proper order of Yeats's poems that has very much intensified since the pub-lication in 1983 of *The Poems of W. B. Yeats: A New Edition,* edited by Rich-ard J. Finneran.[15] This dispute was carried on mainly in the pages of the *Times Literary Supplement* in the summer of 1984, though to understand it one needs also to read Finneran's book *Editing Yeats's Poems,* a subsequent essay in which he attempts to answer his principal tormentor, Warwick Gould,[16] and the last chapter of his *Editing Yeats's Poems: A Reconsideration,* now in press.

The main issue, as far as I am concerned, is the ordering of the text and particularly the placement of six of Yeats's longer poems. The *Book* of Yeats's poems, as I constitute it, has never actually been in print. It differs from the two-volume *Poems of W. B. Yeats* (1949).[17] It differs from the *Col-lected Poems* emanating from Macmillan, the so-called definitive edition of 1956, and from the 1957 *Variorum Edition* of Allt and Alspach.[18] It also differs from the new *Poems* edited by Finneran, but only to the extent that it places the longer poems with the shorter ones. All of these texts differ from earlier volumes published by Yeats. As the *Variorum* documents, in later years Yeats revised his early poems. Further, none of the volumes mentioned above is chronologically arranged by dates of composition or

15. *The Poems of W. B. Yeats: A New Edition,* ed. Richard J. Finneran (New York: Macmil-lan, 1983).

16. Richard J. Finneran, *Editing Yeats's Poems* (New York: St. Martin's Press, 1983); War-wick Gould, "The Editor Takes Possession," *Times Literary Supplement,* June 29, 1984, pp. 731–32. An exchange of letters followed. Finneran summarized his defense of the edition in "The Order of Yeats's Poems," *Irish University Review* 14, no. 2 (Autumn 1984): 165–76.

17. *The Poems of W. B. Yeats,* 2 vols. (London: Macmillan, 1949).

18. *The Variorum Edition of the Poems of W. B. Yeats,* ed. Peter Allt and Russell K. Alspach (New York: Macmillan, 1957).

publication (no Yeats volume ever was). Their ordering and revision has been governed by a principle that I shall provisionally characterize with the Kantian term "internal purposiveness," though more is involved. The distance between Yeats's life and his work may be symbolized by a line in "An Acre of Grass": "Myself must I remake" (332, 301; 341, 576). This remaking becomes a making, the poet (his persona says) having chosen between "perfection of the life, or of the work" (158, 246; 266, 495), only to make a work, in turn, from the materials of life.

The *Collected Poems*, culminating in the version of 1956, the two-volume signed but posthumously published edition of 1949, and the new *Poems* all present different orderings of the poems. In the first and last, the so-called "Narrative and Dramatic" poems are consigned to the back of the volume, safely away from the "Lyrical" poems. In the 1949 text they are mixed in with the "Lyrical" ones, though not in chronological order of composition. (The "Lyrical" poems are not chronologically arranged in any case.)

In a letter from Harold Macmillan to Yeats, much mulled over in the recent controversy, we find one possible explanation of why these longer poems, from 1933 onward, were placed at the back of the *Collected Poems*. The purpose of the changes on this evidence was economic:

> London
> 30 March 1933
>
> Dear Mr. Yeats,
>   I am sorry that I have not been able to write early in reply to your letter of March 17th, but I have had to wait for an opportunity of considering the question of the contents of the complete one-volume edition of your poems.
>   I note that you do not wish to see a specimen page, but that you would like to go over the proofs. I hope that when you see them you will like the form we have chosen.
>   As regards the contents of the volume, I share our reader's view that it would be a pity to omit "The Shadowy Waters." There is, however, one departure from the arrangement of the Edition De Luxe volume which I would like to put before you, as it has been suggested by more than one person. We think it possible that the book would be more attractive to the potential purchaser who glances through it in a bookshop if what first caught his eye were the shorter lyrical poems contained in "Crossways," "The Rose," "The Wind Among the Reeds," etc. rather than a lengthy work like "The Wanderings of Oisin." Our impression is that we might move

the longer narrative and dramatic pieces to the end of
the volume, where they would make a group more or less
related in style, subject, and length, and I wonder if
you would agree to our taking this course with the following longer works:
   "The Wanderings of Oisin"
   "The Old Age of Queen Maeve"
   "Baile and Aillinn"
   "The Shadowy Waters"
   and "The Two Kings"
If this arrangement commends itself to you, and if you
could think of some general title we could use to cover
this particular group, I will instruct the printers to
proceed with the work on those lines. Needless to say,
however, this suggestion is quite tentative, and we
should not wish to do anything of the kind without your
full approval.[19]

Yeats, who had always found it necessary to pay attention to receipts,
agreed to Macmillan's suggestion, even with some enthusiasm: "I am de-
lighted with your suggestion to put long poems in a section at the end. I
wish I had thought of it before." Added to this group was "The Gift of
Harun Al-Rashid," though by whose authority is not known. Finneran
has continued the placement of the longer poems as Macmillan suggested
and as all editions of the *Collected Poems* have placed them. Several critics,
including A. N. Jeffares and Warwick Gould, stand against him on this
matter. They take the view that it was never considered by anyone that
the proposed Edition De Luxe of Yeats's poems, not actually published,
was planned to separate the longer from the shorter poems.[20] The two-
volume *Poems* (1949), which replaced it, puts the longer poems in the positions Yeats assigned to them before Macmillan's suggestion. In this arrangement "The Wanderings of Oisin" becomes the first poem of the *Book*
and of *Crossways*. "The Old Age of Queen Maeve" and "Baile and Aillinn"
begin *In the Seven Woods*, and "The Shadowy Waters" ends it. "The Two
Kings" is restored to *Responsibilities* between "The Grey Rock" and "To a
Wealthy Man. . . ." "The Gift of Harun Al-Rashid" appears just before
"All Souls' Night" in *The Tower*.

Finneran's most recent argument has called seriously into question
whether Yeats ever realized that subsequent to the changes made for *Col-*

19. *Letters to W. B. Yeats*, ed. Richard J. Finneran, G. M. Harper, and W. M. Murphy, 2
vols. (New York: Columbia University Press), 2:552.
20. See A. N. Jeffares, *Times Literary Supplement*, August 10, 1984, p. 893, and Gould,
"The Editor Takes Possession."

lected Poems the Edition De Luxe was not finally to separate the so-called "Narrative and Dramatic" poems from the "Lyrical"—even though in 1933 Macmillan's letter indicated that the Edition De Luxe would not separate the poems into two groups. The argument about the placement of these poems is never going to be resolved beyond all doubt. In my opinion the evidence on this point is inconclusive. The argument of Jeffares, Gould, *et. al.* has been on the ground that the poems should be arranged chronologically—clearly not an argument that will hold, for Yeats's poems were never arranged chronologically, except in the roughest way. Indeed, a strict chronological ordering of the poems would require the printing of the early poems and, later in the book, their reprinting in their new versions. Even this would not be accurate, for theoretically the same principle should be adopted for manuscript versions. The logical outcome of such a view would clearly be a thorough variorum edition using both manuscript and published versions in their chronological places. This will not do. Providing a text for biographers was surely not Yeats's intent. If we cannot blindly trust a poet's interpretation of his own work, we can attempt to constitute the order of his poems on the basis of what intention *to* mean (as distinguished from alleged intended meaning) we can glean from the available external evidence. That evidence always takes precedence, but it is also true that where there is equal doubt about or argument for two different orderings, one has no choice but to constitute two separate texts or to invoke the oscillating method of interpretation (to which I have already referred) to determine whether one or another decision seems to render a more satisfactory result—satisfactory to the presumption that parts and whole have a relation of a certain unity, which is the reason for ordering a text in the first place.

My decision to read the longer poems where they were to have appeared in the two-volume *Poems* of 1949 was not made, then, because I support a chronological ordering. Quite the contrary. The ordering as Jeffares and Gould want it is, as Finneran remarks, only quasi-chronological in any case. I read the longer poems with the lyric poems for three reasons. First, there is some external evidence for Yeats's wanting them placed as they are in the *Poems* of 1949. At the least, there is no final evidence that he did not want them that way. Even Finneran acknowledges this. Second, there is a sense in which it does not matter; even in Finneran's preservation of the arrangement of *Collected Poems*, the longer poems (like the volumes of lyrical poems) are given dates by Yeats that supposedly indicate the years of their composition. These dates are part of the story and show roughly where the longer poems should come in it. Still, one has to decide precisely where, and here I have recourse to the *Poems* of 1949, which followed on the aborted Edition De Luxe. Third, as I hope to show, this ordering makes narrative and dramatic sense. "The Wanderings of Oisin" is an appropriate beginning. "The Shadowy Waters" plays its role in 1906, even though (indeed, in my reading, because), as Finneran points out, it is a sort of throwback to an earlier style. One might note that the year given for "The Shadowy Waters" is a sort of fiction, Yeats having worked on that poem over many years. Indeed, it is difficult to say what a poem's date, when included in a text, means in fact, while in fiction it becomes a somewhat simpler matter. This problem comes up with the various lyrics that bear specific dates in the text.

Alternative and disputed versions of books, even of sacred books, are not unusual, and the existence of more than one text with some claim to authenticity should not deter us from constituting Yeats's *Book* as one book. I accept Finneran's ordering and his decisions about inclusion and exclusion, except for his placement of the longer poems. In a sense, because of the presence of dates in his text, it does not make a lot of difference. To follow Finneran with respect to *Last Poems* is especially important and warrants some comment. The *Last Poems* published by Macmillan were not ordered in either 1949 or 1956 as Yeats desired, and in fact the first thirty-five were entitled *New Poems* when Yeats saw them through the Cuala Press in 1938. The proper order of *Last Poems* ought to be that of the table of contents for the Cuala Press's *Last Poems and Two Plays* of 1939, published posthumously but arranged by Yeats.[21] The order differs significantly from that in Macmillan's *Last Poems and Plays* and *Collected Poems*, apparently arranged by Mrs. Yeats and an editor, and the same arrangement in the two-volume *Poems* of 1949. I transcribe the order Yeats preferred, and hereby adopt it, as Finneran has adopted it in *Poems* (1983):

1. "Under Ben Bulben"
2. "Three Songs to One Burden"
3. "The Black Tower"
4. "Cuchulain Comforted"
5. "Three Marching Songs"
6. "In Tara's Halls"
7. "The Statues"
8. "News for the Delphic Oracle"
9. "Long-legged Fly"

21. In all of this, I accept (as does Finneran) the argument of Curtis Bradford's "On Yeats's Last Poems," in *Yeats's Last Poems*, ed. J. Stallworthy (New York: Macmillan, 1968), pp. 75–97.

10. "A Bronze Head"
11. "A Stick of Incense"
12. "Hound Voice"
13. "John Kinsella's Lament for Mrs. Mary Moore"
14. "High Talk"
15. "The Apparitions"
16. "A Nativity"
17. "The Man and the Echo"
18. "The Circus Animals' Desertion"
19. "Politics"

Anyone familiar with Yeats's work can see that the ordering above (which, among other differences, places the epitaph poem "Under Ben Bulben" at the beginning of *Last Poems* rather than at the end) significantly affects a consecutive reading of the Yeatsian *Book*.

In *Last Poems and Two Plays*, the concluding two plays were *The Death of Cuchulain* and *Purgatory*, which I omit from my text of the *Book* of Yeats's poems with some regret. Also lost are three poems not in *Last Poems and Two Plays* and not in Yeats's notes for the ordering of that volume. They are "Why Should Not Old Men be Mad?," "A Statesman's Holiday," and "Crazy Jane on the Mountain." A suggestion has been made that these three poems be placed in a section between *New Poems* and *Last Poems* and called *Poems from On the Boiler*. Since there is no evidence at all of Yeats's intention here, I have followed Finneran and regretfully decided not to include these poems in the *Book*.

In summary, then, the *Book* of Yeats's poems, as I constitute it, adopts the order of Finneran's *The Poems of W. B. Yeats* with the exception of his placing of the longer poems. Specifically, I divide and order *Last Poems* of *Collected Poems* as they were in *New Poems* (1938) and the manuscript table of contents for *Last Poems and Two Plays* (1939). In this I agree with Finneran's *Poems*. I also follow him in eliminating "Three Songs to the Same Tune" on the ground that "Three Marching Songs" in *New Poems* is a revision of it. I also follow Finneran in changing the title of the section in *Collected Poems* called "From *A Full Moon in March*" to "Parnell's Funeral and Other Poems" and recognize that *Last Poems* is a title not invented by Yeats. In constituting the text as I do, I try to give principal attention to Yeats's intentions as we know them or infer them. These intentions (being only intentions *to* mean) are, if not fully recoverable, inferable in a way that so-called intended *meaning* is not. This is by no means a perfect solution. I confess to completing what I regard as an intention Yeats himself never fully carried out, trusting that what can be understood about

Yeats's poems on the basis of constituting them as a book will make the enterprise worthwhile. In any case I do not believe in perfection as a standard by which interpretations must be made. Every alleged perfection I have heard about is a fiction no more powerful, in my opinion, than mine of Yeats's *Book*.

Now to return to the theoretical question of the book. In a famous essay of 1895, Stéphane Mallarmé made a number of declarations about the book: The world is to end or be contained in a book, and the book, as against the detested newspaper, symbolizes all that is mystery to the mundane intellect.[22] The great book of Mallarmé's dream would be "premeditated, and not a miscellany of chance inspirations." Orphic, it would be, nevertheless, not sacred. To the end there was no such book for Mallarmé, the *Coup de des* being perhaps his most intense effort to marshal all possibilities, including the whitenesses where the page is blank. In "The Book: A Spiritual Instrument," Mallarmé glories in the foldings of a book, which "in comparison with the large-sized, open newspaper, have an almost religious significance." (I note the "almost.") That a book can open and close is for Mallarmé its supreme greatness. It opens upon an unfathomable depth and secrecy, a priceless silence. Yeats, for his part, opens and closes certain of his plays with the ritualistic folding and unfolding of a curtain or cloth. For my purposes what is important in this symbolist way of surrounding the book is the assumption Mallarmé makes that no authentic book is available and that poets must create one. My point will be that a poetically created book will not be a sacred one, unless subjected to a certain historical fate. This Mallarmé seems to have known, hence the "almost" I mention above.

Once upon a time, of course (it is alleged by some), there had been a book, indeed two books, that contained all earthly and extraterrestrial reality. One of these was the Book of Nature. To those who claimed to know how to read it, this book exhibited a definite teleological design. The other book, it was thought, showed how to read the first book and, among other things, delineated beginning and end and provided a meaning for history. This book was, of course, the Bible. Indeed, as book, it seemed to be the expositor of nature, heaven, hell, and all time and space. For a long time, these two books were considered the ultimate and, in a sense, the only true books, or at least the only divine books, as Thomas Browne remarked in his *Religio Medici:* "There are two books from whence I collect my Divinity; besides that written one of God, another of His servant Nature, that universal and publick Manuscript, that lies expans'd unto the Eyes of all;

---

22. Stéphane Mallarmé, "Le Livre: Instrument spirituel" (1895), *Oeuvres complètes* (Paris: Gallimard, 1945), p. 872.

those that never saw Him in the one have discover'd Him in the other."[23] In the case of both, each as a whole was meant to point toward a signified behind it and previous to it—truth—and, in a manner of speaking, a referent—its author.

For Yeats, Mallarmé, and almost all the important poets of their times, both books were lost, decimated, or corrupted. Nature had ceased to be a book and had become a set of mathematical formulae. The Bible had become a code of externally and apparently arbitrarily imposed moral law in the service of those Blake disparagingly called the "Elect." But more than that, both had been desacralized by scientific and historical interpretations that called forever in question the authorship itself, to say nothing of the miraculous symbolic immanence of the author in the text. In his *Autobiography*, Yeats tells us that he longed for a sacred book. Even as a young man he sought out traditional utterance:

> I was unlike others of my generation in one thing only. I am very religious, and deprived of the simple-minded religion of my childhood, I had made a new religion, almost an infallible church of poetic tradition, of a fardel of stories, and of personages, and of emotions, inseparable from their first expression, passed on from generation to generation by poets with some help from philosophers and theologians.[24]

But this does not sound at all like an effort to reconstitute anything like either of the traditional books. Philosophers (among whom we can include natural philosophers) and theologians are declared to be only secondary helpers in its construction; poets, those notorious makers of fictions, are its creators. This is neither a priest's Bible nor the light of Newton. By examining Yeats's many writings we might discover some of the books of this early and somewhat naive effort. One of them would be Shelley's *Prometheus Unbound*: "Half a dozen times, beginning in boyhood with Shelley's *Prometheus Unbound*, I have . . . possessed for certain hours or months the book that I long for."[25] This is a tentative statement, certainly. I have

23. Thomas Browne, *Religio Medici* (1643) (London: J. M. Dent and Sons, 1945), pp. 17–18. For discussions germane to this notion, see Ernst Curtius, "The Book as Symbol," in *European Literature and the Latin Middle Ages*, trans. W. R. Trask (Princeton: Princeton University Press, 1973), pp. 302–47; Sigurd Burckhardt, *Shakespearean Meanings*, trans. Anne Hohenenser (Princeton: Princeton University Press, 1968), pp. 285–313; Derrida, *Of Grammatology*, esp. pp. 15–18; Jesse Gellrich, "The Argument of the Book: Medieval Writing and Modern Theory," *Clio* 10, no. 3 (Spring 1981): 245.

24. *The Autobiography of William Butler Yeats* (New York: Macmillan, 1953), p. 71. Yeats's preferred title, used in a previous edition, was almost certainly *Autobiographies*.

25. Ibid., p. 192.

omitted from it the phrase "in that mood." It is a mood in which Yeats
imagines himself partaking in some "incredible romance." A poet's Bible,
indeed! Some might call it a "Bible of Hell."

Is that not the point? Had not the Bible, from the poet's perspective,
been corrupted from vision into law by interpreters? What sort of law?
Certainly the moral law, but before that the relation of the poetic word to
its referent had been corrupted, and this led to the necessity of making an
allegory of something forever hidden, like Blake's tyrannical sky-god. As
Blake put it in *The Marriage of Heaven and Hell*, is that not the fate of a book
declared sacred?

> The ancient Poets animated all sensible objects with Gods or Ge-
> niuses, calling them by the names and adorning them with the
> properties of woods, rivers, mountains, lakes, cities and what-
> ever their enlarged & numerous senses could perceive.
> And particularly they studied the genius of each city & coun-
> try, placing it under its mental deity.
> Till a system was formed, which some took advantage of, and
> enslav'd the vulgar by attempting to realize or abstract the men-
> tal deities from their objects: thus began Priesthood.[26]

Or if the Bible of imagination had not been corrupted into a text of moral
law by a priesthood of interpreters, had it not been declared irrelevant in
the face of a mathematical law, which had become an abstraction of the
book of nature? There seemed to be two choices for the poet. Find the
original sacred book and restore it, or construct a new one—though
whether either would actually be sacred is a question of importance yet to
be faced.

The myth of the rediscovered or pieced-together lost book informs
Yeats's remarkable work *A Vision*. In the introductory portions of the final
1937 version that have to do with the discoveries made by the fictional
Michael Robartes, the *Speculum Angelorum et Hominum* is introduced. Robartes, it is explained, found it propping up the leg of his bed in sordid
dwellings in Vienna, hardly the proper function for a sacred book. This
book, published in 1584 in Kraków and written by a mysterious Giraldus,

> was very dilapidated, all the middle pages had been torn out; but
> there still remained a series of allegorical pictures, a man torn in
> two by an eagle, and some sort of wild beast, a man whipping
> his shadow, a man between a hunchback and a fool in cap and
> bells, and so on to the number of eight and twenty, a portrait of

26. *Complete Poetry and Prose of William Blake*, ed. D. V. Erdman (New York: Doubleday, 1982), p. 38.

>   Giraldus [looking suspiciously like William Butler Yeats], a uni-
>   corn several times repeated, a large diagram in the shape of a
>   wheel where the phases of the moon were mixed up with an
>   apple, an acorn, and what looked like a sceptre or a wand.[27]

The book had been discovered by Robartes' mistress in a cupboard, where
it had been left by the previous tenant, an unfrocked priest, who had disappeared to join a troop of gypsies. The mistress had ripped out the
middle of the book to light her fire.

Robartes seeks by scholarship to recapture the content of the crucial
lost middle pages, but fails. In misery, he considers pilgrimage and prayer,
but in the end rejects Jesus as belonging to "order and reason." As if this
were a signal satisfying some power that his views were appropriately
"antithetical," on the next day an old Arab appears at his door and takes
up the explanation where Robartes' copy of the *Speculum* was defective,
connecting the whole system to the doctrines of his tribal sect (the Jud-
walis, or Diagrammatists) and tracing all back to a founder named Kusta
ben Luka.

In *A Vision* we are told (through a letter to Yeats from a character called
John Aherne) that the bulk of the work is Yeats's effort to record in orderly
form the words of Robartes taken down by his pupils as Robartes heard
them from the old Arab. This material, in turn, fills up the lost spaces of
Giraldus's expropriation of the Judwali system. John Aherne remarks to
Yeats that he is not surprised that Yeats was able to find what was lost in
the *Speculum* or survives only in the inaccessible encampments of the Jud-
walis. Ever the rational interpreter, he suggests that Yeats's experience
may well have been a "process of remembering," reminding Yeats that
Plato regarded memory as constituting a relation to the timeless.[28] This is
part of a series of sly reminders that we are reading Yeats's fiction.

The whole story plays with the ideas of lost truth, a fall, and timeless
wisdom. The lost book is said perhaps to be timelessly present to the appropriate consciousness—in this case Yeats's "antithetical" man, Michael
Robartes, whose oracular pronouncements are strangely paradoxical and,
in their poetic form (which is their only form), just out of reach of the
"primary" Aherne brothers, who will therefore interpret them. The Yeats
of *A Vision*, as I have shown elsewhere,[29] has to struggle with his own
primary tendencies in order to understand the "system" of *A Vision* and
not turn it into a false form of reason rather than a creative form of fiction.

27. W. B. Yeats, *A Vision* (1937) (New York: Macmillan, 1938), p. 38.

28. Ibid., p. 54.

29. See my *Blake and Yeats: The Contrary Vision* (Ithaca, N.Y.: Cornell University Press,
1955), pp. 164–99, and *Philosophy of the Literary Symbolic*, pp. 312–23.

The myth of a lost, restorable book also occurs in Yeats's expressions of interest in Irish myth and folklore, the "book of the people." But it is always attached to that second choice: Construct the new book. In the *Autobiography*, Yeats wrote: "Is it true that our air is disturbed, as Mallarmé said, by the 'trembling of the veil of the temple,' or 'that our whole age is seeking to bring forth a sacred book'? Some of us thought that book near towards the end of the last century, but the tide sank again." [30]

A few pages later Yeats writes in a somewhat humorous, self-ironic vein about his own desire that Villiers de L'Isle-Adam's *Axel* be that book: "I had read *Axel* to myself and was still reading it, so slowly, and with so much difficulty, that certain pages had an exaggerated importance, while all remained so obscure that I could without much effort imagine that here was at last the Sacred Book I longed for." [31] But, of course, *Axel* was not the book. Indeed, the book was not available even from more promising if less mystifying contemporaries. The result was the necessity of *constructing* one's own book, rather than *collecting* one, as Yeats had tried to do in his youth. The impulse of *A Vision* is the idea of this necessity. In the early section of *A Vision* called "To Ezra Pound," Yeats writes, "I send you the introduction of a book which will, when finished, proclaim a new divinity." [32] This is a radical assertion, certainly. On the one hand, it seems to proclaim a *sacred* book; on the other, it proclaims something entirely new. The speaker of these words is in transition. Speaking in terms of the sacred, he is yet on the way to proclaiming a book that is contrary to the sacred, a book of imaginative energy, an "antithetical" book, to use Yeats's own term.

Sacred books are "primary." Or, at least, when a book is declared to be sacred by a priesthood of interpreters, it is given a "primary," that is to say, an external and fixed, authority rather than the internal authority of an "antithetical" text. In this sense it becomes closed, and there can then be only one such book. As we have seen, Yeats searched for such a book early on, and I shall hold that the *Book* of Yeats's poems incorporates that search into its plot. In the poems of *The Rose*, it is a quite serious, to say nothing of solemn, search for external authority. Later it becomes a search ironically perceived and in the process of change. Still later it is antithetically implied that all true books are profane books, as in "Ribh at the Tomb of Baile and Aillinn."

Yeats's apparently sacred book, *A Vision*, whose main character near the outset says that it proclaims a new divinity, is so full of ironic comedy that

---

30. Yeats, *Autobiography*, p. 189.
31. Ibid., p. 192.
32. Yeats, *A Vision*, p. 27.

the reader comes to recognize that there is nothing sacred about it. The deity it proclaims is a god of discord, similar to the Celtic deity Bricriu, but absent from sacred texts except when made negative like the form of Satan. Discord turns out to be the principle of antithetical order, which is the opposite of the primary order that places authority somewhere behind or previous to the text—what Derrida calls presence. In the 1930 diary, Yeats wrote:

> I am trying to understand why certain metaphysicians whom I have spent years trying to master repel me, why those invisible beings I have learned to trust would turn me from all that is not conflict, from sword in hand. Is it not like this? I cannot discover truth by logic unless that logic serve passion, and only then if the logic be ready to cut its own throat, tear out its own eyes.[33]

Yeats's ambivalence about his "invisible beings," his "daimons," is again an expression of transition, taking place in the drama of virtually all of the books he wrote, from dependence on external authority and belief to antithetical creativity. A few pages later in the diary, he proposes himself as the location of struggle:

> I think that two conceptions, that of reality as a congeries of beings, that of reality as a single being, alternate in our emotion and in history, and must always remain something that human reason, because subject always to one or the other, cannot reconcile. I am always in all I do, driven to a moment which is the realisation of myself as unique and free, or to a moment which is surrender to God of all that I am. . . . Could these two impulses, one as much a part of truth as the other, be reconciled, or if one could prevail, all life would cease.[34]

This assertion of all-encompassing conflict is a myth designed, as Yeats remarks in the introduction to his play *The Resurrection*, to be a reply to a myth—the culturally dominating myth of "grey truth" mentioned in "The Song of the Happy Shepherd"—the myth of the triumph of the primary world of analytic science, Locke's materialism in modern form.[35] It is a closed myth positing an external authority. (Elsewhere I have called it "antimyth" and will do so in this book.)[36] It negates the truth of its opposite, which is the antithetical, poetic way of constituting life as particu-

33. W. B. Yeats, "Pages from a Diary Written in Nineteen Hundred and Thirty," in *Explorations* (London: Macmillan, 1962), p. 301.

34. Ibid., p. 305.

35. W. B. Yeats, Introduction to *The Resurrection*, in *Explorations*, p. 392.

36. See my *Philosophy of the Literary Symbolic*, esp. pp. 330–47.

lar, concrete human experience. The antithetical Yeatsian myth must always remain open to its opposite. In this way it defies the utter dominance of external law, whether natural or religious, even as it includes the existence of such a world as an opposite in its antisystem. Because it does this, it is not a sacred book. It is antisacral, as every poet's book must be. *A Vision* is such a book. The instructors come not with law or "grey truth" but with "metaphors for poetry."[37] The *Book* of Yeats's poems is such a book—a book of metaphor, basic to the poet.

Because myth, in the sense in which I use the term, is potentially open and is capable of challenging closed systems, it must contain a place for those systems and declare at the same time (in a paradox) the limitation of its own point of view at any given moment. (This is the reason we cannot read any particular poem of Yeats as pointing to any external authority, even though each one fictionalizes such an authority for the moment.) Myth is in opposition to "primary" forms of thought while at the same time it can claim to be the container of all thought. Yeats wrote:

> Myth is not, as Vico perhaps thought, a rudimentary form superseded by reflection. Belief is the spring of all action; we assent to the conclusions of reflection but believe what myth presents; belief is love, and the concrete alone is loved; nor is it true that myth has no purpose but to bring round some discovery of a principle or fact.[38]

"Belief" is perhaps not quite the right word here. Yeats claims in the introduction to *The Resurrection* that myth is not "a fiction, but one of those statements our nature is compelled to make and employ as truth though there cannot be sufficient evidence."[39] In *A Vision*, however, what Yeats has called "belief" above is treated as belief's opposite, belief now being associated with proof of "actual existence" and thus antimythical, pointing to an external authority:

> Some will ask whether I believe in the actual existence of my circuits of sun and moon. . . . To such a question I can but answer that if sometimes, overwhelmed by miracle as all men must when in the midst of it, I have taken such periods literally, my reason has soon recovered, and now that the system stands out clearly in my imagination I regard them as stylistic arrangements of experience comparable to the cubes in the drawings of Wynd-

37. Yeats, *A Vision*, p. 8.
38. W. B. Yeats, Introduction to *The Cat and the Moon*, in *Explorations*, p. 400.
39. Yeats, Introduction to *The Resurrection*, p. 392.

ham Lewis and to the ovoids in the sculpture of Brancusi. They have helped me to hold in a single thought reality and justice.[40]

Mythical thought ought always to be met by the contrariety of reason. However, Yeats's reason does not negate his myth, but pulls it into art. Reality is a primary external creation of the reason. Justice is a human cultural creation. The mythic, no longer positing something external for belief, becomes the poetic—an open container. As such it can never be a book of doctrine or law, and it refuses to submit the human to the negating domination of the inhuman or the superhuman. As Yeats makes a strict opposition between the poet and the saint, so he makes one between poetry and religion. The hero of Yeats's *Book* begins by searching for a sacred text, but the real quest that this search becomes is to *create*, including giving voice to the created antisaints Crazy Jane and Ribh. This involves for Yeats a willing acceptance of the earth and the role of Blakean "reprobate,"[41] the contrary of all that is sacred for the sake of life, and even for the sake of the sacred.

Heraclitus declares that Homer was wrong to pray for the disappearance of strife from the world, for he did not realize that when he did so he was praying for the destruction of the world. A poetic, antisacral, mythic, antithetical book would accept and even celebrate life in all its passions, disorders, and capriciousness. It would dwell on particulars rather than the general doctrinal concerns of a sacred book. It would formulate personal experience. This is what Yeats's *Book* does. It presents in the beginning a quest for discovery of an external authority, but it ends by making a contrary to what first was sought.

Perhaps no sacred book was originally really sacred. Perhaps the Bible was not originally a sacred book but an antithetical, mythical, poetical text. Perhaps this explains the uneasiness with which priestly interpreters have faced the Song of Songs. Perhaps this justifies readers who think an editor has tampered with the Book of Job. Priestly interpretation is surely in part responsible for purging the so-called Apocrypha. Perhaps sacred books are made from poetic books by interpreters, who find ways to close them or, like Blake's Urizen, arrange and regulate them in a circle around

40. Yeats, *A Vision*, pp. 34–35.

41. Blake's terms "elect," "redeemed," and "reprobate" originate with Calvin and are employed ironically in *Milton*:

The Elect are one Class: You
Shall bind them separate: they cannot Believe in Eternal Life
Except by Miracle & a New Birth. The other two Classes:
The Reprobate who never ceases to Believe, and the Redeemed,
Who live in doubts & fears perpetually tormented by the Elect.

(I:24:32–36; *Complete Poetry and Prose*, p. 122)

a closed center of doctrine. If so, this is a lesson to literary critics. Criticism must regard the text as closed in the sense that it is a mythic container but open in the sense that such containers can never be contained, that critical closures are acts of desperation, whereas what we need are acts of critical exploration. This is why I say that in the critical constitution of Yeats's *Book* that follows, I accept the fact that my critical constitution is mediatory, heuristic, and temporary, that it wishes to make no further claims for itself, that it dies the poem's life but refuses to live the poem's death.

2

Early Searchings and Irresolutions

"The Wanderings of Oisin" (1889)

[Yeats wrote that he became dissatisfied with "The Wanderings of Oisin." [1] He subjected it to revision and improved it, but his dissatisfaction remained, as it did with much of his early poetry. It is, nevertheless, an appropriate overture, in some ways because of his dissatisfaction, as I shall try to show.]

We read "The Wanderings of Oisin" as the first artistic expression of our main character or hero, a young poet. I take the view here (contrary to Gerard Genette's that mimesis is a form of narration)[2] that narration is a form of mimesis. Yeats's *Book* is a mimesis enclosing both other mimeses and narrations. I use the term "mimesis" in its technical sense of drama only and with none of the ontological and epistemological baggage with which Plato and subsequent literary theorists have freighted it (because Yeats's *Book* includes narrative, Plato would have called it a mixed form). This young poet does not speak directly until the *Book*'s third poem; and in the section called *Crossways* he displays much personal reticence. Nevertheless, each poem in the *Book* is his act, thus a mimesis. In this study I call him "the poet" up to a certain point (when he names himself), distinguishing him at the outset from Yeats, by which name I designate the historical figure, theoretically distinct in turn from the authority of the text or what Charles Altieri calls "intention in." [3] I call the *Book*'s main character "the poet" because the *Book* dramatizes him as such, though he is, of course, other things as well—lover, husband, father, theater director, and politician, for example.

1. *The Autobiography of William Butler Yeats* (New York: Macmillan, 1953), p. 45.
2. Gerard Genette, *Narrative Discourse*, trans. Jane E. Lewin (Ithaca, N.Y.: Cornell University Press, 1980), pp. 163–64.
3. Charles Altieri, *Act and Quality* (Amherst: University of Massachusetts Press, 1981), pp. 146–47.

When the poet speaks directly in the earliest poems, one senses a certain evasiveness quite different from the more vigorous wearing of a mask that appears later on and tends to govern the more mature poet's behavior. It is as if the poet is unsure of his assertions, perhaps because he is uncertain that he has as yet anything positive to say and is uneasy about the world he inhabits or about himself in it. We note also the poet's regret for something he believes lost.

A fictive character, the poet does not have the liberty to suppress his poetic acts, as Yeats did with some of his early works.[4] Further, we are absolutely free to consider this fictive poet's motives and the relation between himself and his works in a way that avoids the pitfalls that would face us were we to attempt the task with the historical Yeats. The reason is that the fictive poet is present only in the *Book*, by contrast to the historical Yeats, who merely wrote it. The fictive poet's intentions are part of the mimesis, though often they must be inferred and interpreted.

The *Book* tells a story, and in that story the poet eventually develops reservations about "The Wanderings of Oisin," as well he might; we know this as part of the story because he expresses them as reservations about his earlier self in the penultimate poem of the *Book*. There he implies that he had indeed been evading direct expression of something very important to him. Of himself and Oisin he says in "The Circus Animals' Desertion": "But what cared I that set him on to ride, / I, starved for the bosom of his fairy bride" (373, 347; 381, 629). These lines we shall eventually read in their proper place, and there we shall understand that the fairy bride stood for someone he could not bring himself to name, such was his own uncertainty about himself.

"The Wanderings of Oisin" appears to be a declaration of poetic roots. It is an adaptation and elaboration of the old Irish mythological story of Finn's son Oisin, the famous warrior-poet. That story has come down to us as a dialogue between Oisin and Saint Patrick, and the poet adopts this traditional form. Temperamentally attracted to the values represented by Oisin, the poet nevertheless acknowledges the reality that Saint Patrick has brought. The dialogue form reflects the poet's sense of a conflict, represented by these protagonists, in the Irish spirit. Absent for three hundred years in the country of the faery, or the Sidhe, Oisin finds the Fenians gone and the new Christian society dominant. He represents the old heroic society, Saint Patrick the modern, the civilized, the rational, and the

4. See *The Variorum Edition of the Poems of W. B. Yeats*, ed. Peter Allt and Russell K. Alspach (New York: Macmillan, 1957), pp. 641–792, and *The Poems of W. B. Yeats: A New Edition*, ed. Richard J. Finneran (New York: Macmillan, 1983), pp. 451–585, for the poems that Yeats never included in the *Book*.

ordered. In the world to which Oisin returns everyone cultivates his garden. Gone is the old nomadic society of hunting and fighting. Oisin laments the loss of the social unity that characterized the Fenians, a brotherhood that abjured organization and lived by passionate loyalties. It was a naive society, and its miraculously anachronistic last remnant, Oisin, is stubbornly naive. Saint Patrick would bring him out of his naiveté could he find a way to communicate with him.

The poem (375, 355; 1, 1) begins with an odd statement by Patrick. It does not directly admonish Oisin, though it may be the beginning of an admonishment that Oisin anticipates and interrupts, a reminder to Oisin of his great age and feebleness. It does not directly call on Oisin to tell his story, though it may obliquely show interest. In any case, Oisin begins his narration. He does this with arrogance, virtually disregarding Patrick while yet taking advantage of the presence of an audience. He is a garrulous old man more interested in an audience in the abstract than in any particular audience as such, and he is irritated by Patrick's power. After Oisin has spoken for a while, Patrick sternly observes, "You are still wrecked among heathen dreams" (375, 356; 1, 4). This verbal gesture of dismissal has absolutely no effect. Oisin proceeds as if he has not heard it, as if he were totally enveloped in his story. Oisin's doggedness in the telling intensifies the sense of his concentration on the past. Though it is Oisin's here, the concentration is also the poet's, and as the *Book* proceeds the unhealthiness of that concentration reveals itself (though Oisin is always to some extent glorified). Indeed, the unhealthiness lies under the surface of all of the early poems; it is made obvious by the pressure of the *Book* as a whole—that is, we more certainly detect its presence as we read on.

Patrick is not a villain, though the poet seems at first to cast him as one. The poet would perhaps like him to be a villain, but retention of the dialogue form deters him somewhat (Patrick must have a voice), and Oisin's naiveté and the curious ambivalences and irresolutions in his story prevent us from siding fully with him. If Patrick represents modern life, he is also the real. The villains of this piece are more likely to be nostalgia and self-pity, which rise to the surface of Oisin's story, perhaps out of the poet's own irresolution, and cause certain disruptions.

It will be worth remembering later that the poet's resistance to full identification with Oisin expresses principally reticence and evasion, while later the creation of fictive voices supports a principle of Empedoclean contrariety between discord and concord that is at the center of the poet's more mature attitudes. Still, we can see a foreshadowing of the discord/concord opposition in Oisin's Fenian passion and Patrick's reason.

Patrick's scathing remark does not deter Oisin. He arrogantly ignores it, or he does not hear it. But at some point he remembers that as a poet he has an audience, and he impertinently addresses it (as did Oisin in the old legend): "O Patrick, by your brazen bell . . ." (375, 357; 1, 7). Further, Oisin proves to be a compelling poet, for though Patrick thoroughly disapproves of Oisin's life, he is moved to interpret Oisin's "text," providing what we might call a remarkably condensed moral allegorical reading that closes the text in the "lesson" of disrespect. It is a reading Oisin certainly did not intend: "Boast not, nor mourn with drooping head / Companions long accurst and dead" (375, 358; 1, 11).

Somewhat later, however, Patrick, unintentionally endorses poetic power, for at a particular point he is interested enough in Oisin's story to say, "Tell on" (375, 365; 1, 24). Reluctantly, perhaps, he becomes for a moment an example of the results of the dangerous power of the poet as Plato saw it. Oisin possesses bardic power, which from Patrick's perspective is something dangerous enough that he must read a moral meaning against the text even as he has become absorbed in the tale as a tale. This is a danger because it suggests that a tale in itself has a power contrary to explicit morality. Patrick is not, however, in serious danger. He continues to hold that Oisin has it all wrong, that he can never go back to his Fenian friends but can only go *down* to them in hell.

I belabor these points because the poet does not emphasize them. He allows them to lie rather unobtrusively in the fabric of the dialogue. I belabor them also because the poet does this more than once later on in the *Book*. We must attend to the dramatic conflict in these dialogues and not leap to consider their content before pausing to consider the enclosing situation.

Sometimes failure to communicate characterizes the drama of these dialogues. One of the problems of communication between Oisin and Patrick is their different world pictures. Patrick's world is threefold and, oddly enough, simpler than the naive Oisin's because it is without unresolved conflict. There is heaven above. There is the world of time, change, and generation in the middle, where society is organized and work is done. There is hell below. These levels are, as I have indicated, vertically arranged. Heaven Patrick does not have occasion to mention; we infer its existence. He threatens Oisin with hell, from which he would save him if he could get its meaning through to him. This he has failed to do as the poem ends.

Oisin's world turns out to be complicated, for the most part horizontally arranged, and ambiguously presented. Because Oisin's world seems to represent both the past and the poetic, it appears that the poet may be uncertain about his own world and his place in it. It is implied that in the land of the faery, or the Sidhe, which belongs to Oisin's world picture, there will eventually be an end of time itself. Oisin is taken to a hall where the god of love, Aengus,

> . . . dreams, from sun to sun,
> A Druid dream of the end of days
> When the stars are to wane and the world be done.
>
> (375, 361; 1, 16)

This assumes a time (actually an antitime) of annihilation and eternal nothingness, projected in Aengus's dream as the apparent completion of desire.
The act of dancing in the land of the Sidhe seems to be either an act of
symbolic projection into that antitime or a ritual forgetting of impending
annihilation. The poet apparently cannot decide which. The dancing is
"wild and sudden" and follows on a speech by a god of joy, who says that
the dance is an expression of mockery of time and death so effective as to
annihilate them both. Oddly, before the dance begins, this god falls into a
"Druid swoon" and presumably misses out on it. But that is apparently all
right, because dreaming has the same power as the dance. This god also
avers that joy is necessary to change and birth, even though the expression
of joy in dream and dance seems to be an effort to rid the world of just
those things:

> And if joy were not on the earth,
> There were an end of change and birth,
> And Earth and Heaven and Hell would die,
> And in some gloomy barrow lie
> Folded like a frozen fly;
> Then mock at Death and Time with glances
> And wavering arms and wandering dances.
>
> (375, 362; 1, 18–19)

Here joy is good, though without it the world would disappear and Aengus would have his dream. (Added to this is an immense fear among those
in the Sidhe's realm of falling into sorrow, joy's opposite.) On the one
hand, the annihilation of earth, heaven, and hell is desired (after all, these
things represent Patrick's world). On the other, the dance is a joyful act
that keeps the earth moving and presumably alive. The land of the Sidhe,
where all of this goes on, must be a halfway place. Indeed, the poet has
created a supposedly timeless area where the gods and dancers are nevertheless still concerned about escaping mundane things. These curious irresolutions must be attributed to the poet, for Oisin's voyage is "real" in
the text and not merely his subjective dream.

There are other curiosities. The land of the Sidhe is made at first to
appear as a conventional lower paradise; but this paradise, we come to
learn, is not above the place of the Fenians, from which Oisin has come,
but level with and opposite to it. That is, in part, because the Fenians have
their own miraculous though mortal qualities, at least when seen through

the lens of nostalgia. The old legend says that the defeated Tuatha de Danaan descended beneath the ground as a result of a treaty with the victo-
rious Milesians, thus continuing to rule over half of the world as the faery,
or the Sidhe. The poet adapts this story to his purposes, giving to the
Sidhe not the lower world but an equal and opposite world somewhere
else. There is no indication that Niamh takes Oisin below ground. At the
moment of meeting Niamh, Oisin seems to find the Fenian society lacking
an adequate object for his desire, and so, smitten by Niamh, he elects to
leave it. But he comes to learn that the land of the Sidhe, for its part, does
not provide the things that he loves in Fenian society. Niamh, on the other
hand, has heard stories of Oisin's exploits among the Fenians and searches
there for him, the land of faery being inadequate to *her* desire. Her land
has apparently three parts. There is a place of dancing and music, where
Aengus and the god of joy already mentioned abide. There is a place of
lovemaking, feasting, and fighting. Finally, there is a place of sleeping,
dreaming (again), and forgetting. Neither Niamh nor Oisin looks long-
ingly toward the world of annihilation dreamed by Aengus. They both
look across to their opposites. There is, finally, within Oisin's world, now
that he has "returned," the world of Patrick, a world of social repression
and spiritual tyranny, which Oisin regards as a sort of hell. Patrick, of
course, believes Oisin's world is the product of delusive, heathen dreaming. What is emphasized in Oisin's world is a clash of opposites. [In connection with all of this, it is interesting to see that, like the instructors of
Yeats's *A Vision*, the faery are no more perfectly content with their world
than human beings are with theirs. The main character of *A Vision* writes
of his instructors as interested in his world. He is not finally certain
whether they instruct him or he instructs them.]

   This opposition [characterized in *A Vision* and elsewhere as living each
other's death, dying each other's life] explains the considerable amount of
anxious talk among the faery about sorrow. Everyone in that place is
trying to avoid it. This perplexes Oisin. When he tells a heroic story to the
faery, he causes sorrow. He thinks his story wonderful, but what has been
heroic and admirable to him becomes its opposite among the faery. Indeed, all thought of his society seems to breed sadness among them. Ultimately, the parallel-opposite is true for Oisin: Niamh is always sorrowful
because she thinks that her world will not please and will eventually sadden Oisin, and she is right. When remnants of Fenian war implements
wash up on the faery beach, his own memory begins to work, and he is
saddened. As the poet projects it, then, the faery place harbors an ambivalence. It is incomplete even for the faery, or at least for Niamh, who impresses us as the only real or interesting figure in it. The others are escap-
ists and either have drugged themselves or desire to drug themselves into

avoidance of sadness, which begins to look like avoidance of life. Certainly the fact that the only really sentient being among the faery is Niamh, a seeker, and that others spend their time in escape or the praise of it gives us pause about what contentment really might be.

Yet Niamh's perspective is curiously presented. When she looks at Oisin she sees sorrow, even before he becomes homesick for the Fenians. She acts like those faery who reject his song. She sees him as sorrowful merely because he is from the other place, yet she desires him. From his own point of view, he is not sorrowful, nor is his song. It is the faery, not Oisin and the Fenians, who equate the Fenian life and temporality with sorrow. Niamh sorrows from the outset of the poem because she senses that she cannot make Oisin completely happy. In this awareness that the Fenians have something the faery lack, she is unique among them. But she is ambiguously presented. On the one hand, she treats Oisin as sorrowful because in the faery view the Fenian life is inferior; on the other, she remains sorrowful herself because she fears she cannot provide a substitute for what the Fenians provided him.

This strangeness, which we shall come to regard as symptomatic of the poet's irresolution, is reinforced by an echo of Keats's "La Belle Dame Sans Merci." In that poem, the poor knight describes himself as the abandoned, hapless victim of a faery, white-goddess figure. We never learn more than the knight tells us. In "The Wanderings of Oisin," however, we are able to grasp the faery Niamh's feelings through Oisin's narrative. It is she who is abandoned. She is projected not as a wicked goddess but as a sensitive lover. The principle of mutual and opposite desire is maintained against the pressure of the Keatsian model.

There is another Keatsian moment in the poem that is perplexing and suggests that the poet has failed to work his way out of an irresolution. As Oisin and Niamh ride into the faery land, they observe a scene of endless pursuit, as if there were a tapestry before them:

> And now a lady rode like the wind
> With an apple of gold in her tossing hand;
> And a beautiful young man followed behind
> With quenchless gaze and fluttering hair.

> (375, 359; 1, 12)

The endless pursuit of the "Ode on a Grecian Urn" is here imposed on a scene from Irish mythology. To Oisin's question about it Niamh only sighs and puts her finger to his lips. There are many questions suppressed in the land of faery, which begins to look like a vehicle for the poet's evasions rather than a true contrary to the Fenian life. The scene offers endless perpetuation of the condition of desire, but Oisin and Niamh are merely observers of a scene treated as desirable (but with reservations) in the drama of Keats's poem. Here its implications are evaded by Niamh, who consummates a marriage with Oisin and lives with him for three hundred years. The poet who has invented this faery land apparently cannot decide what its nature is: desire wrought to its utmost and there eternalized, desire consummated, or consummated desire augmented by a voyeuristic experience of sexual pursuit.

Further, what, we may well ask, is all of the sighing of Niamh about? Sexual passion? Sadness because Oisin is sad? Concern that she cannot hold Oisin? Awareness that her passion for Oisin is for her a "descent" of some sort? The faery world seems hardly very desirable. It is clearly going to become a bore to a warrior-poet. When Oisin acts the bard, his heroic tales sadden his audience, and he is kept constantly on the move by a Niamh concerned about losing him. Her most desperate act is to take him to the place of lovemaking, feasting, and fighting, which is her effort to duplicate in faery land the elements of Fenian life. Here every four days for one hundred years Oisin fights a monstrous opponent in an effort to free a damsel in distress. The working conditions—one day on and three days off—are not bad, but the activity is repetitious and artificially contrived. In time, the illusion of excitement and recklessness dissipates. Niamh plunges rather deeply into the role she has devised for this episode, crying at one point to Oisin to flee and save himself, though it is she who has perpetrated the whole situation, which we may regard as an illusion, despite the energy Oisin must expend. Indeed, the whole faery world has connections with the poet's conception of artifice, but it begins to look like an attractive delusion similar to Spenser's Bowre of Bliss, with its tapestry-like effects.

In addition to its artificial qualities, the faery land is characterized by the petulance of its inhabitants. Niamh is again an exception. All the others are like children. They throw Oisin's harp away when his song saddens them. Even the artifice is finally childish in its evasiveness, offering, as if holding hidden profundities, images that lie undeveloped and are finally more atmospheric than anything else. One passage provoking in this way is the following:

> And with low murmurs, we rode on,
> Where many a trumpet-twisted shell
> That in immortal silence sleeps
> Dreaming of her own melting hues,
> Her golds, her ambers, and her blues,
> Pierced with soft light the shallowing deeps.

(375, 359; 1, 13)

Like the previous, Keatsian image of sexual pursuit, the image of the seashell is a piece of decoration offered portentously. But it merely lies there in the poem.

As things turn out, the next two poems of the *Book* appropriate the seashell and establish its ironic connections to the visionary shell of Wordsworth's dream in *The Prelude*, thus making something of it. As we look back on it from the next two poems and some later ones, it appears to have augured something that the poet at the time of "The Wanderings of Oisin" could not quite grasp or was unwilling to face. This sort of situation is frequently played out in the *Book*, the space between poems having been a time to work out undeveloped implications, the poet making from his irresolutions new opportunities. In the time between "Oisin" and "The Song of the Happy Shepherd," some thinking goes on, and we come to read that time.

But we cannot consider it until we have recognized that the Fenian/faery opposition is presented to us within the Oisin/Patrick opposition and that Oisin's world actually contains the world of faery as an opposite the poet would like to consider equally true. It is a world presented powerfully enough to gain Patrick's attention, though not his belief. The poet has attempted to construct a heroic world that is full of the sort of opposition Blake called contrariety, where each side maintains itself by virtue of the vigorous presence of the opposite. This heroic contrariety, which constantly generates desire, is apparently to be contrasted to the ordered, reasonable world of Patrick, which can only declare the Fenians damned in hell, or, in Blake's language, negated. (My use of Blake here is purely heuristic. I do not declare the poet a fledgling Blakean.)

But the Fenian/faery opposition does not turn out to be a true contrary, because the land of faery is escapist, passive, and artificial in its expressions of desire, therefore negating the real. Only Niamh transcends this, and that makes us willing to give credence to the lines already mentioned from "The Circus Animals' Desertion," which comes at nearly the end of the *Book*. By that time, the poet knows better than he does now. But some part of him knows better even now, though in a curious, irresolute way, for the land of escape is very ambivalently presented. The true object of desire, Niamh, exceeds her false world and threatens already (though we can't know this quite yet) to break into real life as the beloved of later poems, finally named Maud Gonne.

At the end of "The Wanderings of Oisin," we return from concerns about the inner, Fenian/faery opposition to the enveloping, Oisin/Patrick opposition and see an effort to establish a true contrary between the principle of vigorous discord and that of reasoned concord. Oisin possesses a passionate recklessness that the poet would have us value, but we value it less than that of the more sophisticated heroes who appear later in the *Book*. Oisin does not understand the costs that must be counted before one deliberately ignores them. In his choice of passionate loyalty, expressed by his willingness to descend to hell to fight his way out with his Fenian brothers, Oisin reveals the passion that the poet values and praises later on. But Oisin is of the old world and does not understand hell. Unable, therefore, to calculate the enormity of his risk, he lacks the knowledge that would make a modern reckless hero even more heroic, though less pure. In Oisin's view, there has been since the old days a contemptible decline of heroism. But he has not, as we say today, seen anything yet.

For his part, the poet, somewhat hidden behind Oisin's voice and giving Patrick a few innings, is revealed more in the ambivalences of the text than in its bare content. He has not by any means spoken out. He is uncertain what voice is his, though in another, deeper poetic sense he is always present in the performance he has orchestrated. This performance, however, does not speak what it intends, or perhaps it (as the authority of the text) knows itself better than the poet knows himself.

Crossways (1889)

In the *Book*'s second poem, the first of the section called *Crossways*, the poet remains hidden, but in a different way. In "The Song of the Happy Shepherd" (1, 7; 2, 64), he turns to present not an ancient Irish voice but the voice of an Arcadian shepherd. This speaker recalls the world of classical Greek mythology, but he knows the modern world, and so Arcady, like the land of the Sidhe, is located to its side. He speaks of schoolboys, science, and materialism. We infer that he comes from a world of artifice that constructs an ideal image of the past. [Indeed, this poem served as the epilogue to Yeats's early play, *The Island of Statues*, a work not in the *Collected Poems* or the *Collected Plays* but reprinted in *Poems* (1983).] Though he represents and advocates an alternative to the acceptance of modern life, this shepherd is quite different from Oisin. From beginning to end, Oisin granted nothing to Patrick, and he was not content in faery land, though faery land seemed to be tied up in some uncertain way with the poet's own desires. The shepherd is quite explicit about the modern world, and is as disparaging about it as Oisin. He declares that Arcady is over and done with. The old world, which was Arcadian, sustained itself on dreaming. The place of dream, we recall, was one of three places in faery land, the place in which there was the least action. By contrast to the dreaming world, identified with the poetic making of the marvelous, the modern world is dull and colorless, the world of the primary qualities of empirical truth. This world the shepherd regards as trivial. Earth itself is restless, that is, incapable of dreams, or at least dreams of the marvelous.

At this point the opposition is clear enough. Arcadian dreaming is opposed to materialist theorizing, which is its own sort of dream. But now the shepherd introduces a new argument:

> But O, sick children of the world,
> Of all the many changing things
> In dreary dancing past us whirled,
> To the cracked tune that Chronos sings,
> Words alone are certain good.

(1, 7; 2, 65)

Words are favorably opposed to the world of action. Men of action, like kings, were mockers of words, yet they are now reduced to words in history books. But there are bad words, too: the words of the scientists who study the stars. Their hearts are cloven. This shepherd and our poet have been reading Blake and have picked up his notion of the "cloven fiction" of materialistic science, his identification of the world of stars with that fiction, and finally his notion of analogy: everything has its "fallen" parallel-opposite. Thus there are two kinds of words, two kinds of dreams, and (by implication, if we remember "Oisin") two kinds of dancing.

But the shepherd, not a very systematic thinker, is also a somewhat confused one. Speculating, he suggests that

> The wandering earth herself may be
> Only a sudden flaming word,
> In clanging space a moment heard,
> Troubling the endless reverie.

(1, 7; 2, 65)

He toys with the possibility that words are actually the containers of the real, and he comes near to repeating Aengus's dream of impending annihilation. But he backs away from this speculation with a non sequitur: For these reasons do not listen to the words of the "starry men." We are instead advised to pick up a seashell on the seashore and speak our story into it. We recall the narcissistic, dreaming seashells that Oisin and Niamh pass by. We recall also, perhaps, the shell of Wordsworth's dream in *The Prelude* (bk. 5, 50ff.). Wordsworth heard in the shell, opposed to the stone of science, prophetic voices. Clearly these voices came from an inner self, perhaps more than a single self, and were declared by the Arab of the dream to be of immense worth, greater than that of the stone. They were voices of poetic prophecy. The shell advocated by the shepherd is meant also to be of great worth, but by comparison to that of Wordsworth's Arab, its power is pathetically diminished. At best it provides a sea change for our "fretful words," offering temporary, narcotic forgetfulness of the modern world and a vague promise that these words will die away leaving us free of our sorrow:

> Go gather by the humming sea
> Some twisted, echo-harbouring shell,
> And to its lips thy story tell,
> And they thy comforters will be,
> Rewarding ["Rewording" in *Collected Poems*][5] in melodious guile
> Thy fretful words a little while,
> Till they shall singing fade in ruth
> And die a pearly brotherhood;
> For words alone are certain good.
>
>   (1, 8; 2, 66)

Having offered this escapist advice, the shepherd announces his departure. He will seek out the grave of a "hapless faun," which seems to represent the lost world of Arcady, and there he will sing to it, deluding himself into thinking it is still alive. The songs he will sing will be the songs of old, when earth knew how to dream the "unfallen," right sort of dreams. Thus the happy shepherd goes deliberately on his anachronistic way, pretending that he will have an audience.

The *Book* certainly invites us to compare this speaker to Oisin. Both are poet figures, one from the world of Irish mythology, one from that of classical artifice. The poet's movement from one to the other reveals increased bitterness and awareness of self-enclosure in his speaker as well as a diminishment of the desire to act. The heroic, loyal, though futile intransigence of Oisin before Patrick we contrast to a world-weary, cynical view of what telling a story might accomplish. The romantic Wordsworthian seashell is now but a means of narcotic relief, an entrance for a moment into an illusion identified with a past that is treated as if it always had been an artificial dream. There is no dialogue here, for the words dissolve and fade, no ear to hear the fading save one's own; yet the fading is declared good, for in it everything blends together in a "pearly brotherhood" that seems to be the antithesis of language as we know it. The happy shepherd's poetic act is the destruction of his own medium. No voice will respond from the shell's depth, and this is declared to be the best that the world can offer. We shall recall the happy shepherd's advice when, late in the *Book* ("Man and the Echo," 372, 345; 383, 632), a more experienced and wiser man

---

5. Finneran's reading is based on *Poems* (1895), revised and reprinted, 1904, and several subsequent printings, including *Collected Poems* up to 1950.

speaks into a cavern, is gruffly answered, and must engage that voice, albeit only an echo, by rising to a defense of his and all life.

By implication, the poet opposes the happy shepherd's form of escapism in the next poem, where he tells the story of another shepherd and a shell. "The Sad Shepherd" (2, 8; 3, 67) is obviously paired with the preceding poem and is a kind of answer, though by no means a final one, to the happy shepherd. The sad shepherd, not an Arcadian, is from the real world, where there is sorrow, not from the faery world, where it is strenuously suppressed. Indeed, sorrow is this shepherd's friend. And so, on the seashore, that marginal place where most of the important things seem to happen early in the *Book*, he takes up a shell and speaks his story into it. He picks up the shell after seeking and failing to achieve brotherhood with various representatives of nature: The stars, the sea, and the dewdrops that he approaches are all self-absorbed and pay no attention to him. The world's "grey truth" seems to be the Paterian truth of absolute solipsism. The recourse to the shell by the sad shepherd is different, however, from that advocated by the happy shepherd. He wants more than the happy shepherd claims it can give. He wants a shell that will sing his song back to him, that will unburden him of it yet preserve it, objectifying it in the art that the shell seems all along to have represented, though it is strictly a romantic art identified completely with reflected self-expression. This is indeed a greater demand: The sad shepherd wants the opposite of fading to a pearly brotherhood. He wants to hear his words sing out again after they have passed into the shell's pearly heart. There are elements of both purgation and artifice here. But the shell does something closer to what the happy shepherd said it would:

> . . . the sad dweller by the sea-ways lone
> Changed all he sang to inarticulate moan
> Among her wildering whirls, forgetting him.
>
> (2, 9; 3, 69)

The shell performs its act of dissolution, but it fails to combine this with re-creation; only half of the Coleridgean description of how imagination functions is present here. No created song is produced. The happy shepherd promised pleasant, "melodious guile," but the sad shepherd never wanted that, and his experiment is a disaster. He is alone, and his story gone. "Melodious guile," a type of decadent vision of the golden world in Sir Philip Sidney's description of poetry, is not adequate to a true romantic like the sad shepherd. But was the shepherd's view of the shell as a vehicle of personal catharsis ever likely to produce much more than "inarticulate moan"? In any case, the happy shepherd's solution is not quite what occurs and would have been found wanting had it occurred. On the other hand, the sad shepherd may be misguided about what telling a story should amount to. Buried here is the explicit criticism that the mature poet makes of "The Wanderings of Oisin" in "The Circus Animals' Desertion." Making one's personal moan is not sufficient.

At this point, we are invited to take particular note of the pervasive emotion of sorrow, which is perhaps a symptom and not the disease from which the poet and some of his characters suffer. The ways to alleviate the symptoms, offered here and there so far, seem not to have worked. The disease has not been given a name yet, though something like solipsistic isolation has been implied. The dramatic, catechistic dialogue on sorrow that follows, "The Cloak, the Boat, and the Shoes" (3, 9; 4, 69), characterizes sorrow as seductive, ubiquitous, silent, sudden, hidden in a beautiful cloak, traveling in a swift boat, and shod in soundless shoes. Sorrow wears the trappings of this world and seems to have descended into it, provided with clothing by the mysterious speaker. Perhaps sorrow is sorrow simply because it has descended or come from elsewhere. Perhaps anything that comes from elsewhere is sorrow, that is, evokes the sorrow of desire in the viewer, as it does in Niamh when she contemplates Oisin. If it is like Niamh, it is surely also beautiful and a friend, but its effect on man would be hopeless longing, unless one were carried off, and then would one be content? This would return us to the situation of Oisin and cries out for a new departure.

The new departure the poet makes may not be different enough. He writes a group of poems on Indian themes, obviously searching for a different ideal world. It turns out to be a similar world in an exotic cloak. "Anashuya and Vijaya" (4, 10; 5, 70), the first effort to write of an Indian setting, appears to be an aborted dramatic poem about passion and jealousy. Its drama bogs down, and the poem ends in a prayer by Anashuya that does little more than paint an exotic picture.

The Indian landscape, too, proves ambiguous as an ideal and ominous in some of its details. The poet has chosen to adopt voices not his own, a sign that has already led us to suspect tentativeness of commitment (though it will not be a sign of this later on in the *Book*). The theology offered by the Indian who speaks on God (5, 13; 6, 76) can be read in contradictory ways. Either God inhabits all animal and vegetable forms, or each of these forms cannot see beyond itself, forcing God's image into its own shape. If we remember "The Sad Shepherd," we know that the dewdrops to whom the shepherd would tell his story are so engrossed in the sound of their own dropping that they cannot hear him. Something of the same occurs here. The Indian hears the moorfowl, the lotus, the roebuck, and the peacock speak of their moorfowl, lotus, roebuck, and peacock gods. Can they hear the Indian if he speaks to them? Has his journey brought him knowledge of his god or only of the dispersion of God's image into a variety of solipsisms? One is not far here from the old joke about the blind men and the elephant. The Indian merely reports or absorbs the experience of his brief journey; to put a single meaning on it is impossible. The poet's disinclination to comment combined with the poem's ambiguity suggests that the poet, having set forth the issue of isolation in "The Sad Shepherd," will not run the danger of wrecking the Indian's thought with rigorous probing.

"The Indian to his Love" (6, 14; 7, 77) completes the Indian group and does nothing to lessen the ominousness. Here the poet returns to the subject of love, with which the group began. Again there is an Indian speaker, but the poet has returned to the theme of escape that pervaded the first poems of the *Book*, albeit with more sensual suggestion. The Indian has taken his beloved on a sea voyage to a lower paradise. There are some differences from the land of the faery. There is death in this land, and the lover paints an ambiguous picture of that state. Is it a limbo? A condition of disembodied ecstasy? We are uncertain. There are other ominous notes: A parrot rages at its image in the sea, though the ominousness is deflated somewhat by the fact the sea is "enameled," as if it were part of some artifice. Our suspicion by this time is that in these early poems artifice itself is a vehicle of evasion.

What causes the parrot's rage? It is said that these lovers will wander "with woven hands" like Niamh and Oisin and that they will "murmur . . . how far away are the unquiet lands." But why should they dwell on this at all, having escaped it, and will not their isolation in the paradise eventually become a bore? In it there seems to be no hope of change, except that death is said to occur. But in death they will rove the same paths as ghosts.

The Indian experiment is at this point abandoned, certainly in failure. This generates a poem in which the poet seems to speak directly, just as the unsatisfactory advice of the happy shepherd gave rise to the poet's direct telling of the sad shepherd's story. In "The Falling of the Leaves" (7, 14; 8, 79), the poet speaks to his beloved, and none of the earlier alternatives is chosen. "The Sad Shepherd" hid the poet as a teller of someone else's story. This poem hides the poet in a mannered technique, the rolling rhythm and alliteration having the effect of distance. We sense that stealth is necessary to him, even as he appears to speak out. The mood is the familiar romantic agony, the sort of love poem better not sent, the message being that the lovers should part at the height of their passion, before its inevitable waning. Since the moment will not stay, sudden annihilation is preferable to slow decay. Perhaps we have here an attempt to explain the reason for Aengus's not unfriendly attitude toward the sudden annihilation of the world in "The Wanderings of Oisin."

"Ephemera" (8, 15; 9, 79), which follows, continues the theme. The lovers who engage in this dialogue have not taken the advice proffered in the previous poem and now experience the foretold waning, which is described as a general weariness. The whole of the scene in which the lovers speak is beset by it. There are hints of reincarnation and other loves to follow, but no vitality anywhere. Both of these poems may obliquely express a passion that the poet himself experiences but is unable to act out maturely in real life. The heavy technique may hide more than reticence.

Certainly this mood cannot be sustained. There is, indeed, an abrupt break in which the poet obliquely acknowledges a mistaken direction. The mood of romantic agony has led him nowhere in particular, and he returns to Irish materials through the remaining poems of *Crossways*, where problems of unconsummated sexual passion are, if not avoided, toned down. These poems are of various sorts: One is a free adaptation of Irish myth, one invokes the Sidhe, two recall the style of Irish folk songs, and three are ballads.

The first, "The Madness of King Goll" (9, 16; 10, 81), tells in Goll's voice of his sudden rejection of killing, violence, and power in a moment of inner vision that has made him appear insane to others. He travels endlessly and seemingly with no destination, apparently only to escape the fluttering of the beech leaves that torment him. It is uncertain what their message is. Are they a reminder of his own past acts, of aging, of death? Or do they whisper of something to be sought? Probably all of these things, since the desirable no doubt requires a certain abdication. In "Ephemera," dead leaves were identified with the waning of nature by the young woman who

> . . . had thrust dead leaves
> Gathered in silence, dewy as her eyes,
> In bosom and hair.

> (8, 15; 9, 80)

Goll's rejection of kingly power expressed in violence is repeated later on in the *Book*, its next appearance being in connection with Fergus, a king who abdicates to become a poet. It is an attempt to speak about one of the things that most troubles the poet in the world: Goll may seem mad to us, as the poem's title insists, but he believes he has seen a truth or a representation of the truth, suffering for it in being driven by an unappeasable fury. Only music and song quench it, and then only for the moment, with a success no greater than that of the sad shepherd's shell:

> When my hand passed from wire to wire
> It quenched, with sound like falling dew,
> The whirling and the wandering fire;
> But lift a mournful ulalu,
> For the kind wires are torn and still.
>
> (9, 18; 10, 86)

In addition to the sad shepherd's complaint, Goll laments that the bardic harp is now broken, so even that is no solace. There seems to be neither escape from Goll's torment nor consummation of his nameless desire.

"The Stolen Child" (10, 18; 11, 86), which adopts the common folk theme of the child taken away by the Sidhe, reinforces this notion, as if after writing "The Madness of King Goll" the poet has thought again on the matter of escape from conscience and desire and has concluded again, in the manner of "Oisin," that the only escape is into the opposite land of faery. But he has forgotten that there desire is merely reversed. The faery sing their song, and it is ominous. Even as they entice the human child from the world, they capriciously lament that he will no longer enjoy things in that world, even though he is being taken from a world that is "more full of weeping than [he] can understand" (10, 18; 11, 87). A curious ambivalence in the Sidhe echoes Niamh's desire for human love. These Sidhe, like Niamh, are characterized as rather sad. But unlike her, they are also mischievous. They make fun of the child: He is "solemn-eyed" and naive. They give "unquiet dreams" to trout in the pools of the real world. Their opposite would be a fisherman of the real world who seeks to catch an elusive, perhaps supernatural trout. (He actually makes his appearance later in the *Book*.) Here the poet extends his sense of the mysteriousness of the otherworld and its desirability, expressed by the mad Goll. The something that calls from the otherworld is untrustworthy.

Having thought upon the Sidhe and their attitude toward the human child, the poet himself plays with the notion of enticing his beloved to an island apart, of playing the Sidhe-lover, in a sense. "To an Isle in the Water" (11, 20; 12, 89) must be considered not as a thought actually presented to her (such is the poem's gesture) but rather as what the poet thinks he would say were he not as shy as he characterizes the beloved as being. In a voice that he claims as his own, he is not nearly so bold and sensual as the Indian is to his beloved. In the beginning he speaks directly, it is true, but then he speaks only *of* her, and he distances the whole poem by use of folk conventions.

This strategy continues to be played out in the adaptation of a well-known Irish song that follows. "Down by the Salley Gardens" (12, 20; 13, 90) makes clear that the speaker lost out with his love because his youthful foolishness took the form of an excessively ardent seriousness. He did not "take love easy" as she desired him to. If we consider the contrivances and elaborate indirections and posings of some of the previous poems on the theme of love, this is not surprising. (Later we shall learn that at fault are not contrivance and posing in themselves, but the choice of contrivance and posing and the attitude toward them.)

The result is a somewhat bitter and nostalgic poem called "The Meditation of the Old Fisherman" (13, 21; 14, 90), which is clearly a sequel. To this point, the poet has been tormented fundamentally by two things: first, the inadequacy of this world and of certain other imaginable worlds that would possess what this one lacks; second, the fact of growth and decay, both of life and of the beautiful and passionate. Underneath this is a search to discover forms of expression in which to fix these tormented thoughts. Beginning with Irish myth, he passes through Indian and *fin de siècle* stage sets before seeking again to express himself in somewhat sparer Irish materials. Finally, beneath all of this we detect sexual frustration born in part of reticence or shyness, for the poet is frequently hiding himself. "The Meditation of the Old Fisherman" is an important chapter. It dramatizes the thoughts of an old man looking on youth and is obviously paired by the poet with the preceding "Down by the Salley Gardens," which is to be taken as spoken by a relatively young man. This pairing allows the poet to distance himself further from the statement of the earlier poem. "The Meditation of the Old Fisherman" is a poem of nostalgia, but not for a lost love. It is important, especially for the way it introduces into the poet's story an element that has been latently present but is only now given bold expression. The second line of the stanza below offers it:

> And ah, you proud maiden, you are not so fair when his oar
> Is heard on the water, as they were, the proud and apart,
> Who paced in the eve by the nets on the pebbly shore,
> *When I was a boy with never a crack in my heart.*

> (13, 21; 14, 91)

Nostalgia for a lost time of wonder is turned into the idea that beauty, desirability, and greatness must be aloof, as they seemed to the fisherman when he was but a boy. Something of the scenes of endless pursuit in "Grecian Urn" and "Oisin" reappears here, but with immense glorification of the "proud and apart." Simply to have seen such heroic creatures is all that one could expect. Pursuit is not mentioned; only a vague emotion of wonder and respect is conveyed. Now, for the fisherman, everything grand has receded into memory, and nothing in the present can compare. It is because the fisherman does remember that he feels superior to the youths around him. Even to the last poems of the *Book*, the poet is at times susceptible to this sort of nostalgia.

This is the first statement of a theme much dealt with later on and argued from various sides. That the poet himself at this stage is not yet old raises interesting questions about his relation to this text. He will not broach them as yet, and his shift to another poetic form at this point is in part a way of evading the implications of the fisherman's attitude.

The turn is to the ballads that end *Crossways*. The ballad can certainly be interpreted as a vehicle of nostalgia, but it does have distance, the poet adopting a bardic stance. Choice of the balladeer's objective voice seems here a deliberate effort to achieve opaqueness for the statements, a means of hiding behind the appearance of telling a traditional story. The three central figures—the priest, the beggar woman, and the foxhunter—appear here in the reverse order of the importance they later have in the *Book*. The priest figure is not on the whole a heroic one in the *Book*. Here the poet makes the priest's treatment of birds better than his asserted doctrines (14, 21; 15, 91). The tragic Moll Magee (15, 23; 16, 94) enforces the importance of feeling above doctrine. The foxhunter, who calls for the "gay wandering cry" of the hunting horn as he dies (16, 24; 17, 97), foreshadows in crude form a gesture the *Book* comes to glorify and to deem aristocratic and reckless. The foxhunter is, of course, an Ascendancy figure. This cry is the first of a number of sounds in the poems that seem to express moments of intense feeling that break into life, radically changing the situation of the moment. "The Ballad of the Foxhunter" stands in a position of emphasis at the end of *Crossways*. Its glorification of the Anglo-Irish Ascendancy, which the poet will see die in his time, is not yet pressed very hard and certainly not explicitly. Rather, in these three ballads the poet seems to want to identify himself symbolically with Ireland as a whole. Indeed, the next section, *The Rose*, we might regard in one of its aspects as an elaborate deflection from the impending, though latent, Anglo-Irish identification.

Crossways begins in uneasy temptation to escape, moves through search for forms of order in Indian thought and esoteric wisdom, and ends in hope for harbor in Irish folk wisdom. The last is part of a patriotic attempt to recall Irish poetic traditions, but the effort is interfered with to a considerable extent by personal indecision. The epigraph to *Crossways* is from the apocalyptic ninth "Night" of Blake's *Four Zoas*—"The stars are threshed, and the souls are threshed from their husks"—and the collection is dedicated to the Irish mystical poet and painter AE (George Russell). It is obvious enough that the poems do not present an apocalyptic or mystical vision, that both epigraph and dedication express ungratified desire. The poet, standing at crossways, looks down avenues but does not yet really venture forth.

The Rose (1893)

The epigraph to *The Rose* and the first stanza of "To the Rose upon the Rood of Time" (17, 31; 18, 100) indicate that a decision about a direction may have been made. It is not a direction that was among the choices clearly apparent in *Crossways*, but the manner of pursuing it has connections with early ambivalences as well as later conflicts. The decision itself gives rise to a crisis of considerable importance to the *Book*. This crisis, though not explicitly named in the poems and only gradually revealed, we might call the crisis of the poet as mystic and the effort to identify beauty and mystical experience. Beauty is the subject of the epigraph from Saint Augustine's *Confessions*, translated in Finneran's notes as "Too late I loved Thee, O Thou Beauty of ancient days, yet ever new! too late I loved Thee." The epigraph invokes time and the last chance. It is a warning and leads on to the first poem, which seems to seize the moment but is a curious wooing. "To the Rose upon the Rood of Time" is the first augury of crisis, though we might have suspected something earlier; at least, with hindsight we think so. The crisis is generated by the unspoken question of whether or not the poet can be a mystic and yet remain a poet, indeed, whether or not poems can be mystical without undercutting themselves. Since the decision taken in the first stanza is to follow the path of occult mysticism, it is not surprising that the second stanza makes an effort at qualification. With all the discussion that there has been about Yeats's occult interests—discussion that Yeats would have had to think warranted—the poet nevertheless worries about this commitment, sensing a difficulty. At this stage, however, he is uncertain what the issue really is. The *Book* will establish dramatically the difference between mystic and poet, which is a prelude to expression of the relation of the poet to an idea of truth and to God.

It has not often been observed that the rose is an unusual kind of image in the *Book*. It belongs among what I have called elsewhere romantic miraculous symbols.[6] Such symbols are miraculous in the sense that their mystical referents are supposed to be actually immanent in their utterances. The model is the ritual of the Eucharist and certain primitive notions of the word. The problem with this type of symbol is its tendency to

6. See my *Philosophy of the Literary Symbolic* (Tallahassee: Florida State University Press, 1983), pp. 12–23, 140–49.

slip to the level of what I have called "religious" allegory, where it becomes detached from its referent and is thus regarded as "graven" and arbitrary. One sees this beginning to occur even in the title of the poem, where the poet places his rose on the cross of time, which means that its appearance is a sacrifice to its true being, a tragic denigration of its timeless essence. In that sense, the symbol as we experience it is not complete, and we come to question more rigorously the relation of its appearance to its reality.

In spite of the poem's title, the poet does not discuss this crucifixion. The omission is explainable if we conclude that after an initial boldness the poet does not want to face the implications of the crucifixion—neither its traditional Christian implications nor the symbol's diminishment implied by its appearance on earth. This rose is conceived of as having endured a descent. Its sadness, explicitly mentioned in the first line, implies that descent; but, more ominously, it recalls the sadness of others we have already read about when they have even so much as contemplated entrance into this world. Yet the poet regards the descent as good because he can identify his aspirations with at least this somewhat defiled spiritual beauty and can hope to be freed thereby from the world of determinism that the happy shepherd criticized so strongly but for which he had no effective antidote. This would make it possible for the poet to see things as they really are. There is a sort of neoplatonism here. Poetry in the *Republic* is regarded as dangerous because it is blinded by passion and by the process of mimesis; but a neoplatonic theory, as in Plotinus on "intellectual beauty," would save poetry by making the beautiful image a vehicle or passageway to the imageless truth.

The title of the first poem suggests a connection to Rosicrucianism. In the space between *Crossways* and *The Rose*, the poet has studied still another rose. When the poem is remembered with later ones like "The Two Trees" (37, 48; 38, 134), the cross on which the rose hangs comes to suggest a tree, which in turn is a reminder of the upright, flourishing tree of life and the inverted tree of the knowledge of good and evil that William Blake, and later Yeats, had discovered in various occult iconographic designs, including the Cabalistic and Gnostic. The poet turns this inverted tree into the tree of love and hate. Some of this I shall return to. Here we see that the poet asks the rose to approach him as a muse. What we have noticed as a direction, implying travel or quest, seems to have taken on the form of conjuring by means of poetic incantation. The poet thinks that he requires the inspiration of the rose in order to "sing the ancient ways." Occult mysticism is alleged to be the way to bring alive once more the heroic Irish past. Since this past of Druids, Cuchulain, and Fenians was pagan, the poet must apparently suppress the Christian side of his Rosicrucianism, even as he evokes it in the cross, particularly if he is to be true to Oisin and the "ancient ways." The mystical way is put to curious use. Meanwhile, the poet has revised the role of the stars in his poetry. We recall that when the sad shepherd called on them, they merely laughed and sang on undisturbed. Here, though still alone and above man, they sing of the rose's sadness for having descended.

It is actually "eternal beauty" that the poet seeks. This beauty is treated as feminine, though he would see it in "all poor foolish things that live a day." This raises difficult questions. Was the rose a rose before its descent? We know, of course, from a modern pythoness that a rose is a rose is a rose; but that is a statement made from a strictly poetic—and secular—stance, whereas here we have the dramatization of a poet seeking the muse of mysticism. Is the rose's femininity, like its sadness, something that in its descent it takes on by necesssity? Or is what the rose stands for (incarnates?) feminine in essence? "Eternal beauty wandering on her way" is what the poet would seek, presumably through his poetry. He seems to say that this would be achieved by retelling under inspiration the ancient Irish legends, which have fallen from favor. If he could properly express them, he would bring beauty into miraculous presence on earth. This means that these legends are, in his telling, the rose. They are in some sense aloof, to themselves, "wandering on [their] way." This aloofness perhaps expresses the aesthetic qualities of the legends. But on what ground the femininity of the rose is squared with the indubitable masculinity of the Irish saga material is not clear, unless it is the outer form this material is given or unless something deeper troubles the poet.

This deeper thing is, I think, twofold. First, the poet is forced into confusion by his own mystical symbolism. Is the rose in essence a rose? Is the rose in essence feminine, or is it feminine only in appearance? Is the ultimate object of veneration and desire feminine, or is sexuality only fallen appearance? If the rose is feminine, how can this femininity be made to inhere in "all poor foolish things that live a day"? Second, the poet at some level of consciousness recognizes the problem these questions point to and appeals with some anxiety to the rose to back off. This is a curious way to treat a muse or a symbol of the desirable. It is a sign of a crisis that the *Book* exploits in drama. The poet expresses, in the poem's second stanza, fear of being so enveloped in the symbol that he will no longer be able to identify himself with the world of individuals, which becomes transparent and secondary when treated merely as appearance. Specifically, he wishes to maintain his identification with the world of desire ("common things that crave"). Anything else, he confesses, would make him speak a language no one could understand, would be to go beyond language into the mystical, forsaking poetry.

The desire to stay in the realm where he can "sing of old Eire and the ancient ways" causes him to remain on the level of sexuality implicit here and to live with a desire that cannot be consummated without loss. Turning to the rose and assuming that his poetic activity is identical to mystical search, the poet nevertheless finds himself qualifying his mysticism, almost calling it in question. At the same time, the undertones of sexual passion (very near the surface in, for example, the renaming of the tree as the tree of love and hate) suggest that the poet's true object of desire has been displaced and its real name has not been uttered. Further, the poet, trying to speak of both the mystical and the aesthetic independence of the rose, seems to will his own frustration. It is interesting that in the last poem of *The Rose* the poet speaks directly not only of his effort to combine the rose with Irish legends and Irish patriotism but also of his love. He says that he writes for Ireland "the love I lived, the dream I knew," acknowledging the intrusion of his frustrated love for the beloved into his poetry and still trying to accommodate both without strife.

If we turn to that poem, "To Ireland in the Coming Times" (39, 50; 40, 137), we can observe how far the poet has come. Here the poet expresses concern that his occult mysticism may be taken by some as an abdication of poetic patriotism. If we read the space between the first and this last poem, we can infer that either someone has raised questions or the poet himself has become increasingly self-conscious about the matter. He therefore deliberately identifies himself with poets who "sang, to sweeten Ireland's wrong." This is somewhat oddly or ambiguously put. Surely the poet does not mean that he and they have tried to sugarcoat Ireland's terrible history in order to make it more bearable. Surely he means that he would help to overcome that wrong. Or does he mean that to put this history into poetry creates a beautiful sadness? Perhaps the poet himself is uncertain. A descended rose must be both beautiful and sad, like Niamh contemplating Oisin. The poets with whom he identifies himself—Davis, Mangan, and Ferguson—were all Irish poets; but none was a mystical occultist, and Ferguson identified himself strongly with the Union. This will not bother the poet, whose sense of "Ireland's wrong" is as much on the artistic level as on any other. Ferguson's use of ancient Irish material apparently qualifies him no matter what his politics. Later on it is clear that with the poet's identification of himself with Anglo-Irish culture, this is no problem. Indeed, it seems here that the poet has already attempted to disregard certain political differences in an effort by will of imagination to make Ireland one and whole. With Mangan the matter appears at first easier: The poet is perhaps able to identify Mangan's "Dark Rosaleen" with both Ireland and his own rose, but for Mangan the poem was strictly one of political devotion written as a subversive allegory and was not occultist.

The poet's rose is regarded as having descended into time. She is declared to have generated the life of Ireland (as she must have generated all life). The poem plays on the word "measure," identifying measure in all its meanings with the world of time. Included here are temporal measurement and the rhythms of dance and poetry, both the mathematical and the artistic being links to otherworldly, measureless truth. The hope is that Ireland itself will find ideal measures to "brood" upon. The word "brood" implies a certain moodiness, the passion under which this thought will have to survive in a situation of political suppression. Measurement, as for Plato, is for the poet here the closest possible worldly thing to truth. The term foreshadows a famous remark in the late poem "Under Ben Bulben" ("Measurement began our might" [356, 326; 386, 638]), and we shall recall its use here when we come to that poem, which recasts present issues.

This poem seems a recommendation to mystical meditation with a Platonic undertone, which, passing through "measures," unmeasures the mind and conjures up the faery muse. At this point the poet refers to the shortness of life and to the possibility—offered with characteristic tentativeness—that the faery are a means of passage into a place where there is "no place for love and dream at all" (39, 51; 40, 139), both being lower forms. Such a place would seem to be the nonworld of annihilation dreamed by Aengus. The faery are now seen as a mediation between the poet's world and a place of nothingness or pure being, or at least a world where, without love and dream, there would be no activity for the poet. It is not an opposite world of desire like that of Niamh but beyond desire. The poet avers that he will follow the faery in the sense that to do so will be to follow the rose. The rose is never described, never given a body, the hem of her garment being the only trace of her being. The rose we see only as the metonymous garment. [As such it behaves much as the sphere does in *A Vision*. It is a symbol, merely a symbol.] The miraculous, incarnate, crucified rose of "To the Rose upon the Rood of Time" is here disembodied, revealing a perhaps unresolvable contradiction.

This may be why we notice the poet protesting so much that his mystical, Rosicrucian way is also the poetic and patriotic way, yet the intervening poems reveal much uncertainty about identifying poetry and mysticism and some repressed questioning of the world of pure being as nothingness. If we look forward to "The Circus Animals' Desertion," we again remind ourselves that the poet later thinks these early poems clothed not mystical truth but sexual desire. We must see how things go in *The Rose*.

After the introductory poem, the poet turns to a dialogue between Fergus and a Druid (18, 32; 19, 102). Fergus was a king in the Red Branch sagas. In Ferguson's nineteenth-century version, which the poet here adopts, he abdicated in favor of Conchubar, having better things to do than be king: to seek after truth as a philosopher-poet. In "Fergus and the Druid," it is said, he abdicates to "cast away . . . sorrow." He has been a closet sad shepherd. Further, in his opinion Conchubar was a better politician. This abdication, though more thoughtfully made, has something in common with King Goll's, of course. "Sorrow" is the world of time and experience, the product of desire. Fergus seeks "dreaming wisdom." Remembering the happy shepherd, we know that the poet has played with kinds of truth. Fergus's desire is expressed in the formula "dream equals truth," and we already have cause to be suspicious of it because of the happy shepherd's reasoning.

The Druid would dissuade Fergus, who seeks his wisdom: "No woman's loved me, no man sought my help." His wisdom has isolated him. Fergus's reply to this is interesting: "A king is but a foolish labourer / Who wastes his blood to be another's dream" (18, 33; 19, 103). In his view, the man of action merely dies into legend. Of what value these legends might be is clear to him; they are but dreams, presumably of the wrong kind because not of truth but of the acts of this world. But if this is so the "ancient ways" are not worth singing about, so we must wonder whether Fergus has it right. [We are reminded of an entirely different approach to this point, which is of heuristic value here, in Yeats's *On Baile's Strand*, where Cuchulain accepts his role to act as the mythological figure he will become. This would make him, in Fergus's language, the dream of someone else. Cuchulain also asserts: "I make the truth." Fergus only seeks it, and that may be the problem. Perhaps the opposition making/seeking is a false one. One might say that the Druid knows this.]

The dreams that the Druid reluctantly gives to Fergus make him even more sorrowful. This sorrow can be identified with the sadness of the rose as a result of its knowing its former state. Knowledge in this world does not cast off sorrow but is merely the absolute recognition of the existence of the cloak sorrow wears. So at this point, though the issue has been distanced into dialogue, the poet has explored both solipsism and universal identification, which becomes loss of identity, and discovers only metaphysical sorrow, which is a cloak in the poems for frustrated sexual desire. This last is much suppressed and will continue to be suppressed for a while in personal and borrowed poetic styles.

Cuchulain's madness in the next poem, "Cuchulain's Fight with the Sea" (19, 33; 20, 105), is unlike Goll's, and his behavior is opposite to that of Fergus, as if the poet has deliberately chosen to make a contrast. Here we have the tragedy not of the thoughtful seeker but of the passionate doer. There is nothing the least bit ascetic about Cuchulain, and he is involved in sexual jealousy and revenge. A man under oath, he expresses passionate, not reasoned, loyalties. As such, he is the political pawn of the subtle, worldly Conchubar, who uses him until his passion exceeds his usefulness and poses a danger to the state. At that point, Conchubar orders the Druids to cast a spell on him. On his side, Cuchulain, who is without subtlety of thought, is particularly susceptible to Druidical magic. His struggle with the sea is heroic madness. [In an earlier version of the poem Yeats had Cuchulain die fighting the sea, but he later revised the final lines to leave Cuchulain's actual death in doubt so that he might be restored to life in *The Only Jealousy of Emer* and suffer a different death in *The Death of Cuchulain.*]

The poet has now sung twice of the "ancient ways," as he said he would; and two quite opposed figures have been his subject. Both have been tragically dramatized. What has driven these men? Some mad ideal? Fergus sought impossible knowledge; Cuchulain followed a passionate commitment symbolized by an oath. Are both of these acts forms of beauty in the telling? Are they the poet's expression of rosiness? If so, they are roses of *this* world.

"The Rose of the World" (20, 36; 21, 111) marks a typical stepping back from the bold dramatic efforts we have just observed. We are inclined to two readings of the space preceding it. First, we may conclude that the poet, having ventured into the dramatic, feels he has lost his way or has said more than he meant to and recovers by trying to subsume the events of these poems under the domination of his governing symbol. Second, we may conclude that the poet has indeed "sung the ancient ways" and writes a footnote demonstrating the connection to the rose (perhaps we did not notice her hem in the previous poems) that he will insist on again at the end of *The Rose.* Both readings seem right to me. The "ancient ways" remain present here in the reference to the Deirdre legend, which is buttressed by identifying Irish mythology with the ancient Grecian, a form of cultural patriotism frequently indulged in at the time.

The poem tells us that beauty appears in many guises, that dreams have been dreamed about her and great tragic actions taken in her name. Clearly, the answerer in "The Cloak, the Boat, and the Shoes" was the poet's own archetype of the poet, who, in providing a vehicle for sorrow, provided one for beauty.

But here a new element is introduced. In the past, beauty has been ephemeral. Now the poet claims that it is we and all things that are ephemeral, beauty (the rose) having been at God's side even before the archangels were created and already "weary" then, as the angels later become from having to spend so much time with the "whimpering dead." The weariness came presumably from countless descents into sorrow. The rose referred to here is the rose of the world because it descends as sexual beauty. The examples are Helen, Deirdre, and a "lonely face" of pure passion, perhaps along Pre-Raphaelite lines appropriate to the poet's historical moment, the poet being a bit nostalgic for his own lost youth.

In the poem that follows, "The Rose of Peace" (21, 36; 22, 112), this idealized or archetypalized sexual beauty (though somewhat distanced and idealized) becomes the beloved, directly addressed as "you" and identified as the contemporary form of descended beauty that Helen and Deirdre anciently represented. As one might expect of a poem of direct address to a beloved at this stage, there is something tentative about the poem, principally in that it is surrounded by poems that do not speak of peace. It suggests the intrusion of some wishful thinking into the situation. As we later learn, this poem expresses an attitude as far as is imaginable from what the poet later comes to believe about the beloved, for in his eyes she turns out to be a creature of strife and political passion. It becomes unbelievable that the angel Michael, who is the nearest thing to a war god that the poet can find in the Christian "pantheon," would take up weaving in emulation of someone whom the poet finally names Maud Gonne. The poem wishes for peace, perhaps as a relief from the conflicts of the preceding poems.

One senses, in spite of the direct address (perhaps actually because the poet has chosen that route and is reticent), a regression that dominates even "The Rose of Battle" (22, 37; 23, 113), obviously paired with it for contrast. The poet returns to the idea of strife that seems fundamental to him but is greatly tempered here by the languid technique that suppresses the violence of battle, even as it is expressed. The poem's ostensible subject is obscured also by vague symbols and syntactical difficulties that frustrate our search for the poet's real position. The scene, however, is the familiar seashore where the sad shepherd walked. The battles are spiritual ones, and all spiritual ones are searches for the rose, which has descended only to entice its followers to defeat on the sea, symbolizing the human condition. We are reminded that under enchantment Cuchulain fought the sea, though thoughtlessly by comparison to the unfortunates of "The Rose of Battle," and that Fergus's life drifted like a river once he opened the bag of dreams. Ultimate defeat is the theme of all these searches, whether intellectualized or not.

It is no wonder, after this, that the poet should think wistfully of quiet. In "A Faery Song" (23, 38; 24, 115), the faery, who watch over the sleeping, hidden Diarmuid and Grania after their flight from Finn, speak of rest far from men and ask rhetorically if there is anything better; observing tragedy in the lives of both the active and the contemplative, the vastly

experienced faery give to Diarmuid and Grania what they deem best—
silence, love, and rest far from men. We know their fate from the old legend. Their love and rest is but momentary, their fate tragic.

The faery have been returned here to some form of lower paradise.
Thousands of years old, they remain gay, but their gaiety is much tempered with sadness or perhaps ennui as they contemplate the lovers. Indeed, that they seem able to enchant the lovers for only a little while is in
the end a good thing. For the lovers to remain in that state indefinitely
might very well turn it into hell, though the poet does not explore this
possibility, except perhaps by the tone of weariness he gives the faery. The
poet has, in fact, returned to issues previously dramatized. We sense regression.

That is why "The Lake Isle of Innisfree" (24, 39; 25, 117) is a startling
statement, not because it too is a poem that looks favorably on retirement
from the world (it does, of course), but because the poet suddenly speaks
out strongly and directly and because for the first time we sense that he is
speaking from a real place. It is a poem directly about his own situation.
He is far from the lake isle in a city of "pavements grey." He declares that
he will act. Though the act is one of withdrawal, it is also one of deeply
felt identification, and the statement is of a quality we have not heard before. The assertion is deeply resonant. The poet speaks as much about a
real place to which he is drawn as he does about alienation from the grey
world of concrete about him. There are those who will say that the poem
is not in the poet's true voice. [Yeats was among them, at least in his later
years, when he came to hate the poem, partly because he was so often
asked to recite it.] That is so if the poet's true voice is the later voice or one
of the later voices. But the poem's difference from the preceding work is
what is important to the *Book*. Its powerful rhythm is the young poet's way
to express a deep feeling we have not yet heard. Up to this point we have
been presented with all those mythological and/or mystical poems in
which the poet has rarely spoken forth in a voice that has not seemed eva-
sive. Here he turns oratorical and assertive. This may still be escapism,
but it is as personal an utterance as the poet can make at this point.

He does not, of course, go to Innisfree, as we know he would not. "The
Lake Isle of Innisfree" is an important moment not because he says he will
go and does not, but because he takes a stance. The stance may be ab-
stractly implicit earlier, and it may be full of conventional romantic iconography, but this does not matter as long as we view it as a gesture that
does not *intend* to hide anything.

But stances are hard to hold. New events intervene. Old loves reassert
themselves. The poet has certainly not escaped nostalgia for his youth and
for a favorite place. He is pulled toward composition of the song of expe-

rience that follows, "A Cradle Song" (25, 39; 26, 118). The poem is distanced from the mannered "reality" of "Innisfree" by virtue of its use of certain conventions, yet it has its own simple directness, new to the *Book:*

> I sigh that kiss you,
> For I must own
> That I shall miss you
> When you have grown.

(25, 40; 26, 118)

Here, under the domination of adult affection for the child, the poet toys with the idea that the child and the child-become-adult are not really the same person. If this is so, the nostalgia of "Innisfree" must be a deluded one, and perhaps the juxtaposition of the two poems has to do with some such recognition. The simplicity of this poem is also qualified by traces of a not quite conventional theology harking back to the poet's having projected dissatisfaction on those who inhabit other worlds. The angels here are treated with a certain wit, a quality we have not seen in the *Book.* It is consistent, I think, with the tendency that the poet has recently shown to speak out more boldly. They are weary of their life with the "whimpering dead," and they joy in descending to observe the child. Who these "whimpering dead" are is not entirely clear, but the suggestion that the other world is not satisfactory in the angels' slightly comic irritation is not new. The poet keeps to his notion that all may not be perfect in the supernatural world. But this is a song to a young child and must not be taken as proposing a purgatory. The remark is slightly impertinent, hardly the theology a child would hear from the elect. Its gesture suggests a certain new freedom in the poet, following upon his having spoken out in "Innisfree."

The poet's new sense of himself is yet quite tentative and grows but gradually through *The Wind Among the Reeds* and into *In the Seven Woods.* The next poem, "The Pity of Love" (26, 40; 27, 119), remains directly spoken in the poet's voice. To speak directly of his beloved creates in him a powerful anxiety. It is to have made her real; and now everything becomes a threat, not only the world of commerce and the "pavements grey" but also nature itself. The poet here dramatizes with insight his own state of mind, which is one of extremity. It is not surprising that he backs away and distances his situation with the beloved in "The Sorrow of Love" (27, 40; 28, 119), which follows. [This distancing Yeats effected in revisions, where direct address to the beloved is eliminated, so that the woman is not actually identified.] The poem refers to a mysterious, Helen-like woman. Before her appearance man's "image" and "cry" are blotted out by natural events. At the moment of her appearance, all of nature "composes" what has been blotted out. We learn that the woman is of mournful countenance and is or seems to be doomed like Odysseus and Priam. The poem is one of those elusive statements that we have come to expect when the poet suppresses or formalizes into an excessive politeness an expression of sexual desire. The backing away is reflected in the tendency to mythologize the loved one and to see her as the cause of some nearly cosmic change. Whether or not we accept John Unterecker's notion that "arose," twice used, is a pun to be read also as "a rose,"[7] the loved one is meant to be so beautiful in the Pre-Raphaelite style that she represents the rose of spiritual beauty. But to consider such beauty in this world is to imagine it the cause of strife. The connection with Helen and strife is repeated later, but with the important difference that the rose symbolism has been abandoned.

The next poem, "When You Are Old" (28, 41; 29, 120), which returns to direct address, finds the poet more composed. He has been reading Ronsard and performs his version of a Ronsard poem in English. His poem reminds his beloved of the transiency of physical beauty. The sense of "doom" here is different from that previously expressed. She is also reminded of his love, which he claims is a true love because it accepts the changes of her face and the sorrows they foretell. Three things are unspoken here. First, the poet has recovered from the reticence that caused him to hide in the deliberate vagueness of "The Sorrow of Love." Second, the poet predicts the sad outcome of his love. Third, there is a touch of resentment, suggesting threat, about his treatment at her hands and possibly as a result of her lack of sensitivity to the profundity of his feelings. Look, he says, you are going to grow old, and superficial loves will desert you. He avers that he will accept this transiency because he has loved the "pilgrim soul" of the beloved, that part of her that has descended to this world. Yet he threatens her with his knowledge that she will not always have the power of disruption she now possesses. We shall recall the poem when in *In the Seven Woods* we find the lover and beloved older. Before then, we shall notice further threats.

This mood, too, does not hold. It has been to some extent a piece of bravado. Quite hopelessly in love, the poet sends his beloved the passionate "The White Birds" (29, 41; 30, 121), based on a spiritual principle that would transcend all earthly passion and capture the beloved as a "pilgrim soul." The poet is somewhat didactic and seems to be trying to convince the beloved of the existence of a spiritual life. Perhaps desperately, he boldly asserts that both he and she are of one mind. He desires that together they be two white birds, and then he avows,

7. John Unterecker, *A Reader's Guide to William Butler Yeats* (New York: Noonday Press, 1959), p. 81.

> We tire of the flame of the meteor, before it can fade and flee;
> And the flame of the blue star of twilight, hung low on the rim
>   of the sky,
> Has awaked in our hearts, my beloved, a sadness that may not
>   die.   (29, 41; 30, 122)

This is a spiritual seduction that takes liberties with the beloved's views, attributing his own to her. She is forced into the attitudes of many of the poems we have read to this point: ennui and sorrow. The poet speaks again of the land of the Sidhe, this time of "numberless islands" where time and sorrow will no longer torment them in their transformed shapes. This is certainly a regression when we consider the skepticism with which the life of the Sidhe has been treated. The poet's high emotion is clothed in expressions of conventional escape to a lower paradise. The desire to be a hermit on Innisfree has been suppressed. The poem indicates a love affair not going well, and the next poem, "A Dream of Death" (30, 42; 31, 123), reveals that the beloved, referred to only as "one," is apart from him either physically or spiritually or both. Imagining her dead, the poet turns in the next poem to think of the Countess Cathleen dead and sent to heaven ("The Countess Cathleen in Paradise," 31, 42; 32, 124). The countess was a saintly radical who sold her soul to the devil in order to obtain food for starving Irish peasants. In the countess's heaven there is no repose. Rather, she is a dancer among seven angels, having carried "earth's old timid grace" into heaven. She is a powerful personality, identified by juxtaposition of this poem and the previous one with the poet's beloved. The poet seems to be admitting with obliquity that the beloved's capacity for radical action has not squared with his insistent romantic spiritualization of her.

The turn back to Fergus in "Who goes with Fergus?" (32, 43; 33, 125) is as abrupt as that marked by "Innisfree" and has something in common with it in that the path of Fergus is lonely, contemplative, and apparently identified with nature. It is surprising that the poet now ignores the earlier, unsatisfactory conclusion of "Fergus and the Druid." The impulse to release oneself from brooding on "love's bitter mystery," which has possessed the poet's recent life, seems to have been so strong as to blot out thoughts of Fergus's own disappointment. Fergus is treated as the ruler of all that is yet valuable, which is offered as a world of enchanted nature. Partly in the form of a question, the poem is more or less an invitation. Yet the question remains: Will the poet himself follow Fergus or pursue his beloved, the two possibilities apparently being opposites that cannot be resolved?

However, the enchanting quality that the poet claims to exist in common things is made ominous again (we remember "The Stolen Child") in

"The Man who dreamed of Faeryland" (33, 43; 34, 126). To this man everyday objects of nature sing of the world of enchanted islands and dancing. The imagery of silver and gold that runs through the poem suggests enchantment rather than its fallen form of material wealth. Yet the poem is about the man's discontent. His experience of tender love is disrupted by singing fish. His monetary success is disrupted by a singing lugworm. His anger at his mockers is dispelled by the singing of the knotgrass. Always his success in this world is transformed into desire for another. Even in death there is no comfort. Perhaps his story explains in part why in "A Cradle Song" the dead whimper. The poem clearly carries on the frustrated mood of "Who goes with Fergus?"

At this point, the poet executes a commission—a book of stories selected from the works of Irish novelists—and writes a dedicatory poem to Irish exiles (34, 45; 35, 129). In it there reappears a bell branch like that which enchanted Oisin. The ancient Irish bell branch is said to have performed a communal function, but the branch that the poet here presents is torn from a different tree, for Ireland's boughs are now declared to be barren and wintry. We hear in this poem a voice so much more direct and colloquial that we are startled into recognizing a commitment by the poet to his opinions. Though the branch is "full of ease," Eire is

> That country where a man can be so crossed;
>
> Can be so battered, badgered and destroyed
> That he's a loveless man. . . .
>
> (34, 45; 35, 130)

[These lines, a product of revision by Yeats, are a deliberate effort to infuse his poetry at this point with a bitter speaking voice.] This voice yet insists that the branch, the stories collected here, will bring bells of laughter, sadness, and "memories of half-forgotten innocent old places." The bitterness of which the poet has spoken is not in these stories, for they express the real world of "Munster grass and Connemara skies."

Again there is a contrast, but not so much of two worlds as of two different parts of this world: the country world of the novelists, near to nature and innocence, rather like the lake isle, as against the present sociopolitical world of Ireland. In these poems we see the gradual replacement of the emotion of sadness with a harder, colder bitterness. Certain forces have convened to produce "The Lamentation of the Old Pensioner" (35, 46; 36, 131) and "The Ballad of Father Gilligan" (36, 46; 37, 132). If the stories of novelists have no bitterness in them, that is not true of the poet's characters, and the contrast seems deliberate, for the old pensioner is bitter indeed.

The imagery of the tree, a part of the cluster that includes the rose, appears here and later. Ireland has just been identified as a tree with barren boughs. Now the poet, intending to write a poem like those "saddest chimes" that are "best enjoyed," shelters the old pensioner beneath not merely a barren tree but a broken one. The pensioner, who once was in the thick of love and politics, now bitterly spits at time and identifies himself with the broken tree under which he sits. What has driven the poet to offer this voice? Certainly there is the bitterness with which he has just looked on contemporary Ireland as well as his sense of time passing in his own unhappy love affair, though that is not directly treated here. Still, the poet may be imagining his future indirectly.

"The Ballad of Father Gilligan" is closer to being a song of "saddest chimes" that are "best enjoyed," complete with a miraculous vision. In its context, this accomplished balladic poem has, nevertheless, an aura of forced simplicity on the poet's part. In contrast to the voices we have recently heard, the priest's is perhaps too innocent, and the poem is perhaps a condescension.

In this it has something in common with "The Two Trees" (37, 48; 38, 134), addressed to the beloved. The poet delivers an occultist sermon, warning her against the external tree, which the poet treats as her reflection in a mirror, in contrast to the holy tree that grows inside her. Like Blake, the poet has turned the upright and upside-down trees of occult tradition on their sides.[8] The internal tree is the tree of romance. It is to be identified with the tree of the ancient bell-branch. It specifically represents spirit, innocence, love, circling movement (perfection), and organic complexity. The external tree is appearance, the beloved's own possibly self-bewitching beauty, and the external world of Irish politics and the bitterness that it evokes in the poet. Why does it do so when the poet is a patriot writing, he says, in Ireland's behalf? Because it tempts his beloved and threatens to keep her apart from him. The poet has brought some of his occultist knowledge to help him in an argument that would, he hopes, influence her. As in "The White Birds," anxiety presses upon him a didactic intent that the beloved, we imagine, might well feel compelled to resist. [I am aware that some people have claimed that this was one of Maud Gonne's favorite poems, but in fact she did resist.]

The penultimate poem of *The Rose* is a dedication not to Ireland, as is the concluding one, already discussed, but to those who have dedicated themselves, like the poet, to Irish folklore. "To Some I have Talked with by the Fire" (38, 49; 39, 136) refers to his poems as "fitful Danaan

---

8. On Blake's two trees, see my *William Blake: A Reading of the Shorter Poems* (Seattle: University of Washington Press, 1963), pp. 35–44.

rhymes." Perhaps this presses a point; they are not all Danaan, but they have been fitful, as I have tried to show, in their movement from attitude to attitude. The poet here acknowledges certain friends and what he has talked about with them. He mentions particularly "the dark folk who live in souls / Of passionate men, like bats in the dead trees" (38, 49; 39, 136). He himself is a passionate man. He has not said that his body harbors a bat-soul, but there *has* been talk of a dead tree or a potentially dead one. The imagery of the previous poems hangs over into this one with ominous overtones suggesting the tormented state of his own being.

The poet also mentions, as subject for talk,

> . . . the wayward twilight companies
> Who sigh with mingled sorrow and content,
> Because their blossoming dreams have never bent
> Under the fruit of evil and of good.

> (38, 49; 39, 136–37)

These are, of course, the Sidhe, whose freedom has been so ambivalently portrayed throughout *Crossways* and *The Rose*. The poet, without any hesitation or obfuscation, now portrays them as ambivalent because they miss life: They do not have to make the choice of one of the two trees. But it works the other way too. The third group that the folklorists have particularly spoken of are those who give men just enough premonition of exalted being that men are made hopelessly full of desire.

Thus we come to the last poem, already discussed. To the question we posed at the beginning—can the poet be a mystic and remain a poet?—the answer is deferred. A somewhat different one is posed and answered: Can the poet write of the rose and remain in the tradition of Irish patriotic verse? The poet declares that he can do that much. Yet there may be a price. Further, the beloved's absorption in political life causes the poet to hate that life in her even as he declares for a version of that life himself.

The Wind Among the Reeds (1899)

The most interesting and thorough book devoted to a single volume of Yeats's poems is Allen Grossman's *Poetic Knowledge in the Early Yeats: A Study of "The Wind Among the Reeds."* [9] Grossman does not consider the poems as composing a fictive order. His interest is in Yeats's development as a poet, and he is therefore concerned with the original 1899 version of

---

9. Allen Grossman, *Poetic Knowledge in the Early Yeats: A Study of "The Wind among the Reeds"* (Charlottesville: University Press of Virginia, 1969).

The Wind among the Reeds, before Yeats made certain revisions, changes of titles, and one most significant change in the poems' ordering. Grossman acknowledges Yeats's attempt to make a single work of his collected poems. For him the structure is "predominantly" autobiographical (p. 11). He has some interesting things to say about the Yeatsian symbol, which he thinks conflicts with Yeats's concept of a poem and must be resolved with it:

> The symbol derives its validity and importance from its relation to an unchanging reality, it can only be integrated into a changing structure as a series of successive discrete closed systems or moments. But in the Yeatsian conception of *the poem* . . . the symbol does indeed become structural. . . . Thus we have the paradox in Yeats's work of a vast, everchanging system of conflicting assertions solved from moment to moment by symbols pitted against the flux. (p. 12)

For a moment Grossman has tried to turn a real conflict, which Yeats actually dramatizes as such, into a paradox; he reveals this in his next sentence, where the paradox has shown itself only as a problem: "One such evidence of this problem is Yeats's vacillation between the simplicity of the one and the energy and disorganizing power of the many within the self." For Grossman, whose interest is finally biographical with emphasis on Yeats's growth as a poet, the conclusion is that Yeats, incapable of a complete mysticism, remained able to sustain "that continuous personal development which is essentially alien to the achieved mystical consciousness" (p. 12). This seems to me a correct view of Yeats's creative life. It explains Yeats's continuing to be a poet. Yeats remained interested in the truths that might be achieved through dramatic performance.

But Grossman is not interested in the *Book* as such a performance. Someone interested in that must study the revised *The Wind Among the Reeds*, the order of the poems, and how Yeats's treatment of symbols like the rose is internalized dramatically as conflict within the *Book*. Perhaps it would be accurate from Grossman's biographical perspective to say that conflict is displaced artistically from the historical Yeats to the central character of the *Book*, the fictive poet who does not utter his own name, Yeats, until more than halfway through his story (203, 190; 210, 406). One of the prolonged events of this story is the poet's emancipating himself from the dominating idea of the "miraculous" symbol (the sense of symbol employed by Grossman)[10] and the adoption of a "secular" stance foreshadowed in "The Fiddler of Dooney," the last poem of *The Wind Among the Reeds*. [It was not always in that position. In 1899 it was approximately in

---

10. Contrasted to the "secular" symbol in my *Philosophy of the Literary Symbolic*, pp. 17–23.

the middle of the text. Clearly, Yeats moved it to the end for emphasis and to suggest a development of some kind.]

Although *The Wind Among the Reeds* begins with an evocation of the Sidhe in "The Hosting of the Sidhe" and we know the Sidhe to have become connected in the poet's mind with the mystical rose and a world out of human time, in the poems that follow we see a series of events that might be expected to presage emancipation from the quest for mystical wisdom under the rose's domination. What change does occur takes place slowly and with great difficulty, expressed in a maddening repetition of error suggesting that the poet is sometimes on the verge of mental collapse. He seems to be searching for or desperately trying out roles, and some may be evasions of reality and thus retrogressions. [Indeed, in the original versions, as Grossman's careful study reminds us, Yeats distributed the speaking of many of the poems among several characters, some of whom he took the trouble to describe in prose comments. Thus poems were spoken by characters named Hanrahan, Robartes, Mongan, Aedh, and Breazil, in addition to the characters who remain: Aengus, an unnamed woman, an old mother, and the fiddler of Dooney. In the poems where titles were changed the speakers are "the lover" or simply "he." It seems to me that this signifies in the revised text Yeats's desire to make the poet acknowledge his own problems more directly.] At bottom, his effort has been all along to discover the appropriate poetic stance toward life and death; and this, though he does not know it completely at the beginning, requires him to separate himself as poet from abstraction and mysticism, in short, all efforts to escape from particulars, including the wish for death and even for the death of his beloved—all the wishes that at times make the reading of *The Wind Among the Reeds* so painful.

That this struggle is of the greatest importance is demonstrated by "The Hosting of the Sidhe" (40, 55; 41, 140). The poet collapses ancient mythological Ireland into the Sidhe, Caoilte being in legend one of Finn's men and not among the Tuatha de Danaan. This host inhabiting the wind calls once again to "empty your heart of its mortal dream." We seem to be back with the happy shepherd and the stolen child. We are back with ambiguity, too, for there is a threat in the beckoning:

> *And if any gaze on our rushing band,*
> *We come between him and the deed of his hand,*
> *We come between him and the hope of his heart.*

(40, 55; 41, 141)

The appearance of the Sidhe in the world of mundane experience merely intensifies a desire that turns out to be frustrated by their intervention. The Sidhe here seem to be sexual and to frustrate not only knowledge but also the consummation of sexual passion. We recognize that Oisin was victim to this sort of beckoning: "And Niamh calling *Away, come away.*"

The poem is seductive, a tour de force of incantation. It is as if the poet has leapt nearly into the Sidhe's position, only to reveal their charming duplicity once again. In "The Everlasting Voices" (41, 55; 42, 141), he is back in place, however, and speaks *to* the Sidhe, not so named but now regarded in their occult mystical rather than Irish mythological forms. Acting the conjurer, he asks for silence from them. He wishes no more to hear the cry of Caoilte or Niamh to mortals but rather wants them to turn their attention in the opposite direction, working their magic of desire on the guardians of heaven, causing those guardians to wander from the gates, presumably so that he may enter. If they were to do this, not only would the gates be open, he would not have to face their frustrating mediation, for their own attention would be elsewhere. One is tempted to think that he would then slip into heaven unseen, as does George III in Byron's *The Vision of Judgment*, a poem whose tone is about as far from this one's as possible. The question of lines 5–7 indicates a certain irritation, the poet complaining that he has had enough and that the Sidhe should realize his need for relief:

> Have you not heard that our hearts are old,
> That you call in birds, in wind on the hill,
> In shaken boughs, in tide on the shore?
>
> (41, 55; 42, 141)

This exasperated view, offered with slight humor, is different from what has preceded it, providing the new possibility that the everlasting voices are not conscious of the problems they create, perhaps not even aware that their acts are callings. The degree of confusion, nay, even incompetence, that this implies is perhaps not quite so far as we had thought from Byron after all. [It is also not so far from the strange, sometimes blundering, sometimes possibly malicious mediators of Yeats's *A Vision*.] It is, in fact, close to the poet's growing tendency to multiply possibilities and increase mystery while gradually calling in question his own capacity to achieve mystical knowledge.

The slight lyric "The Moods" (42, 56; 43, 142) seems an odd moment in the *Book* until we realize that it is meant both to summarize and to introduce. It is called by Grossman Yeats's "first dogmatic poem."[11] I think that this dubious honor must be reserved for "The Two Trees" or even "The White Birds," but the search for Yeats's didacticism is somewhat quixotic if we are willing to accept the notion that all statements in the *Book* are

---

11. Grossman, *Poetic Knowledge*, p. 67.

being made by a character in a context and the *Book*'s authority does not allow us to take any one of them as the *Book*'s dogma. This is, of course, not to say that the poet here does not assert something. He does. First of all, he subsumes the Sidhe and the everlasting voices under the umbrella term "moods." He is attempting to summarize, though arcanely and with the mysterious power of the poem's cryptic wording, what he was trying to evoke in the two previous poems:

> Time drops in decay,
> Like a candle burnt out,
> And the mountains and woods
> Have their day, have their day;
> What one in the rout
> Of the fire-born moods
> Has fallen away?

(42, 56; 43, 142)

Are we asked to consider and answer? This host or rout of moods seems to be the Sidhe as they appear to man: immortal mediators between man in time and timeless truth. Fire-born, the moods represent the immortal passions. Fire, which is passion and which also consumes, is identified frequently with a final conflagration, a burning up of the world and of time. The moods seem to be emanations from some timeless place identified very strongly with pure feeling.

Who has been taken away in the rout of the moods? Stolen children? Goll, perhaps? Fergus, in a sense? All passionate lovers? Or passion itself? Do such people "fall away" as do time, the mountains, and the woods? Or are they immortalized by being taken up by the moods? Very strong value is given here, though with questioning hesitation, to pure passion, which now appears to be the source of all motivation and the state to which everything returns. The hesitancy of the question preserves mystery even as it seems to require the answer, "No one of passionate intensity falls away but is gathered into the eternity of which the moods, sometimes in the form of the Sidhe, are appearances." I deliberately employ some of the poet's later phrases in this answer to point up how this poem foreshadows later concerns as well as summarizes earlier ones. The presence of a question *almost* rhetorical, since there is ambiguity here, expresses the poet's sense of dislocation, enforced later in *The Wind Among the Reeds* by a variety of adopted voices and styles. The ambiguity is advanced further by the poem's having a relaxed tone even as it questions. In "The Hosting of the Sidhe," there was a hint of something frightening which the poet has perhaps not put to rest by the turnabout of "The Everlasting Voices." "The Moods" attempts to level all of the fear, though the poet wishes to preserve mystery, which is for him desirable and not frightening. [Yeats revised the poem to make it end in a question. The *Book's* version maintains conflict. The original leveled both fear and mystery:

> But kindly old rout
> Of the fire-born moods
> You pass not away.]

In any case, the doctrine of "The Moods" is that of essences of emotion, identified with the condition of truth, knowledge, or ultimate spirit. Collected under this term as mediatory between man and these essences are all of the intimations of the immortal world heard in wind and birds, the Sidhe, the everlasting voices, and, of course, the rose, which is reintroduced at this point, in "The Lover tells of the Rose in his Heart" (43, 56; 44, 142), as if the poet were reminding us of its continued symbolic presence.

This poem, which seems simple enough at first glance, raises a severe problem. It is a very curious love poem. All common things, the poet claims, are "wronging" her image, which is blossoming a rose in his heart. But if this is what is happening, is it not her image, being lesser, that wrongs the rose in his heart? And can this glorification of what his imagination produces out of, indeed at the expense of, the beloved's living being be anything finally but a disaster? Actually, it is and already has been, as we shall see in *In the Seven Woods*, where the poet faces the failure of his idealized love affair. The poet declares here that in his heart her image has been etherealized into something superior to her *earthly*, to say nothing of *earthy*, self. It is as if he thinks of his heart as an alchemical crucible that has refined her into pure spirit. What would happen, we might ask, if she should suddenly appear before him in her mundane form? What choice would he make between that form and the rose in his heart? Under this poem's surface its antipoem interferes in the form of life itself, just as the poet asked life to do in "To the Rose upon the Rood of Time." It seems that at best he is making one step backward for every two steps forward. Indeed, we can say that the poet is dramatized here and later as learning by descent.

When the many steps backward occur, the poet tends to adopt a persona, tell a story, and/or return to the haven of folk material, where he hopes that truth is at least latent and where contradictions can be dramatized and embodied. Perhaps we are, by now, a little suspicious of their use as solace. The "truth" of "The Host of the Air" (44, 56; 45, 143) is the ambiguous piping that O'Driscoll hears. It is *both* sad and gay. As we think on this it occurs to us that in the preceding poem the poet was suppressing or blithely unaware of contradiction.

"The Fish" (45, 58; 46, 146), which follows, has been variously interpreted, but it is clearly an allegory of the poet's relation to the beloved, the
fisherman's net being his strategy, including his poems, to capture her. The
poem is a tacit admission that the gambit of the rose has failed. Actually,
the poem is a threat to her that his future readers will think her unkind.
This is not the only statement of this sort that we shall read and is one of
the slight signs of resentment that build to the crisis of *In the Seven Woods*,
where there are efforts to try to understand what has gone wrong.

For a while that matter is suppressed in, or rather displaced to, the
fearful speech of a mother cradling her child in a storm, either symbolic,
natural, or both (46, 58; 47, 146). She expresses the familiar blends of fear
of and attraction to the flying Sidhe, who laugh, she thinks, to appease her
child's fear of the wind. But she also says that they are cold of heart. The
fear is not quite mitigated by the final lines: "O heart the winds have
shaken, the unappeasable host / Is comelier than candles at Mother Mary's
feet" (46, 58; 47, 147). [The poem's title, "The Unappeasable Host," revised by Yeats from "A Cradle Song," intensifies expression of the mother's
fear.] The host is substituted for the mediatory candles of prayer and sup-
plication and is not the host of the Eucharist, the play on the word pointing this up. This unappeasability coupled with comeliness hardly offers
succor equal to that of the Holy Virgin, and it seems odd that the mother,
even under pressure to calm a frightened child, would make such a comparison unless behind it were bitterness. In any case, the decision is for
Ancient Ireland against Holy Ireland, the choice of Oisin.

"Into the Twilight" (47, 59; 48, 147) supports this decision in the poet's
own voice (or is this Mother Eire herself singing another sort of song?) by
declaring the heart's mother to be the ever-young Eire, which is really
Ancient Ireland still present in spirit. The mother of the previous poem
chooses to play that role for her child. This poem tries to move beyond
fear. The heart is called upon to move back past the "nets of wrong and
right," the religion Blake ironically perceived as angelic and which must
be identified as that of modern Holy Ireland, to the "mystical brotherhood" of the natural world. The Fenian brotherhood was not mystical, but
the poet so identifies it, and he also identifies it with nature. At this point,
it is not a pastoral, Wordsworthian Triton who blows a wreathed horn but
instead God blowing a lonely one. It is an odd turn because some Irish
counterpart of the Wordsworthian figure might have been expected. But
the poet, who protests against the rights and wrongs of his culture, is not
finally seeking nature but instead relief from the love and hope that have
so depressed him.

This is a beautiful piece of protest, but it turns out to be inadequate and
unacceptable to its author. Though he next hides himself in the name of

Aengus, the god of love, he speaks of endless search, endless desire, end-less love (48, 59; 49, 149). In the name of Aengus he indicates that he embodies the mood Aengus represents. The poet has apparently been thinking about Blake's poetry, for here, too, the echoes of Blake are strong, particularly "The Mental Traveller" and "The Crystal Cabinet," both with sexual themes. The "nets of right and wrong" of the previous poem have a connection with Blake's "Golden Net," which connects right and wrong with sexual morality and sexual repression. That the fisherman has sought to trap the beloved in a net is but the other side of the coin, not a true contrary to the awful nets of Blake's women. This desire to capture may be part of the poet's trouble. In "The Fish" the poet imagined himself a fisherman in search of the beloved, who is also wisdom. This blending of the beloved with wisdom has been the trouble all along. It is abstracting the beloved from herself. "Into the Twilight" seems to pass beyond any concern for the living beloved. Aengus, however, brings in the opposite. At first he attempts to achieve the state of "mystical brotherhood" with nature because "a fire was in [his] head." When he has caught a trout (this time the fisherman has not a net but a hook), he discovers that it has meta-morphosed into a "glimmering girl," whom he follows into old age with continuing hope that she will lead him to "the silver apples of the moon / The golden apples of the sun." This is a turn of the sort seen before but not with such decisiveness, though the poet has displaced his words to Aengus, confessing to a more secular form of desire.

Perhaps Aengus's persona was too close for comfort. In any case, the poet is next engaged in a series of exploratory poems in different voices. He treats of the sexual opposite, an old mother, who accepts her working lot while the symbolic fire, which is sexuality, desire, youth, and comfort, dies away (49, 60; 50, 150). The contrasting young woman of "The Heart of the Woman" (50, 60; 51, 151) does not describe herself in terms of fire but certainly does so in terms of sexual passion, which is for her a moment beyond life and death, being, in the poet's terms, the moment of an im-mortal mood.

These poems have explored, by opposites and with relative detach-ment, love and age. One sees, however, that in them the poet attempts to will a state of miraculous sexual passion that is beyond right and wrong, life and death, and even love and hope, all opposites offered for transcen-dence in "Into the Twilight" and "The Heart of a Woman." The use of a dramatized voice seems to occur at moments of crisis in the poet's life that are connected with his own desperate passion. The voices are employed to work out a problem.

The particular problem here is one of relation not only to the beloved but to another woman as well. In "The Lover mourns for the Loss of

Love" (51, 61; 52, 152), the poet lets us know that another woman has been present. In desperation she leaves him, convinced that she cannot compete with the beloved's image, which she sees in his heart. She does not see a rose blossomed there, just the image, which is quite enough to send her "weeping away." He laments because he had hoped that in time she would have banished that image.

This marks a renewal of crisis and gives rise to an extremely troubled poem in which the poet imagines himself calling to the beloved, allegorically represented as a white deer with no horns (52, 61; 53, 153). He had been changed into a hunting hound by a wizard while he was "looking another way," presumably in the direction of the woman of the previous poem, who has just left him. He is reduced by these events to a sheer ravenous passion. He has been governed by "hatred and hope and desire and fear." Suddenly changed into the hound, and she imagined as a white deer, he enacts a tableau from "The Wanderings of Oisin," where "now a hornless deer / Passed by us, chased by a phantom hound" (375, 359; 1, 11). It is the Keatsian scene of endless desire. But now there is nothing pleasant about it. In the hound's body, he yet hopes for the traditional last battle in the Valley of the Black Pig which will destroy the world and, in turn, himself and his passion. That the poem is spoken to the deer indicates that it is a desperate cry to the beloved for aid or mercy.

The effort seems to have brought her to him for a short time. In "He bids his Beloved be at Peace" (53, 62; 54, 154), the poet has not lost his vision of tumultuous disaster, but now he speaks to her about this event with foreboding rather than perverse affection. They are together, and he calls to her for protection from shadowy horses and devouring time, which can never be defeated by "vanity of Sleep, Hope, Dream, endless Desire." It is the poet's "Dover Beach," spoken out in a moment of passion; he asks not for them to be "true to one another," as did Matthew Arnold, but instead,

> Beloved, let your eyes half close, and your heart beat
> Over my heart, and your hair fall over my breast,
> Drowning love's lonely hour in deep twilight of rest,
> And hiding their tossing manes and their tumultuous feet.
>
> (53, 62; 54, 154)

These last are the Sidhe as horsemen of the apocalypse. Hidden under the protective tent of his beloved's hair, the poet will receive a moment's respite from anxiety and ambivalent desire for extinction, but no more than that. Violence will surely ensue and destroy all varieties of escape into passion.

"He reproves the Curlew" (54, 62; 55, 155) tells us that the beloved did as he asked, but now it is all merely a troubling memory. The curlew is reproved because it reminds him of her absence; the wind, which gradually takes on a more and more forbidding quality in the *Book* and which was not heard when he was protected by the beloved, cries quite enough evil. Also ominous is how the poet seems to distance the beloved into an archetype or icon of worship in the poems that immediately follow. In "He remembers forgotten Beauty" (55, 62; 56, 155), he speaks of embracing her, but he claims that when he does so he embraces a lost perfect beauty: "the loveliness that has long faded from the world." In "A Poet to his Beloved" (56, 63; 57, 157), he addresses her as "white woman," a sort of goddess to whom he brings poems in ritual tribute. They are poems that, he next says, in "He gives his Beloved certain Rhymes," "[build] a sorrowful loveliness / Out of the battles of old times" (57, 64; 58, 158). They too identify beauty with something from the past, as he has indicated before.

He now faces a beauty that he has identified with both a heroic past and perfection. It is his only protection against a universe he seems now to regard as full of impending doom or at least a forbidding knowledge that will require perhaps an infinite effort to attain. His heart trembles. He is again at a moment of decision, and in "To his Heart, bidding it have no Fear" (58, 64; 59, 158), he encourages himself, as if he were some knight in a dark wood, to go ahead. Toward what? Toward his beloved, who may reject him, and toward wisdom, we presume, which is beauty, which he identifies with her. Wherever he turns, she is the object of desire. He regards the situation as perilous, and indeed it is, because he sets a difficult goal for himself and an incredible ideal for her to live up to.

"The Cap and Bells" (59, 64; 60, 159), which follows this, internalizes in a wish-fulfillment dream the problem of his desire and his knowledge that she is not really his. To this point, his offer of spiritual love, his various forms of encouragement to her, and finally his abasement of himself before her, his treating her as a goddess, have not been successful, except for a period of brief liaison. The poet is now even more hopelessly smitten, even more willing to make her the archetype of all wisdom and beauty. In this dream-poem the jester offers his soul, then his heart. Both rise to her window in the evening, one to speak, the other to sing love. Neither is successful. The jester then offers her his identity in the form of his cap and bells. This she accepts.

The poem has been interpreted as a sexual self-immolation, but that is at best a recognition of an overtone and at worst a case of Freudian symbol hunting. It should first be seen as one of the earliest steps in a dramatic movement toward the notion of the mask that later appears in *The Green Helmet and Other Poems*. What the jester has offered is his appearance, his role in life, the thing he has made himself into; and this, the dream implies, is the most important thing of all. The notion of the mask as role is somewhat ahead of our story and not yet consciously formulated by the poet. We have here only a dream of it, which prophesies the importance of locating true being not in the body or the soul or some combination of the two, but in an achieved role. Only when the role is offered up are the heart and the soul allowed to come into the beloved's presence.

But, of course, the dream, despite its happy ending, results in complete submission, and this may be why we do not discover the idea of role or mask exploited in the poems that immediately follow. Indeed, a violent dream replaces this one. It is so vivid that the poet offers it in the present tense and actually declares it an awakening: "The dews drop slowly and dreams gather: unknown spears / Suddenly hurtle before my dream-awakened eyes" (60, 65; 61, 161). It is a dream of the battle the poet had hoped for in "He Mourns for the Change that has come upon Him and his Beloved, and longs for the End of the World." Here the submission is not *in* the dream, nor is it to the beloved. Rather, it is to the master of the keepers of the gate of heaven, who in "The Everlasting Voices" were asked to abandon their posts. This dream marks a sudden return of the purely spiritual, which imposes itself after moments of more or less sexual concern. It appears that the poet would have us see these two dreams dissolve the worlds of sexual and spiritual passion into each other, but the latter dream seems to act as a suppressor of the former.

Certainly the two dream poems offer different moods in both the mundane and the esoteric senses of "mood" special to the *Book*. Under the guise of "lover," the poet next apologizes for his many moods ("The Lover asks Forgiveness because of his Many Moods," 61, 66; 62, 162). He declares that these moods, which make him appear to have an "importunate heart," are really the archetypal sources of poetry, a great memory that he has brought to expression. Central to such moods is "murmuring and longing."

Then the poet reveals yet a third dream, which is one of longing to recapture the moment of the protective tent of hair that he once experienced:

> I cried in my dream, *O women, bid the young men lay*
> *Their heads on your knees, and drown their eyes with your hair,*
> *Or remembering hers they will find no other face fair*
> *Till all the valleys of the world have been withered away.*
> ("He tells of a Valley full of Lovers," 62, 67; 63, 163)

The young men to whom he cried are a displacement of himself. He calls to women for relief from the torment of his desire for his beloved. But we remember from an earlier poem that one such woman has gone weeping away, that the solace he seeks here did not work then. It will not now. In "He Tells of the Perfect Beauty" (63, 67; 64, 164), he as much as admits this, once again identifying the lost love with perfection, which puts both the solace and the lost love out of reach. "He hears the Cry of the Sedge" (64, 67; 65, 165) summarizes. She is indeed out of reach, but not merely as perfect beauty. The poet is in despair at his failure to win her:

> I wander by the edge
> Of this desolate lake
> Where wind cries in the sedge:
> *Until the axle break*
> *That keeps the stars in their round,*
> *And hands hurl in the deep*
> *The banners of East and West,*
> *And the girdle of light is unbound,*
> *Your breast will not lie by the breast*
> *Of your beloved in sleep.*
>
> (64, 67; 65, 165)

If we had questioned the connection in the poet's mind between his own situation and that of the Keatsian lover of "La Belle Dame Sans Merci," this should eliminate any skepticism: We recall Keats's lines, "The sedge has withered from the lake, / And no birds sing," and surely the poet is "alone and palely loitering," apparently unable to act. Not birds but the wind cries a song that the poet now has the temerity to translate into the most stark language. It appears that finally he must accept the reality that the wind cries. The alternatives to this are both regressive: return to the mystical or continuation of a hopeless, debilitating passion.

There is a pause before the battle involving these three choices is once again joined, for the poet cannot escape mulling over these themes. He expresses his faithfulness to her in the only way left to him, a poem. In "He thinks of Those who have spoken Evil of his Beloved" (65, 68; 66, 166), words alone may not be professed certain good, as the happy shepherd claimed, but there is a declaration that their ideality made from "a mouthful of air" will outlast those who have criticized her. The poem contrives to be one of comfort; beneath its surface is perhaps resentment at her failing to appreciate his own sort of magical conjuring power.

The poet is now plunged back into the regressive effort to dissolve his mystical and his sexual desires into each other. In "The Blessed" (66, 68; 67, 66), he presents to us an apparently ascetic Irish wise man speaking of a knowledge beyond knowledge that is blessedness. In "The Secret Rose" (67, 69; 68, 169), he calls once more on the mystical rose. The last time that this happened he implored it to keep its distance even as he asked it to

advance toward him. Now he seems not at all concerned about its prox-
imity and the danger to poetry that he earlier saw in it. This indicates an
intensification of the struggle beyond what we have seen before. It includes a strong effort at mystical identification with Irish heroic mythology. There is also a continued effort, carried on under great stress, to believe that mystical and sexual desire can be conflated. The poem ends with
hope for apocalyptic destruction, the appearance of the ultimate wind that
will destroy everything. This wind has, of course, been blowing lightly all
through *The Wind among the Reeds*, carrying unsettling messages of frustration.

Now the pressure of the poet's frustrating task generates a desire for
destruction under its aegis. In "Maid Quiet" (68, 70; 69, 171), he must
turn to lamentation over departure of a lover, perhaps the one with whom
he had tried to forget the beloved. He is puzzled by his calmness at the
time, for now the words that he remembers she spoke disturb him terribly.
Then, we surmise, his own knowledge that his beloved's image dominated
his heart prevented him from being able to respond to the woman's words.
Now those words thunder in his heart, tormenting him by reminding him
of his passion and his failure with both women.

The pain that this caused the poet is next considered at a greater distance in "The Travail of Passion" (69, 70; 70, 172), which he imagines as
spoken by unnamed creatures apparently both sexual and spiritual. We
find here a curious effort by the poet to speak in the voices of moods which
or whom he imagines having invaded him in the form of sexual passion
and who describe themselves as "immortal." They treat their descent from
heaven as if the descent were a crucifixion, reminding us of the rose upon
the rood of time. In the last three lines comes the abrupt turn to sexual
passion, yet mixed with intimations of the rose:

> We will bend down and loosen our hair over you,
> That it may drop faint perfume, and be heavy with dew,
> Lilies of death-pale hope, roses of passionate dream.
>
> (69, 71; 70, 172)

This ambiguous treatment implies that any time sexual passion occurs the
moods descend and enact the Passion of Christ and that the descent is the
Passion. This is certainly the poet's ultimate effort to conflate the religious
and the sensual, but he looks away from the bold general assertion and,
instead, returns at once to the more mundane theme of the loss of his beloved. Yet he deliberately obfuscates the theme by insisting in his title that
he is speaking to a "friend," not the one person who is more than a friend.
The poem, "The Lover pleads with his Friend for Old Friends" (70, 71;
71, 172), can be read as a veiled threat, implying that she will regret having

left him. He appeals to her vanity: When she is older, she will still be beautiful to him, though, it is implied, not to others. This theme is carried into the next poem ("The Lover speaks to the Hearers of his Songs in Coming Days," 71, 71; 72, 173). Those who will read his work in the future will be women whose thoughts of his love poems will disrupt their prayers. He asks them to "pray for all that sin I wove in song," thus to rescue him and his beloved from purgatory.

What sin is this? Or do poets *always* sin in song? Perhaps the poet's effort in "The Travail of Passion" to join spirituality and sexuality in the ambiguous word "passion" is doomed to failure and is itself the sin the poet fears. A decision he has been putting off is required. In pleading with the elemental powers in the next poem, the poet steps back from the entirely Christian (specifically Catholic) imagery he has been using and prays to the forces of *this* world, as a magician might, calling on air, water, and fire to protect his beloved ("The Poet pleads with the Elemental Powers," 72, 72; 73, 174). Yet this secular piety is immediately replaced by the startling "He wishes his Beloved were Dead" (73, 72; 74, 175).

If the poet's thoughts are truly these, perhaps that is the reason he anticipates a place for himself in purgatory, a penance for such thoughts, though this does not explain why the distant beloved is there with him, unless the scene in purgatory is a perverse wish fulfillment.

This poem and those that have preceded it indicate that the poet has indulged himself in an impossible fiction and that he now pays the price for it in violent vacillations of attitude. The fiction has been that his vision of the beloved can be fully grounded in something entirely other than human sexual desire. In first calling for her protection and then wishing for her death, with its overtones of the famous quotation from Villiers de L'Isle-Adam's *Axel*, "As for living, our servants can do that for us," he forces the fiction to its bitter extreme. He is willing to do imaginative violence to her (and perhaps to himself) in order to keep intact the fictive role he insists that she play. His celebration of her and his offering of himself and of his poems threaten to become domination, even destruction. We have watched the accumulation of bad faith and vacillation that has led to this. His pleading with the elemental powers, for example, was a pleading to protect the fiction he has attempted to make of her.

The poet as well has watched, and this is his saving grace. In "He wishes for the Cloths of Heaven" (74, 73; 75, 176), which follows, he would make amends, though somewhat obsequiously but, I think, in good faith bolstered by a serious effort to rethink his situation in what follows and concludes *The Wind Among the Reeds*. One might say, though, that the poem, lovely tribute to her that it is, is also yet another appeal to protect the dreams of her that have made it so difficult for him to see her clearly.

Yet the poem marks a moment that steps back from the extremes of the preceding ones. "He thinks of his Past Greatness when a Part of the Constellations of Heaven" (75, 73; 76, 177) is extreme in its way, but it does mark an attempt to step back from the desires for annihilation and his beloved's death. Ultimately this attempt fails because of the intensity of the poet's depression. He is far worse off than the philosophical Fergus, though not nearly as far gone as the mad Goll. Fergus, we recall, journeyed through various incarnations to a tragic understanding. But Fergus perceived the truth without the egoistical involvement with it that this poet has. Fergus discovered that the Druid's bag of dreams contained "great webs of sorrow." These sorrows remained unnamed, and Fergus seemed philosophically detached from passion; but we know the poet's sorrows, and there is desperation in them. "He thinks of his Past Greatness," following expression of a desire to possess heaven's cloths, sends the poet meditating on the wizardry that might be the condition of such ownership.

The poem marks a severe crisis in that it presents an attempt to step into a persona representing the detachment or disinterest of philosophical knowledge, but the attempt fails. It is also nostalgic, indulging momentarily in the fiction of having passed through all identities, as did Fergus, only finally to become a man and reach the knowledge he now has, the one piece of knowledge that blots out all else:

> I became a man, a hater of the wind,
> Knowing one, out of all things, alone, that his head
> May not lie on the breast nor his lips on the hair
> Of the woman that he loves, until he dies.
> O beast of the wilderness, bird of the air,
> Must I endure your amorous cries?
>
> (75, 73; 76, 177)

He hates the wind because he now knows that when it cried in the sedge (in an earlier poem) it spoke the truth, that this truth is the answer to the question that has always really possessed him and has made everything else of secondary importance. It is only as a man at the end of all his transmigrations that he learns what he had already heard but not accepted as the message in the wind. There is bitterness and resentment against nature here. At the end of *The Wind Among the Reeds* the poet has turned unequivocally against the wind, now definitely a sinister force symbolizing all that his hope to spiritualize his desire has brought him to. In "The Hosting of the Sidhe" the wind was equivocally presented as the vehicle, perhaps even the miraculous presence, of the mediating Sidhe. It is now identified only with his frustration both in love and in the search for knowledge and also in the attempt to join them. Nature is now suddenly only nature, not a crucified rose or spirit in a lower degree. The sounds he hears remind him of the uncomplicated sexuality of animals and birds and, of course, of the complications of man's. Rather than wish directly for his beloved's death, he now recognizes that life will always include bitter knowledge.

This is an abrupt change and recognition, and it requires the search for another ideal. One senses that there *must* be change, that the tension of his self-delusion about the beloved *must* be broken.

In the position of emphasis that it assumes in the *Book*, "The Fiddler of Dooney" (76, 74; 77, 178) represents a turning away from much that has gone before. [This last poem of *The Wind Among the Reeds* was shifted to its position after the first appearance of the volume. Originally, it had been somewhere in the middle.] Unlike any persona the poet has yet presented, the fiddler is a happy, thoughtless person. Identified with folk customs and contrasting himself as a sort of artist to his two brothers, who are priests, he claims heaven as a reward for all three of them. His route there is secular. His thoughtlessness leaves him concerned only with performance. His book is a secular book of songs, perhaps an antithetical book, as against the religious book of his brothers. He is, to use one of Yeats's favorite later words, his own mask. He is content with his role, and he remains with the world. He seems to have escaped the poet's frustrations, though he remains within the realm of desire, where he leads a secular dance. The dancers he identifies with the sea, which is life; and goodness he identifies with merriment "save by an evil chance."

The poet views this fiddler from the outside. He has not himself achieved the role he dramatizes here. But he has been able to formulate it. This small victory—but a step toward self-definition—makes possible some movement. The fiddler remains an ideal that is perhaps too dangerously sentimental in itself, but a step has been taken toward psychic recovery. (The poem is certainly much more important when read in the *Book* than when read outside it.) Yet with a powerful, self-directed honesty from which the *Book* of Yeats's poems taken as a whole does not shrink, the next step is backward before forward. The result will be, in the space before *In the Seven Woods*, severe depression, as if the whole experience has stripped the poet of whatever role he had managed to make out of his misery. He next attempts, with only moderate success, an analogy to the role of the fiddler, a storytelling role, in two longer poems.

"The Old Age of Queen Maeve" (1903)

The crucial poems of *In the Seven Woods*, which soon follow, reveal the toll that all of this has taken on the poet. We have seen a series of events that might have been expected to presage the poet's gradual emancipation from the quest for mystical wisdom under the rose's domination. What change has occurred has taken place slowly and with great difficulty, expressed in a maddening repetition of error suggesting that the poet has been sometimes on the verge of collapse. *In the Seven Woods* begins to tell the story of a life rebuilt. But first the poet endeavors, if not exactly to be a fiddler of happy songs, at least to be a singer of tales, a sort of Irish bard.

This effort does not result in merriment or dancing. "The Old Age of Queen Maeve" (376, 389; 78, 180), a turn to Irish mythological materials, is yet given a frame that is a transparent allegory of the poet's desire to move his beloved. "A certain poet in outlandish clothes" sings in a Byzantine lane to his stringed instrument. He gathers a crowd of listeners, yet at the outset seems to be singing to someone hidden behind a window above. Indeed, the singer, whose subject is Queen Maeve and Aengus, the love god, soon admits that his real subject is someone else:

> O unquiet heart,
> Why do you praise another, praising her,
> As if there were no tale but your own tale
> Worth knitting to a measure of sweet sound?

> (376, 390; 78, 181)

He must goad himself back to the story of Aengus and Maeve, who is in some way the beloved in disguise, as is the listener behind the window. This beloved, however, is not the Pre-Raphaelite beauty of the poems we have just read. The poet has redrawn her in Maeve's image:

> She could have called over the rim of the world
> Whatever woman's lover had hit her fancy,
> And yet had been great-bodied and great-limbed,
> Fashioned to be the mother of strong children;
> And she'd had lucky eyes and a high heart,
> And wisdom that caught fire like the dried flax,
> At need, and made her beautiful and fierce,
> Sudden and laughing.

> (376, 389; 78, 181)

The "unquiet heart" passage, quoted above, follows, and this same heart speaks out later in *In the Seven Woods* without the same elaborate disguise. "The Old Age of Queen Maeve" ends with the singer addressing the beloved as an old friend; he goes so far as to insist that it is not he alone who interprets all heroic stories to be about her. All heroic stories *are* about her.

The tale tells of Aengus's desire for the daughter of Caer and his enlisting Maeve's aid in a subterfuge to gain her. Aengus is, of course, immortal;

Maeve and Caer's daughter are mortal. Once again we have before us the theme of immortal desire for mortal beauty, as in "The Wanderings of Oisin." What we had seen for a while was the poet's mortal desire for the immortal rose under the guise of the beloved, but this effort was plagued with difficulty. The fact is that the beloved has always been quite mortal indeed, quite physically desirable. Now she is described in the guise of a young Maeve as "fashioned to be a mother of strong children." The etherealization of the beloved under the pressure of frustration at her failure to respond fully to him is abandoned, and the poet speaks out with greater assurance in a "secular" role. But some things have not been simplified. There is a cost of some self-assurance; he recognizes that his youth has been lost in unrealistic expectations, that his will is not sufficient to transform things. The beloved is now "friend of these many years." In the early poetry we were told how their love had aged. We were not convinced: The poet had been speaking melodramatically and evasively. But by now time really *has* passed, and he acknowledges it with a new form of address. As we shall see, however, to do so does not help him as much as he perhaps had hoped, for she remains to him more than a friend, as she was when he first so addressed her in "A Lover pleads with his Friend for Old Friends."

"Baile and Aillinn" (1903)

In the second longer poem, which follows, the poet retells the old tale of Baile and Aillinn (377, 398; 79, 188), but again he dwells on his own situation. The theme involves two lovers kept apart in life by the sort of "evil chance" mentioned by the fiddler of Dooney. Yet this evil chance is turned into eternal good luck and has indeed been so engineered by the god Aengus, for the lovers are united in death. Of them the poet writes:

> *Their love was never drowned in care*
> *Of this or that thing, nor grew cold*
> *Because their bodies had grown old.*

(377, 397; 79, 189)

The poet steps away from the story from time to time to comment generally on it. The tone of these speeches is suddenly far more mature. Again the wind is the villain or the vehicle of frustrated desire, but now the poet seeks to see things as they are:

> *O wandering birds and rushy beds,*
> *You put such folly in our heads*
> *With all this crying in the wind;*

> *No common love is to our mind,*
> *And our poor Kate or Nan is less*
> *Than any whose unhappiness*
> *Awoke the harp-strings long ago.*

(377, 398; 79, 190)

The theme of impossible desire remains, but it is now seen in terms of folly:

> *Yet they that know all things but know*
> *That all this life can give us is*
> *A child's laughter, a woman's kiss.*

(377, 398; 79, 190)

These things are acknowledged as important in themselves, and they are not treated as sad in themselves. Baile and Aillinn are imagined as together in the familiar world of passion beyond mortality, but that world and their story are treated more or less as fictions. The poet's commentary expresses the real.

It is told us now that poets say there sprung from the graves of the two lovers an apple and a yew tree that intertwined their branches. The poets who have maintained this old story apparently insist on keeping their lovers in some way in this world—as apple and yew and as vehicles of the poets' secular love tales:

> They wrote on tablets of thin board,
> Made of the apple and the yew,
> All the love stories that they knew.

(377, 402; 79, 197)

The world of the wind can cry Aillinn's beauty, tempting man to that other world, but the poet asserts his freedom from its crying and from the cry of the birds, whose cries, we know, he deems amorous but other than human. They can cease to cry now. His beloved is their equal, and she is also real, though he admits that all lovers would, if they could, love as Baile and Aillinn did.

The poet cannot finally be a bard of the old school. He cannot escape self-expression, but self-expression, he is learning, can take more or less mature forms. To express the struggle for self-control is to be more knowing and perhaps to escape being the hapless victim of impossible desire.

3

Crises of Love and Responsibility

In the Seven Woods (1904)

The stories the poet has told are poetical, not historical, idealizations; we have seen these idealizations take a somewhat different direction from those of the earlier poems. They have suggested a stronger grasp on reality; something apparently connected with this change has taken place in the space between these poems and the beginning of *In the Seven Woods.* Events causing severe depression seem to have occurred, as if the poet has been stripped of whatever role he has managed to create out of the misery of his love. *In the Seven Woods* begins in the shock of having put aside certain illusions on which he has foolishly fed.

The poet is now at Coole. It is August of 1902. The title poem sets a scene of apparent contentment. At least it so asserts, but it is a momentary and superficial contentment. The poet says that he has "put away / The unavailing outcries and the old bitterness that empty the heart" (77, 77; 80, 198). This marks a recognition that his previous work can be so characterized, and he implies that it is all behind him. At Coole he has brought order to himself. He has even momentarily laid aside his personal sadness, his old regret for the disappearance of ancient Celtic Ireland, and his disgust at the ascension of the new English king.

But the poet has, nevertheless, a certain anxiety. "Quiet" is personified as wandering "laughing and eating her wild heart." This is hardly the quiet of contentment that the poet claims to enjoy, but rather is a distressed, wild, even perhaps mad Quiet, gone to cannibalistic lengths to silence the heart, which we soon learn has, after all, not been silenced. Furthermore, something impends in the image of a Great Archer, imagined in the sky, who is but waiting to shoot. The poem's assertions are plagued by their opposites. The suggestion is of a deep psychic unrest.

The Great Archer's arrow is not, however, shot. Rather, in the next poem, "The Arrow" (78, 77; 81, 199), the poet remembers that he had made an arrow from the thought of the beauty of his beloved, now directly addressed. Playing his own Cupid, he has aimed his thought at her but has accidentally shot himself. Time has passed since this occurred. The wound—indeed, the impaling thought—remains as a remembrance of her former beauty. The poet declares that this beauty is not apparent to men today and is now replaced, he claims, by a "kinder beauty," though he admits that he could weep for the disappearance of the old. These remarks support the idea that the calm quiet of the first poem of the group was indeed but a surface quiet. It is significant that the poet does not weep but only declares that he *could*. The depression is too deep for easy purgation, the situation too prolonged for tears. The poet has described the sorrow as "made out of a wild thought," implying that his act was reckless. It also seems to have been almost comically incompetent. Whether or not the statement is self-castigation is not clear and probably is not clear to the poet, who is seriously querying his own past actions, so costly to his psychic and physical well-being.

The friend who speaks in the next poem, "The Folly of being Comforted" (79, 78; 82, 199), is unnamed, but it may be inferred that it is Lady Gregory.[1] The beloved's aging is still the subject, but the poet's stance has changed somewhat under pressure of the conversation that the poem recalls. Like the new beauty of the beloved, this friend is kind, and she begins in a patient way to reason with the poet about his feelings. Her language is deliberately prosy and has the character of a friendly lesson or an old precept from a wise elder: Time heals all wounds because one becomes wiser with time. Who is to become wiser, the beloved or the poet, is not specified, perhaps deliberately, by the friend. She recognizes that he cannot now see it this way.

Indeed so. Now the poet divides himself into his heart and his detached, observing, apparently rational self. The heart, in its resistance to kind advice (and in a show of stubborn, courtly faithfulness to the beloved

1. As the *Book* proceeds, the poet becomes less reticent about naming actual historical people. What does this do to my claim that the *Book* is a fiction? These historical figures are drawn into the fiction as characters, much as in a historical novel. In this respect it is not different from Moore's *Hail and Farewell* or Joyce's *Ulysses* or any other fictive text that locates itself in some historically recognized era or place. But I go farther and claim that as the book proceeds and the poet names himself in "To be carved on a Stone at Thoor Ballylee" (203, 190; 210, 406), the book becomes an autobiographical fiction, though the need to distinguish author, the authority of the text, and the poet, now William Yeats, remains.

We infer the friend here to be Lady Gregory, there being sufficient indications that this is so. The case of Maud Gonne, the beloved, is more complicated. She is mentioned by name only once and then in a late poem ("Beautiful Lofty Things," 334, 303; 343, 578). The connection back to the beloved is never spelled out, there being great reticence about naming her, which is itself part of the story.

or perhaps to a vision of the proper Petrarchan stance), goes so far as to qualify or perhaps even deny the observation made in "The Arrow": It declares that the beloved is more beautiful than ever, not merely that her beauty is kinder. Hers is now a noble beauty. In the concluding couplet, the observer side of the poet sadly addresses the heart: "O heart! O heart! if she'd but turn her head, / You'd know the folly of being comforted" (79, 78; 82, 200). The observer is presumably the rational one, the one who *can* know. The heart, it appears, can but feel. However, this rational one has been moved in his observation and recognizes that his knowing is not merely rational. If she would "but turn her head" (toward him, acknowledging his heart?), in that moment the heart would *know*, not just feel, that the friend's comfort was for nothing. The beloved's gaze would destroy all argument, and the poor heart, overcoming the opposition of knowing to feeling, would be hopelessly enveloped in this passionate knowledge. The rational observer speaks here in a lamenting, resigned, wise tone. Part of the reason, he implies, that the heart does not know everything right now is that it is anxious, in a passion, and a little irritated at the friend and perhaps at the split in himself. This accounts for the vociferousness of the heart's protest and for the observer's repetition in response: "O heart! O heart!" But further, we notice that the division between the reason and the heart breaks down. It just isn't that simple, and an important part of the poem is the attribution of deep feeling to the reasoning self, as if the passion were so powerful that even the reason is captured by it.

There is an important technical development here toward dialogue and drama, both external and internal, the beginning of a deliberate identification of poetry with the dramatic in the *Book* as a whole, and we shall see more of it. Indeed, this development is a major part of the poet's story.

Meanwhile, we recognize that the heart has insisted on building a new image—that of nobility—for the beloved. Will the observer be able to control this image, or will it too wreak its havoc on the whole poet? Has the heart relapsed into the lovesickness of the earlier version of romance, or can this apparent hyperbolic tendency be channeled into another mode of behavior more akin, let us say, to that of the Renaissance courtier? This issue is in doubt, particularly since the division between reason and heart has been called in question and the reason's capacity to control apparently lessened.

The poet returns to the theme of the arrow in "Old Memory" (80, 78; 83, 201). Here our Cupid directs the aim of his thought to "her," taking up her new image of nobility. It is evening, and he feels the wound in his marrow still. He directs this second arrow more carefully than he did the first, however, and at the outset it has the quality of a barb. Her nature is that of the special nobility that he has previously praised in Queen Maeve.

It is this, not the apocalyptic archer, that "might call up a new age." But he himself, the poet claims, can take half the credit for this wonder, for he half created her strength over the years. Now bitterness overcomes him, and he discovers that all his words of creative praise have come to nothing. She has still not turned her head. The poem changes abruptly in midline; rather than proceeding to its couplet close as a sonnet, it ends in a sentence with an off-rhyme. The gesture of these lines dismisses the complaint uttered in the first part: "When we have blamed the wind we can blame love." The wind as a vehicle of mystical causality built up in the earlier poems is dismissed here. It now seems but a part of nature and chance. Love, simply love, is the culprit. But this move does not dispel the poet's bitterness or resentment toward the beloved. He characterizes her with malicious obliquity as a child who has strayed away. The bitter conclusion and covert accusation are also childishly wishful. Children may return, chastened; they are supposed to be under adult control; and they must not, being children, be treated too harshly. The poem is condescending and wishful at the same time, and the condescension is bitter.

That the bitterness is deep is emphasized in "Never give all the Heart" (81, 79; 84, 202). The poet's arsenal of arrows seems now exhausted. The whole situation collapses yet again. He characterizes passionate women as dissatisfied with the certainty of a lover's love. For the moment, he imagines his error to have been his unquestionable faithfulness. He proposes that such women know that loveliness is radically temporal and ephemeral and that their treatment must assume this. Such women, he imagines, are like actors. A play does not last forever. It involves a role. "Play" is ambiguous; it can be a game. One can give one's heart to the play and not hopelessly lose it, as he, not a player, has.

We find here intimations of the dramatic mask, which is later developed; the point is that the poet does not seem to have a sufficient mask, while others apparently do. The poem is an effort to generalize from the poet's experience, to establish some principle by which to bring himself out of his situation. He seems to be offering general advice to lovers; he would play the wise role that his friend did in "The Folly of being Comforted," but the advice here is far different and full of self-pity. Not to have masked himself in a role, he implies, was a mistake, and yet he seems to feel that his own honesty and innocence were virtues not appreciated. But was he not playing a role after all? The mannered nature of so many of the early poems suggests that he was, but that the role was an inadequate one adopted from without, an imitation, so to speak. Perhaps the truth is that there are always masks and that he must come to know this. But has the beloved really been playing a part? Has she been more self-aware than he? Is his theory of play merely an illusion? Has he forced a purely male imaginative vision of behavior on women as a rationalization for his difficulties? These are questions that he does not face.

In "The Withering of the Boughs" (82, 79; 85, 203), the poet describes the result of his own allegedly naive, unmasked sincerity. It is not the wind, object of his hatred earlier (a sort of scapegoat), that has withered the trees; it is his own open self-expression. This knowledge has come to him in a dream of witches, Danaan dancers, and a wandering pair of lovers, a king and a queen. The poem is ambiguous and unsettled, for while it seems to formulate a clear reason for his failure—the forthright assertion of his dreams—he contrives to state that this new wisdom itself arrives as a result of dreams, forthrightly asserted.

The aura of withering and dying love is extended into the next poem, "Adam's Curse" (83, 80; 86, 204), but the scene and imagery suggest some psychic recovery. It is an effort to make a more subtle explanation for failure than the one he has just offered. "The Withering of the Boughs" has seemed a regression that develops naturally out of his expression of the utter loss of his heart in "Never give all the Heart." [Actually, Yeats broke chronology here, apparently to gain this effect. "Never give all the Heart" was written in 1903, "The Withering of the Boughs" in 1900, before any of the previous poems of this section were written.] In "Adam's Curse," it is the love relationship that is described as having slowly died. In "The Withering of the Boughs," nature sympathetically responded to his mistaken actions; in "Adam's Curse," nature is part of the scene on which the actors of the poem gaze, and the waning of day seems to reflect their state. When we read this poem in its place, we suspect that its more or less dialogical form indicates its importance, for dialogical form tends more and more to signal the most important moments in the *Book.*

"Adam's Curse" begins with a scene of three people—the poet, the beloved, and another woman, a friend. The scene is appropriately evening, and the poet distances the scene in time by locating it at "one summer's end," though it seems to have been quite recent. The talk reported begins in a desultory way, with the poet speaking about the difficulties of poetic composition: One's hard work must *appear* to have been momentary and easy. The friend implies that women have always known about this problem because they "must labour to be beautiful." Actually, this talk has not been as desultory as it seems. The poet's remarks have been purposively directed toward the beloved, to whom the whole poem is implicitly addressed. He is defending himself against (and attacking the views belonging to) the world of action, with which he identifies her. There remains here some malice and resentment built up in the previous poems against a world that he now thinks has been his rival in love. The friend is deliberately described as "beautiful," "mild," and, by the implications of this last adjective, different from the beloved. She also seems wise in her remark; at least, the poet would like to think her so. His response to her is also a statement to the silent beloved. He describes obliquely his own labor as a lover under the guise of lovers of the past who were schooled in courtesy; but in a show of ennui he declares that to behave today in this way (as he has) is "an idle trade enough." His effort has failed, and he is clearly depressed and showing off his depression, in the form of an indirect accusation, to his beloved.

Moments of quiet follow as twilight comes and a worn moon appears, reflecting the state of their love. The romantic image here emphasizes the poet's subjectivity. He declares that he had at this moment a thought for her ears only: He had tried to love her "in the old high way of love," and they had become "weary-hearted." Why had it gone wrong? No answer is offered, but the poem at this stage sets off speculation. The poet has claimed to have striven to love her according to a certain traditional role, but this is not exactly what an earlier poem had said. There the problem was that he had been but himself, had given all of himself, had held nothing back for the play. But here he claims he had striven to achieve a role. The role, as he now remembers it, is that of a courtly lover. The Renaissance handbook for such behavior is Castiglione's *Courtier*, where "recklessness" (as *sprezzatura* is sometimes translated) is requisite for the courtier in all things. The lover has certainly been reckless with his heart, as we have seen, but this was hardly Castiglione's notion of recklessness, for Castiglione's is a *studied* recklessness, a discipline to be learned like that of the poet or of the achievement of female beauty, as described by the friend. It is a dramatic mask. In "Adam's Curse," the poet attempts in hindsight to transform one recklessness into another. The "old high way of love" is a role he seems either to have failed to achieve or to have achieved in the wrong way. But he does not abandon the notion of poetic and courtierlike behavior that is the subject of discussion here; we shall see it again in elaborate development. What we recognize is that it now appears as a movement beyond the naive idea of either an unmasked or, if that is actually impossible, an inadequately masked lover. There is more than a hint that the world must be a world of actors. Drama is coming to seem the model for life, the authority here being a Wildean notion of life as an imitator of art. Whether an active or a more sophisticated *choice* of a dramatic mask would have won the beloved is a question not asked.

It has always seemed to me that the next poem in the *Book*, even when read apart from the *Book*, has an undercurrent of bitterness, though it has always, as far as I know, been read as a straight patriotic poem. [Yeats placed this poem, written in 1894, among poems written in 1902 and 1903.] Following "Adam's Curse," it invites being read as a poem of a parallel bitterness. The poem is "Red Hanrahan's Song about Ireland" (84, 81; 87, 206), and in this location it appears to be about another bitter and exhausting love affair, that of the Irish with Cathleen ni Houlihan. That the poet should make this parallel is a measure of his deep feeling. We learn later, of course, that the beloved is a radical Irish patriot, and he has resented this Ireland as a rival, even an unnatural female rival in this case. "Red Hanrahan's Song about Ireland" is also about what love has wrought over long years. Each of the three stanzas of the poem takes the same form, suggesting description of either a dogged commitment of the spirit or a stubborn fanaticism or both. We are not allowed to decide whether or not the bitterness that the context invites us to read into this poem is caused by the poet's sense of a worthy political commitment frustrated by ill luck or a fanaticism that has grown in excess of anything to be gained. There had, of course, been a long history of commitment to Cathleen ni Houlihan in Ireland. The bitterness of the poem could be interpreted free of this context as simply against the traditional enemy, England, but here the poem seems equally to suggest bitterness at what this commitment has internally wrought. The theme arises later, of course, in "Easter 1916" (193, 180; 200, 391) and governs the way that poem develops. The juxtaposition with "Adam's Curse" suggests that the poet's unmasked or insufficiently masked devotion to the beloved mirrors and is mirrored by the devotion of Irish patriots to Cathleen, who is treated with a certain ambiguity, being powerfully idealized virtually as a religious icon (perhaps an unapproachable ideal) with similar dire results, from folly perhaps to madness or to the mental exhaustion and illness suggested by the conditions under which this section of poems began. I cannot think of another poem in the *Book* the placement of which so influences our reading. [Maud Gonne, of course, played the title role in Yeats's *Cathleen ni Houlihan*.]

If we take "Red Hanrahan's Song about Ireland" to be bitterly ironical, it is not at all difficult to move to "The Old Men admiring Themselves in the Water" (85, 82; 88, 208), but even if we attribute less irony to its predecessors, this poem continues the theme of idealization and its discontents: ". . . the old, old men say, 'All that's beautiful drifts away / Like the waters'," the term "admiring" being an ironic reference to the myth of Narcissus. The parallel, of course, is to the beauty that the poet's love for the beloved once had or was thought to have had.

Beauty is now regarded as transient, in contrast to the ideal, eternal beauty of the earlier poems. The poet tacitly calls in question the arguments his heart has previously made for his beloved's persisting beauty. In "Under the Moon" (86, 82; 89, 209), he also calls in question his earlier use of myth and legend, heretofore identified with eternal beauty. In the past he had gone to these, he thought, to renew the real world. Now, in a

mood burdened by the sense of loss through time's erosion, he rejects
them. As he has previously admitted, when he had written of the old legends he had really been writing about the beloved. He recognizes also that
myths and legends are unbearably prophetic when they tell of betrayed
lovers. The scene of the waning moon from "Adam's Curse" is evoked:

> Because of something told under the famished horn
> Of the hunter's moon, that hung between the night and the day,
> To dream of women whose beauty was folded in dismay,
> Even in an old story, is a burden not to be borne.
>
> (86, 83; 89, 210)

Under the worn moon on that earlier evening, something must have been
said that was left unreported in "Adam's Curse." The moon in these poems
is a dominating force, as if the poet were trying to discover reasons for the
betrayal of love by recourse to some theory of fate. He and the beloved are
moonstruck, he seems to imply.

But he cannot give her up, and in "The Ragged Wood" he addresses her
passionately, calling her to the wood's edge, where he will drive away all
other lovers. They are unreal; only he and the beloved, he declares, have
truly loved. This seems to be the final dismissal of the myths and legends
of lovers on which the poet has tried to model his relationship to the beloved. It is accomplished dangerously, not only by dispatching the old stories but also by declaring for a new myth of their own uniqueness. The
new myth, however, cannot hold. Too much truth was uttered in "Adam's
Curse," to say nothing of its title; the waning of love becomes the theme
once again. True, in the remembrance of their love in "O do not Love Too
Long" (88, 83; 91, 211), the myth of uniqueness nearly dominates:

> Neither could have known
> Their own thought from the other's,
> We were so much at one.
>
> (88, 84; 91, 211–12)

But they, like everything, are subject to time, and the fashion changes.
The "sweetheart" addressed here is not the beloved. This sweetheart is
warned not to love too long. Still, the poet does not admit that he has
changed; he admits only that the beloved has changed and (in hindsight)
changed in a minute. He, for his part, was steadfast. And so his advice to
a new sweetheart is advice he should have taken; perhaps it is really addressed as a reminder to himself. Certainly he is absorbed not by this
sweetheart, but instead still by the beloved. The poem is virtually an assertion to the new sweetheart that this is so.

What of his art? Is it also moon-crossed, subject to dissolution? In the next poem, "The Players ask for a Blessing on the Psalteries and on Themselves" (89, 84; 92, 212), the poet creates three voices, who speak a sort of prayer before they play and sing. The third voice sings,

> O kinsmen of the Three in One,
> O kinsmen, bless the hands that play.
> The notes they waken shall live on
> When all this heavy history's done;
> Our hands, our hands must ebb away.

> (89, 84; 92, 213)

We have, indeed, been reading a heavy history. The hands of the players, like the hands of the old men admiring themselves in the water, must ebb away. But, the singers tell us, the "proud and careless notes live on." The concluding poem of *In the Seven Woods* is what they play: The fictive singers of "The Happy Townland" (90, 85; 93, 213) appear either to be immortal or about to be made so, for they are going to a place of immortality. The notes and words project carelessness. In the *Book* this poem and its predecessor constitute a play within a play. The turn to explicit interest in plays and dramatic performance, which is suggested by these two concluding poems, has considerable importance for the poet's future development. Not only are the players examples of a kind of recklessness that identifies art with heroic gesture, but the appearance of the dramatic presages its growing importance in the poet's eventual conception of life and the world as held together by conflict.

When the "heavy history" is done there will remain a work that dramatizes personal conflict. It is as yet unfinished. Later on in the *Book* a thematic opposition appears between life and the work. Has there ever been a body of poetry more ruthless (and reckless) with its persona?

The Shadowy Waters (1906)

[The textual history of *The Shadowy Waters* is complicated enough to have made a book. The play gave Yeats much trouble over an extended period of time. He performed several revisions of it. From his remarks about it, one clearly understands that it meant a great deal to him. The meaning was personal; I suspect that because of this he thought it belonged as a dramatic poem in a *Book* that creates a dramatic autobiographical fiction of personal development. There are different versions of the play, of course, and some critics prefer earlier ones. Yeats published the 1906 version in *Collected Poems;* it properly follows *In the Seven Woods* in the *Book*.]

The interest in drama evident at the end of *In the Seven Woods* continues

with *The Shadowy Waters*. Successful drama must have conflict. *The Shadowy Waters* is a play, but it is only a step toward the later, more sophisticated embodiments of conflict. The main character, Forgael, seems to be a
projection of the poet's desires. The poet does not divide this projection
into various characters or even into two opposed parts. What contrasts
exist are rather simple—that between Forgael and Aibric, for example.
Forgael is not only the archetype of the poet but also the poetic magician
and lonely subjective hero. His magical power over others comes from the
harp he plays. This power he puts in the service of his extreme romantic
desire, which is infinitely beyond the capacity for desire of the sailors he
commands, including that of his first officer, Aibric. His desire does not
stop short of the ultimate:

> Miracle, ecstasy, the impossible hope,
> The flagstone under all, the fire of fires,
> The roots of the world.

(380, 413; 96, 227)

All of this is expressible for him in one word, "love," but love "of a beautiful, unheard-of kind / That is not in the world" (380, 414; 96, 228). Such
a thing, he asserts, "must be substantial somewhere" (380, 415; 96, 229).
Forgael seeks to enter bodily into his dream.

The birds that are his ship's guide in this quest seem to him harbingers
of a possibly achieved desire. At one point, he convinces himself that they
are not leading him to his death; but then he asserts that if in death he
discovers the love they seem to promise him, he will accept even that. The
birds circle above the ship's mast in an activity that puzzles him. We
quickly learn that this signals the coming of Dectora from a ship captured
by his sailors. When she appears and when the birds have indicated by
their actions the significance of the event, Forgael is momentarily uncertain. He sees that she casts a shadow; she should be entirely spirit. But he
quickly comes to believe that she is his fated companion, the Shelleyan
prototype of his desire. Convinced of this, he sets about convincing her,
whose husband and king has just been murdered by Forgael's men. She
wishes to be released, but he argues that it would be futile for him to free
her because fate would return her to him. They belong to each other.

In *The Shadowy Waters* fate is controlled by the play's author through the
magic of his surrogate, Forgael. The poet has constructed a fictive situation that is the opposite of the events he has brooded over in *In the Seven
Woods* and explained there as fate decreed by the moon. In the play, fate
brings Forgael into complete control over the object of his desire. "Both
you and I are taken in the net," he declares to Dectora (380, 420; 96, 237).
Here Forgael is capable of controlling even time; in *In the Seven Woods*, time

eroded everything, including the poet's relation to the beloved. It was she, he claimed, who changed in a moment, while he remained faithful. Here Forgael declares that the past is dead and that Dectora will quickly forget her husband. Stung, no doubt, by his remembrance of his own futile constancy, the poet has Forgael gain revenge by successfully erasing Dectora's declared constancy:

> The movement of time
> Is shaken in these seas, and what one does
> One moment has no might upon the moment
> That follows after.
>
> (380, 421; 96, 237)

We suspect that Forgael is a dangerous casuist. He does not confess to his magical power; he concentrates on convincing her that they both are pawns of a superior power. It is *they* who are caught, he says; but the fact is that she is his captive: "Do what you will, / You cannot leap out of the golden net" (380, 422; 96, 238). The lines recall Blake's poem "The Golden Net," which describes an innocent man trapped by three deceptive, aggressive women. Here the poet transfers control entirely to the man. It is Forgael, claiming that the net is their fate, who actually casts it about her.

The poet must be well aware of the turn he has made on the Blake poem. Indeed, it is fulfillment of the desire expressed in "The Fish":

> The people of coming days will know
> About the casting out of my net,
> And how you have leaped times out of mind
> Over the little silver cords,
> And think that you were hard and unkind.
>
> (45, 58; 46, 146)

One of the sailors goes so far as to remark that Forgael has "caught the crescent moon out of the sky" (380, 423; 96, 239). This is a moon similar to the one that presided ominously over events in "Adam's Curse" and "Under the Moon," dictating the waning of his relationship to the beloved. Here the moon becomes but a weapon of Forgael. Dectora, of course, succumbs to his enchantments.

Forgael's speech to the clamoring, wheeling birds expresses what seems to be the poet's own bitterness:

> . . . if it be reproach, I answer this:
> There is not one among you that made love
> By any other means. You call it passion,
> Consideration, generosity;

> But it was all deceit, and flattery
> To win a woman in her own despite,
> For love is war, and there is hatred in it;
> And if you say that she came willingly—

(380, 426; 96, 244)

He does not complete this statement. What does it mean? His argument is that all love is aggression (we shall see this notion later in the *Book*, but in a different context of ideas) and that pleasure is in the taking. Would this statement's completion have been that if she came willingly the triumph would not be worthwhile? Her ego would be diminished in relation to his and thus no longer the adequate object of his desire. It appears that she must be won against her will in order that his own ego be adequately satisfied.

At this point Forgael is unable to complete such a statement and turns from her in grief. It seems that in a moment of conscience he admits to having deceived her and that, in truth, he has nothing for her but "desolate waters and a battered ship" (380, 428; 96, 246). Yet this proves to be the final success, as if he had planned it all along. Her capitulation is now complete, for she gives herself to him entirely, embracing even his deceit and declaring that she wishes there were "nothing in the world / But my beloved" (380, 428; 96, 246). In this moment, she speaks a line very close to the last line of "The Ragged Wood," which ended, "No one has ever loved but you and I" (87, 83; 90, 211). Dectora's line makes her play the role that the poet plays in real life, but the result is achieved desire, not the frustration that "The Ragged Wood" actually expresses.

The poet has turned the tables on his beloved; Dectora seems to be the poet's revenge in symbolic wish fulfillment against the beloved's behavior. True, there is a moment when Aibric reasons with her, claiming that Forgael is taking her to their death. She hesitates; but in the end, unlike the real beloved of the poet's life, she gives herself entirely to Forgael's quest.

> The world drifts away,
> And I am left alone with my beloved,
> Who cannot put me from his sight for ever.
> We are alone for ever.

(380, 431–32; 96, 251)

She seems now, in fact, to control the situation, but her control has been completely ordained by Forgael's magic. He dominates her yet possesses at the same time a willful, powerful mistress. It is the both-and of his dream of desire. In the conclusion, she orders him to bend down: "Bend lower, that I may cover you with my hair" (380, 432; 96, 251). Her hair

becomes the golden net, and it envelops both of them. This is the fulfillment of a wish uttered more than once by the poet of *The Wind Among the
Reeds*. In this dream, the poet has it both ways, but in life, neither.

The Green Helmet and Other Poems (1910)

The poet's interest in the drama continues, the title of this next group of
poems implying their appearance together with a play, *The Green Helmet*.
The curious wish-fulfillment drama of *The Shadowy Waters* is followed by a
dream poem about death. "His Dream" (91, 90; 97, 253) is connected the-
matically to *The Shadowy Waters*, for the hero and heroine of that play are
surely headed for death, and both works are studies of death; "His
Dream," much condensed and confusing in the picture it presents, appears
to place the dreamer, who is the poet, in the position we found Forgael at
the beginning of *The Shadowy Waters*—steering a ship. But here the
dreamer is partly an observer of death, oddly detached even as he steers
the boat and is drawn into the situation of clamor and praise by a crowd,

> Crying amid the glittering sea,
> Naming it with ecstatic breath,
> Because it had such dignity,
> By the sweet name of Death.
>
> (91, 89; 97, 254)

What is this death? The poems that follow in this section help, perhaps,
to answer the question.

The section is framed by "His Dream" and the concluding "Brown
Penny," which is about the mystery of love that is also the subject of *The
Shadowy Waters;* but it offers a contrast. It recommends the study of love,
but the morbidity that threatens in *The Shadowy Waters* and "His Dream"
seems to have been purged and life to have triumphed. It is safe to say that
what has died in "His Dream" is the whole false vision of his relation to
the beloved, which has been brought to allegorical expression in *The Shadowy Waters*. This expression has a curious decadent beauty. In "His
Dream" the poet seems compelled to praise death even though he would
have hushed the crowd. He is uncertain of what he should do. Is he acknowledging in his dream that his praise of death was in some way forced
on him by what he thought the crowd wanted of him? Looking back, we
can see that the whole manner of his courtship of the beloved has had the
character of a role accepted from without. It has been carried on, in
expression, in the adopted manner of post-Pre-Raphaelite decadence. The
introductory dedicatory verses of *The Shadowy Waters* are dated in the *Book*

September 1900. The play itself is dated 1906. There is, under allegorical guise, a great deal of the poet in it, and it was long in the making. One is tempted to regard it as the death that is dreamed of in "His Dream." Now the play has at last been finished, and it summarizes fully the complex of his attitudes toward the beloved; here, that complex is named "death," as if the poet's conscious self were insisting that his old manner, including his artificial vision of the beloved and his elaborate sorrow, is to be put behind him.

This is a resolve that may or may not be effectively carried forward. Clearly, "A Woman Homer Sung" (92, 89; 98, 254) has a recessional quality that seems a deliberate celebration of something departed. There is a certain deliberate distancing. The beloved is treated as she *was*, and the poem is about writing about her. The poet reviews his treatment of her in his poetry. There is an overtone of agitation in the word "wrought": "Whereon I wrote and wrought" out of jealousy and yet anger at anyone indifferent to her. Now, however, he declares that he has achieved a new power. With it comes a new myth of the beloved that will enable him to rewrite his past relation to her and explain satisfactorily the situation he has been in. Now she is a modern Helen, "a woman Homer [would have] sung" (92, 89; 98, 254). That makes the poet her modern Homer. Homer was, of course, the chronicler of Helen, not her would-be lover, so it will not be easy to play this role. The effort is to distance her to the past and treat her as strictly a literary subject. On top of the fact that the poet is still in love with her is the risk of nostalgia, and "A Woman Homer sung" ends on a nostalgic note. Without it, he is unable to sustain completely the healing, distancing emphasis on his art, reached at the poem's midpoint. By the end both "life and letters seem / But an heroic dream" (92, 90; 98, 255). However, the matter is treated as past, and that is at least a step toward emancipation of himself from his old role and of her from hers, though the new myth may have its own danger.

In "A Woman Homer sung," the poet hopes that he has gained greater poetic power. In "Words" (93, 90; 99, 255), his depression comes to the surface once again. He states that he has many times thought himself successful in making his beloved understand his work, for (as he has claimed in the previous poem) he has thought that finally "words obey my call" (93, 90; 99, 256). But apparently she has not understood. The sun is evoked as governing the world of everyday work and the condition under which he must struggle. The moon is not mentioned but must, by the implication of its previous appearances, stand in contrast as the condition of passion and of poetic composition not controlled by mundane external purposes. This opposition is, of course, much employed later. Here the poet goes on to ask what might have happened had he been successful in explaining his own work to her. What might have occurred? "I might have thrown poor words away / And been content to live" (93, 90; 99, 256).

The statement is deeply ambivalent. On the one hand, it might mean that had the beloved understood he could have had a life with her. Contentment to live, on the other hand, seems to be treated with slight contempt. He is, after all, a romantic; and for the romantic poet contentment is an abdication of creative effort. Romantic heroes, as we well know, quest endlessly. The romantic quest had earlier been interpreted by the poet as a quest, possibly ending in death, for the beloved. But now it appears to be turning into a quest for greater and greater poetic expressive power, which power the poet will come to regard as in the service of celebrating life.

Later on, he puts the issue more clearly, for he understands it better: One chooses between perfection of the life and perfection of the work (258, 246; 266, 495). Here he recognizes that his work has become more powerful and that it gains at least some (maybe most) of its motivation from his desire to explain himself to the beloved. However, real purposive success with words would have resulted in the triumph of life over work. From this point onward in the *Book*, the poet's realization of the strange situation of his creativity grows and becomes the second myth by which he distances himself from his crisis of love. Here, as yet, there is still regret and bitterness.

Who might be blamed, other than himself? The beloved, of course. In "No Second Troy" (94, 91; 100, 256), the poet struggles with the desire to externalize and assign blame. The new myth of the beloved as Helen (which has some poetic sanction in a tendency, characteristic of the Irish literary revival, to identify the Irish with the ancient Greeks) is invoked in order to seek an explanation for what went wrong between them. There is much bitterness against the sun-world that she has inhabited, the world of politics and life (as against work). He regrets her trying to influence "ignorant men" and "little streets" and implies with contempt that she failed in this because such people did not have courage equal to their desire and she was above them. But the poem is all questions, a Yeatsian, truncated sonnet of Shakespearean form, preparing us for a summary couplet but withholding it. The questions remain. There is an implicit answer, though the form requires us to regard it as tentative, despite the powerful rhetoric of the last two lines: "Why, what could she have done, being what she is? / Was there another Troy for her to burn?" (94, 91; 100, 257).

The implicit answer is, of course, that she is a Helen born into an unheroic age (the later poet would characterize her as out of phase); thus she had no choice in playing out her role but to do as she did. The poem brilliantly combines rationalization and bitterness, as is quite appropriate to the condition of mind being presented in this section. The growing intensity of the questions displays the poet's stress in attempting to rationalize a behavior and series of events that he has hated. An interesting question that this poem and certain subsequent ones raises is to what extent the dislike of the "little streets," which is connected to certain class and political views attributable to the poet, is generated out of the need to rationalize away the failure of his love affairs. To put it too simply, is this a political poet in love or a love poet politicized?

A brief reconciliation that must have been on the whole painful for its clearly transient nature follows. "Reconciliation" (95, 91; 101, 257) continues to express bitterness and contains an only partially hidden tendency toward accusation, in spite of the previous effort to avoid just that. The poem powerfully rehearses the past: "Some may have blamed you"; "you went from me." Did some actually blame her for leaving the poet without his main subject matter? A likely story. But it is true that

> . . . I could find
> Nothing to make a song about but kings,
> Helmets, and swords, and half-forgotten things
> That were like memories of you.
>
> (95, 91; 101, 257)

His barren thoughts have chilled him, and she must warm him. One suspects that *The Shadowy Waters* is one of the works alluded to here.

This reconciliation does not return things to a previous state. The poet has passed into new experience, and he no longer complains about a love he seeks. Rather, he regrets the time that has been lost. There is yet another poem about a king, but it is quite different from poems of romance. In "King and no King" (96, 91; 102, 258), which refers to the play of that name by Beaumont and Fletcher, he reminds her of two things. First, they (probably only he) had hoped to live as if in a romance with a happy ending, but something she did, discreetly left unstated, frustrated this. [The act was Maud Gonne's vow never to marry.] Second, her religious faith promises an afterlife of recompense; his skepticism does not. This is the first overt admission of ideological differences between them and must be regarded as part of the poet's gradually coming to terms with the real.

Two more poems about the beloved follow, and they are paired. The first, "Peace" (97, 92; 103, 258), laments that peace should come to her only when time has touched her beauty. It was in her storminess that painters found the beauty of form that always suggests peace and repose. Behind this short poem there threatens to emerge a theory of opposites encompassed by art. In the second poem, "Against Unworthy Praise" (98, 92; 104, 259), the poet bids his heart be at peace and satisfied with his poetry, which has been written for her who has renewed his strength. Between the first and second stanzas, the poet's heart seems to have sought the praise of others, whereupon the poet tries to silence the heart by reminding it that it was others—the "self-same dolt and knave" that are the world—who slandered her. This is the "haughtier text" that the heart is commanded to read. She is at peace; the implication is that his heart should be, too.

With a somewhat more realistic idea of the beloved, and with the poet's absorption in new concerns, particularly the theater, it seems that the heart does achieve some peace. Obsession with the beloved no longer consumes the poet. Now, external subject matter enters the *Book*. Dolt and knave appear to obstruct not the beloved's activity but his own work in the theater (99, 93; 105, 260). A group of short, epigrammatic poems also signals this broadening of interest, attacking both conservative Catholic students who would ban "immoral" literature (102, 94; 108, 262) and poets who have slavishly imitated him (103, 94; 109, 262). These scornful poems are preceded by two that express possession of a certain wisdom (100, 93; 106, 261, and 101, 94; 107, 261). The poet begins to acknowledge here a public role and reputation, in contrast to the stance of "Against Unworthy Praise," where the heart is asked to be content with poems that are virtually a secret between it and the beloved.

These are followed by "The Mask" (104, 95; 110, 263), which expresses a very important development. The poem is a dialogue between two people of opposite sex. Who is male and who is female are not clear. [The poem appears in the play *The Player Queen*, where the wearer of the mask is a woman, but in this context there is no way to reach a decision.] The conversation has no parallel preceding it in the *Book*, and it leads to much that follows. The poem is one of a seduction quite different from anything in the love poetry previously addressed to the beloved. It is also an early formulation of a notion of the mask that will absorb the poet through the rest of his career. The masked person here attempts to convince the naive auditor not to look behind the mask to discover whether its passionate beauty masks coldness. The auditor wants truth behind appearance and would discover whether this is an enemy or not. But the masked person declares that these matters are irrelevant to their relation; only the mask is important.

This particular mask seems to be a glorification of a mask worn at a masquerade ball. We note, however, that it appears in the *Book* at the same time that the poet expresses interest in the theater, where masks are sometimes employed and where roles themselves can be thought of as masks. The dominant speaker of the dialogue identifies passion with the mask, and passion has been real for the poet, often more important than the advice of reason. But the idea of the deliberate creation and charging up of passion in performance is certainly enough to put the auditor on guard. How are we to take all of this? As a suave seduction in which all the power is with the seducing masked figure? The other person apparently does not have a mask. It seems unfair. Is there more to it than that? Yes, there is, potentially, for the *Book*. The seducer, wily and ruthless as he or she may seem here, has offered the germ of an idea not far from the poet's own thoughts. Several times he has attempted to force the beloved into what might be called a mask or role, albeit often a passive one: the languid, Pre-Raphaelite beauty, the white goddess, Dectora the queen, Helen of Troy, Maeve, even Cathleen ni Houlihan. He has never been successful, these masks being enforced from without. What of the possibility of a mask that one actually becomes by choice? The notion here is the opposite of that of a fundamental self hidden by acculturation or by will, further and further hidden over time. Rather, it is the result of the action of a life, the making of a role. In "The Mask," the seducer identifies the mask with passion, as if passion were free and reckless, the means by which a true self or mask is created. The dominant speaker of the poem has a design on the auditor and perhaps on the world. There is still too much of the magician here and perhaps not enough of the actor or actress. But it is possible at this stage that the idea of the mask, if developed further, might clear the poet's mind of the need to dominate that is present here—or the need to be dominated, for the impossibility of assigning sexes to the speakers suggests the same ambivalence present at the conclusion of *The Shadowy Waters*.

The main principle of the mask might be described as the *making* of a life that in its artfulness is real. The mask is not a disguise or an imitation but the reality being made. From now on the poet is never far from expressing this notion. The drama becomes the model for life, and everyone must make or accept a part.

The considerable respect that the poet holds for Lady Gregory, to whom *The Shadowy Waters* is dedicated, and for her home, Coole Park, is a respect for the artful role both have played. In the next poem, "Upon a House shaken by the Land Agitation" (105, 95; 111, 264), the poet honors the unity of "passion and precision" that he feels characterizes Coole. To the pure "passion" advocated in "The Mask" the poet adds the precision of aesthetic order and discipline and the characteristics of "high laughter, loveliness, and ease." But the life of the achieved mask that Coole embodies is now, he fears, in jeopardy. He finds it difficult to imagine the world better off were Coole razed and "mean roof-trees" in its place.

All through his career, the poet seems to have been absorbed with the situation of isolation. The new identification of Coole with a certain kind of mask tends to produce a new kind of isolation—that of the intellect struggling against the leveling of all things to some common denominator. The poet believes this leveling occurs in life when houses like Coole come under threat of demolition and in the arts when the public governs taste. The next poems take up this concern, identifying the life of Coole and of art with "horsemen" ("At Galway Races," 108, 97; 114, 266), and align all against the encroachment of "merchant and clerk." Perhaps, the poet hopes, a "new moon" will rise and the earth will "change its tune." The current tune is not exactly the "cracked" one that Chronos sings in "The Song of the Happy Shepherd"; that was the tune of a culture that had arisen in the wake of Arcady and ancient romance. Now the song is that "breathed on the world with timid breath" by "merchant and clerk," spoken against the Abbey Theatre plays ("At the Abbey Theatre," 106, 96; 112, 264), and responsible for the poet's fear that "all things at one common level lie" ("These are the Clouds," 107, 96; 113, 265). The poet hopes wistfully for a rebirth of all the things now grouped together in his imagination under the aegis of the moon: art, poetry, Coole, horsemen, passion, precision, recklessness, and the created mask. On top of these concerns is the poet's worry over the health of his friend, presumably Lady Gregory ("A Friend's Illness," 109, 97; 115, 267).

At this time he recognizes that new interests, which, it must be observed, have emancipated him from his obsession with the beloved, have also tempted him away from writing verse. One part of him, at least, even wishes to be "colder and dumber and deafer than a fish" ("All Things can tempt Me," 110, 97; 116, 267). He recalls that as a young poet he had strong views about poetry; he had

> . . . not given a penny for a song
> Did not the poet sing it with such airs
> That one believed he had a sword upstairs.
>
> (110, 98; 116, 267)

The image or mask of the cavalier swordsman he obviously never achieved in his own early work. Now he succumbs too easily to external things.

"Brown Penny" (111, 98; 117, 268) appears to be expression of an effort to restore his poetic voice to himself; in it he tosses a penny to see whether he "might love." It has, after all, been love that up to now has inspired so much of his work. But now the attitude toward love and toward himself is different. He treats himself with a certain ironic humor. With humor he projects himself as timid and indecisive, then comically reckless:

> I whispered, "I am too young,"
> And then, "I am old enough";

Wherefore I threw a penny
To find out if I might love.

(111, 98; 117, 268)

The dream of death with which *The Green Helmet and Other Poems* began is replaced by this comic recklessness, which is followed by contemplation of love as a most curious mystery, a "crooked thing." The language is different here, more colloquial: "'There is nobody wise enough / To find out all that is in it'" (111, 98; 117, 268). A familiar romantic imagery of stars, moon, and loops of a beloved's hair remains, but the degree of self-absorbed subjectivity is different.

Responsibilities (1914)

Love, at least sexual love, is not the main subject of this new section. Rather, responsibilities are recognized, the poet having been freed in the previous section of his "barren passion." The untitled introductory poem (112, 101; 118, 269), addressed to his ancestors, acknowledges a responsibility to carry on the line. He has nothing to show to them but a book. The reason has been the "barren passion," which he is now able to name as such. The poem is dated January 1914 (the poet declares himself to be almost forty-nine years old): It frames *Responsibilities* as a whole, being written after the poems that follow were collected.

Another responsibility recognized here is to confess to failure, and the poem does this, yet the two epigraphs to the section salvage something from the failed and barren dream. The first, "In dreams begins responsibility," is ambiguous and makes the dream either a valuable part of growth or the phenomenon that requires confession. The second epigraph, from Khoung-fou-tseu, seems in this context to imply that the speaker has lost his inspiration in some way, perhaps indicating here the need to face responsibility: "'How am I fallen from myself, for a long time now / I have not seen the Prince of Chang in my dreams'" (p. 100; p. 269).

John Unterecker has listed the various types of responsibilities addressed in this section: supernatural, social, personal, and aesthetic. To this list may be added the responsibility of recklessness that is in a special way the responsibility of poets.

"The Grey Rock" (113, 103; 119, 270) makes the book he has produced and half apologized for an expression of responsibility after all—responsibility to his art and to his old companions among the Rhymers. If he has not carried on the family line, he has carried on a poetic one. "The Grey Rock" thus continues the thought of the introductory poem, offering by opposition an example of his poetic faithfulness. The poem moves between address to dead ancestors and the telling of an old story. The poet begins by picking up the notion of "barren passion" in the introductory verses. The Rhymers, being dead and beyond earthly passion, may, the poet imagines, be bored with hearing about it. Therefore, he will tell another story. Love plays a role in it, but it is love that meets the competing demand of commitment. The story is about the supernatural woman Aoife, who before the Battle of Clontarf gave to her mortal lover a magic pin that made him invisible at his will. Meeting the severely wounded Murrough, he removes the pin:

> ". . . I will not take
> The fortune that had been my shame
> Seeing, King's son, what wounds you have."
>
> (113, 105; 119, 274–75)

He is subsequently killed, and in anger Aoife reports the whole story to the assemblage of the gods. The mortal lover has betrayed her love by a reckless act of symbolic identification with another mortal. The gods merely smile and drench her with wine, whereupon she is plunged into forgetfulness and stares at them "with laughing lip."

The text that punctuates this one is addressed directly to the dead Rhymers, praising them for having kept to "the Muses' sterner laws" when they could have had money and a troop of friends. In this, they were "unrepenting." The word is powerful here, especially in light of the notorious dissipation of these poets. All of this is against the grain of middle-class respectability. Keeping to the "Muses' sterner laws" means not merely allegiance to the classical structure of verse; it means putting poetry ahead of getting ahead. The faith that the poet claims he has kept is not to ancestors, living friends, or a goddess-lover but to his own version of "that rockbound, rock-wandering foot," the poetic muse itself. This has left him vulnerable to criticism, but later in the section he gives as good as he gets. It is to be noticed that the kind of faithfulness the poet claims is different from either kind treated in Aoife's story. Hers are the forms of faithfulness traditionally treated in "old stories." The poet chooses to emphasize a third one, which is for that reason alone harder for people to comprehend and about which he will therefore have more to say later.

In neither of these poems is any type of faithfulness denigrated. Caught between the demands of two types, the friend of Murrough chooses one, and the gods choose not to answer Aoife's angry question, "Why are the gods by men betrayed?" except by inducing forgetfulness. The problem is one of contending forces.

The contending forces in "The Two Kings" (381, 435; 120, 276) are the worlds of life and death. Queen Edain is committed to her husband of this world; King Eochaid is pursued by a supernatural figure who declares himself her husband before her birth. In a dialogue with this death king, Edain says that she will remain true to Eochaid and argues that love depends for its power on the knowledge that it is between those who pass away and is thus built "upon a narrow ledge / Above a windy precipice." She fights off the death king, who suddenly disappears at the very moment Eochaid sees a supernatural stag with which he is fighting elsewhere also disappear. It has been Edain's commitment to nurse to health Eochaid's brother, Ardan, that has brought her to a place where the death king can attack her. The commitments here are to a human love that knows its object must eventually be lost and to promises kept. In both "The Grey Rock" and "The Two Kings" the world of death fails to overcome the passions of life as long as there is life. It can be said that in "The Wanderings of Oisin" this was also the case, but in that poem the notion of heroic commitment to oath or ideal was not as strong as lamentation for a lost way of life. Here the loss is acknowledged as inevitable, and commitment to values is emphasized.

Mindless commitment to middle-class self-interest, however, is clearly villainous. The next five poems explore this with a bitter rhetoric worthy of Aoife herself. The poet gives more specific designation to that "loud host before the sea," who are the critics mentioned in "The Grey Rock." The host is composed of those of the merchant class in Dublin who, given the opportunity, failed to play the role of patrons of the arts that true aristocrats would have embraced. The title "To a Wealthy Man who promised a second Subscription to the Dublin Municipal Gallery if it were proved the People wanted Pictures" (114, 107; 121, 287) tells the story. This man is scornfully encouraged to emulate the Renaissance dukes of Ferrara and Urbino (the latter is praised in Castiglione's *Courtier*, a work that influences the poet's idea of appropriate behavior).

"September 1913" (115, 108; 122, 289) locates itself during the controversy over Hugh Lane's proposal to give his art collection to Dublin provided suitable housing could be found. (Lane was Lady Gregory's nephew.) The poem indicates that the campaign has been a failure. The poet's response to this is full of sarcasm and anger. He ironically couples moneymaking and religious piety in the lives of those who have failed to support art. Against them are massed with scorn past revolutionary heroes of Ireland. Particularly interesting is the description that the poet gives of true heroic, patriotic activity: "All that delirium of the brave?" (115, 108; 122, 290). This identification of heroism with a sort of madness recalls the recklessness of Murrough's friend or, for that matter, the Rhymers. Such delirium, being without self-interest, comes to seem to the poet the art of life, parallel to the art of art. Yet this delirium has its cost, and there can be other attitudes toward it, as we shall see when we come to the poet's having to respond to the events of 1916.

The person most deeply involved with the Lane pictures, Lady Gregory, has had to face failure. The poet addresses her in "To a Friend whose Work has come to Nothing" (116, 109; 123, 290). He encourages her to play the role of someone "bred to a harder thing / Than triumph." She is invited to "exult" in the midst of failure. The poet foreshadows here his reservations in "The Tower" (205, 196; 212, 411) about triumph itself and even later, where triumph is seen as dangerous to both the poet and the hero. He foreshadows also thoughts common to several of the *Last Poems*, which recommend exultation in the face of tragedy.

Why should exultation be the proper response to this failure? Because she was in the right, has proved her superiority to the victors, and has been faithful to her heritage. To exult is the most difficult thing to do in the situation and proves her mettle. But the exultation must be secret because anything else would be vulgar histrionics that descend to the common level.

Scornful anger is acceptable, and the poet indulged it in "September 1913." It was controlled and haughty there, but now he reports in "Paudeen" (117, 109; 124, 291) his own uncontrolled anger. At that moment something happens: There are the simple cry of a curlew and another curlew's answer, and his mind is cleared for a calming vision:

. . . and suddenly thereupon I thought
That on the lonely height where all are in God's eye,
There cannot be, confusion of our sound forgot,
A single soul that lacks a sweet crystalline cry.

(117, 110; 124, 291)

Neither exultation nor madness is quite the right word for this. The moment is purgative of the "confusion of our sound" and of the "loud host" of "The Grey Rock." It is the first intimation of a notion that comes to play an important role later on: the idea of the cleansing power of anger that influences the poet's attitude toward Jonathan Swift and engenders the lines of "Under Ben Bulben":

. . . when all words are said
And a man is fighting mad,
Something drops from eyes long blind
He completes his partial mind,
For an instant stands at ease.

(356, 326; 386, 638)

The next poem of this group remains bitter. The poet does not achieve the state of secret exultation he has advised, but "To a Shade" (118, 110; 125, 292) does recover the scornful composure of "September 1913." The shade is Charles Stewart Parnell. Lane's plans were destroyed, it is implied, as Parnell's were—by the same enemy, "an old foul mouth." It is better that the shade not witness this return of the same, and the poet waves the ghost back to the tomb in a gesture of utter contempt for what has occurred.

These poems have revealed a side of the poet that suggests he is making a mask. The voice seems more natural, less mannered according to some recognizable fashion. At the same time, it plays a role of the Irish poet adept at uttering curses and invoking *that* traditional magical power, not the manipulative, magical power of Forgael.

But the poems, as invective, have perhaps been one-sided. As often before and later, the poet suddenly for a moment sees things from a different angle, imagining in "When Helen lived" (119, 111; 126, 293) that had "we" been onlookers in Troy at the carrying on of Paris and Helen, "we" might have treated the matter with "a word and a jest." He sees it for a moment as not at all surprising that an onlooker does not take as seriously as does one deeply involved the "beauty that we have won / From bitterest hours" (119, 111; 126, 293). However, this magnanimity is momentary; an angry memory of a few years before floods in, and the short poem "On Those that hated 'The Playboy of the Western World,' 1907" (120, 111; 127, 294), scorns again "the loud host" that caused riots in the Abbey Theatre and thereby implied impotent jealousy.

A sequence of an apparently quite different kind follows, but it is generated by the feelings that have recently been expressed. Questions have been implied about the relations among delirium, madness, recklessness, reason, and responsibility. The shape of the first of these poems connects it to "The Grey Rock" in that two stories are present. Here, however, one frames the other. In the frame of "The Three Beggars" (121, 111; 128, 294), an old crane stands in the water encouraging itself to be a patient fisher. Inside the frame is the story of King Guaire and three beggars. He offers a fortune to the first one who can fall asleep "before the third noon sounds." The beggars frantically keep each other awake. Exhausted, they finally all fall asleep, but too late. Meanwhile, the crane, disturbed by their noise and relieved that they are finally silent, declares: " '*Maybe I shall take a trout / If but I do not seem to care*' " (121, 113; 128, 297). This treatment of an effort at nonchalance, identified with *sprezzaturra* by Castiglione, is a comic rendition of the idea of the mask. Even the purposive crane can seem to have a mask of nonchalance, though putting it to such mundane use may compromise its purity.

In "The Three Hermits" (122, 113; 129, 298), two hermits argue vociferously over a matter of theology. The third hermit sings "unnoticed like a bird," his purpose apparently purged. He seems mad, but is he mad? Or does he but seem mad to us? What does he sing? Has he achieved the mask of madness? Is this what achievement of the mask looks like to "the loud host before the sea" (113, 106; 119, 276)? Has it some connection to the advice in "To a Friend whose Work has come to Nothing"?

> . . . Turn away
> And like a laughing string
> Whereon mad fingers play
> Amid a place of stone,
> Be secret and exult.
>
> (116, 109; 123, 291)

By contrast, the desires expressed by the beggars in "Beggar to Beggar cried" (123, 114; 130, 299) are entirely mundane and secular; in the light of the surrounding text they seem the expression of base or vulgar values. "Running to Paradise" (124, 115; 131, 300) is perhaps a comment on such values from the opposite extreme. Here the speaker is apparently a mad beggar. He speaks a sort of wisdom, but at the same time he is so detached from the real that he seems to have no role in life, at least no social role except as the object of charity. His actions predict those of the late phases of Michael Robartes' lunar wheel, yet to be presented in the *Book*.

The issues generally raised by the beggar-hermit sequence are addressed in "The Hour before Dawn" (125, 116; 132, 302), the last and most complex of the group. Here, in the debate between the "cursing rogue" of a traveling man and the "great lad with a beery face," the whole question is one of purpose. The scene has some vague ironic suggestion of Wordsworth's "Resolution and Independence" and similar overtones from "Michael" and *The Prelude*. In "Resolution and Independence," the old leech-gatherer possesses both qualities named in the title. In "The Hour before Dawn," these qualities are split, and both are ironically perceived. The "great lad" has lost resolution, having crawled into a cave with a tub of Goban's beer, and now would "sleep away all time." His original purpose in entering the cave was temporary shelter, but now he is content with sleep itself. The "cursing rogue," who has come upon him and interrupted his slumber, is outraged at this, but the sleeper persists to claim that all purpose is really reducible to the same thing:

> "You cry aloud, O would 'twere spring
> Or that the wind would shift a point,
> And do not know that you would bring,

> If time were suppler in the joint,
> Neither the spring nor the south wind
> But the hour when you shall pass away."

(125, 119; 132, 306)

Even more angered, the beggar accuses him of robbing his life of "every pleasant thought" and pummels him severely; but he is already asleep. The beggar goes away after praying, and cursing, and finally thanking God that the dawn has come.

Perhaps the sleeper speaks truth. Later on, in a poem called "The Wheel" (214, 211; 221, 434), the poet himself utters similar sentiments. But it is also true that the beggar speaks life. Perhaps purposive activity cannot be defended against the skeptical mockery of the sleeper; but desire, the beggar tacitly understands, is necessary to life. Free of desire, the sleeper rejects life, as Aoife forgot her anger when she was drenched with Goban's wine. Still possessing desire, the beggar also possesses a kind of responsibility that causes a comic surge of moralistic outrage from a man whose morality is hardly impeccable.

It may be that here the poet has been displacing into a sort of allegory the problem of whether or not writing poetry is action and life. What, it may be asked, is the true mask of poetry—the dreamer (sleeper) of the early works or the rogue full of desire and life? Perhaps the extremes of vulgar purposiveness, which is the utilitarianism of the "loud host," and the total achievement of a purposeless singing madness are both unacceptable, and some third position is necessary: the purposeful, perpetual creation of a mask of recklessness, nonchalance, and only internal purposiveness. Such an action must not come to completion or stasis, for then it would sink into complacency. We are observing early stages of the development of such a notion.

To appear to side with the beggar, therefore, would mislead, suggesting advocacy of a practical realism. The poet seems to guard against this in the next poems. A song from *The Player Queen* (126, 120; 133, 308), which is a farcical drama of masks and performances, follows. It is sung by a young woman whose mother imagines that she will be a queen. The song seems to be balanced against "Running to Paradise" and especially its refrain, in which the ascetic beggar sings out *"and there the king is but as the beggar."* Here a young woman becomes a queen. Realists are next addressed in a poem with that title (127, 120; 134, 309), where myth and legend are described as awakening "a hope to live / That had gone with the dragons." In the paired poems "The Witch" (128, 121; 135, 310) and "The Peacock" (129, 121; 136, 310), the fate of the mundane toiler is compared negatively to that of the artist, completing the theme of responsibility to art begun in "The Grey Rock."

The cryptic, mysterious poem that follows, "The Mountain Tomb" (130, 121; 137, 311), introduces a new subject—the esoteric or occult (in this case Rosicrucianism), which plays a role later in the *Book*. Study of neither occult documents nor the placement of this poem has unlocked its secrets for me. All I can say is that it presages a series of somewhat elegiac poems as thoughts of the beloved flow back into the poet's consciousness. *Responsibilities* has appeared up to this moment to have marked a movement beyond these formerly compelling concerns, but in the *Book* moments of regression and setbacks are not always avoided. The first of these poems is a remembrance of a child dancing in the wind (131, 122; 138, 312). The wind, invoked earlier in *The Wind Among the Reeds*, where it was first a harbinger of some marvelous truth and then a sinister natural phenomenon, remains "monstrous." Dancing, from the time of "The Wanderings of Oisin," has often been associated with an absolute freedom and continues to be so here, with suggestions of innocence added. It too will reveal a darker side eventually, though on the whole it remains associated with a radical internal purposiveness. In "Two Years Later" (132, 122; 139, 312), the poet is more pessimistic and predicts in experience the same suffering that the child's mother, unnamed, has endured. The poems that follow suggest that the mother here is the beloved. The poet next recalls, by contrast to her present state, a moment of his and her youth in which he had unaccountably been able to play the role of a courtierlike lover.

Through the *Book* the poet has emphasized as part of a personal iconography the moon, sun, stars, wind, and birds. These images are by no means static in meaning. Rather, each generates a wealth of possibility limited in each context. The moon can wax and wane, appear and disappear; it is not a fixed image of imagination, subjectivity, and passion. The wind can sigh in the reeds with suggestions of another world, other creatures, voices of a strange truth; but it can cry monstrously. Birds come in different species, from the seabirds suggesting passionate knowledge and freedom to the "ridiculous little bird" (133, 123; 140, 313) of "A Memory of Youth," which cries out just as the moon appears from behind a cloud and saves a situation between the lovers that had been full of darkness. The way that the poet introduces the moon here makes it for a moment uncertain whether the moon as first introduced is or is not merely a symbol: "A cloud blown from the cut-throat north / Suddenly hid Love's moon away" (133, 123; 150, 313). As the poem proceeds, it becomes clear that the moon is a real presence in the sky, as it was in "Adam's Curse." The relationship of the lovers suffers until the moon reappears:

We sat as silent as a stone,
We knew, though she'd not said a word,
That even the best of love must die,

And had been savagely undone
Were it not that Love upon the cry
Of a most ridiculous little bird
Tore from the clouds his marvellous moon.

(133, 123; 140, 314)

One cannot decide whether the relationship is one with which nature sympathizes, whether it is fated, or whether chance (in the bird's cry and the simultaneous reappearance of the moon) rules. The reason for this is, I think, the poet's inability finally to explain anything about this relationship, though as a love poet he would like to invoke, as he does here, the poetic convention of a god of love working behind the scenes. As the poem ends it is this god, a sort of fate, who seems to control things. Any other explanation may still be too hard to bear. This accounts, perhaps, for the "most ridiculous little bird," which plays the role that the poet might have earlier given to some more dignified member of the class. The event is given a quality of unlikelihood by virtue of its inappropriate herald.

Plunged now back into remembrance, the poet, knowing his own somewhat ridiculous position, describes himself, singer of praise of one now grown old, as "some last courtier at a gypsy camping-place / Babbling of fallen majesty" ("Fallen Majesty," 134, 123; 141, 314). This self-description, in a poem that recognizes he is but recording the irretrievable past, seems to cause him to compose himself. "Friends" (135, 124; 142, 315) begins as a formal poem of praise with no tone of lament or nostalgia, in contrast to "Fallen Majesty." It would try to be a poem expressing formally the theme of responsibility in the way that a proper laureate would behave. Three women are to be praised. The first presents no difficulty: Lady Gregory is praised for the meeting of their minds. The second, with whom he must have had a first or at least an early sexual experience, is also easily praised. But then both the tone and the whole established aim of the poem break down, for the third woman is the beloved, and his feelings toward this friend are ambivalent and tormented. He faces the matter squarely, however, and puts an end to the formalities of praise. Yet in the end the description of himself as he remembers her is a form of praise after all, though it must come after these bitter lines:

And what of her that took
All till my youth was gone
With scarce a pitying look?
How could I praise that one?

(135, 124; 142, 315–16)

The praise is in the form of confession that he still is passionately moved:

. . . up from my heart's root
So great a sweetness flows
I shake from head to foot.

(135, 124; 142, 316)

This poem, which was to have set him back on the path of responsibility, engenders another, more searing remembrance ("The Cold Heaven," 136, 125; 143, 316) of what must have been their estrangement and his sense of blame (responsibility) for it. He imagines now the soul after death naked on the roads and suffering punishment. The speculation anticipates later ideas about the afterlife. Here, for a moment, he suffers in an anticipatory way, riddled with the daylight that he will later come to associate with the blinding otherworld of bodily annihilation, the ultimate primary phase of the great wheel of life and death.

The next poem attempts once again (as in "No Second Troy") to rationalize the beloved's behavior by attributing to her an excess of "desire / For what proud death may bring" ("That the Night come," 137, 125; 144, 317). The return to the beloved, the nostalgia, and the attempt once again to explain why it all went wrong suggest compulsive, neurotic repetition. (It will not be surprising that we discover the poet back at Coole after this—at the beginning of the next section.) Nevertheless, there is something more conclusive about "That the Night come" than about "No Second Troy." First of all, it does not end in a question. Second, the beloved is treated elegiacally as belonging to the past, even though memory can deeply move him. Third, he is discussing an aspect of her that would have been entirely foreign to Helen, who brought about the fall of Troy simply by her beauty and the strife it caused. Here the poet ceases to suggest anything that might possibly indicate passivity or lack of action. With this goes the last vestige of his efforts to force her into some traditional mold of femininity. So some change, and perhaps progress, has occurred.

The section ends with a group of ironic poems. The poet's mind returns to the political world in the slight "An Appointment" (138, 125; 145, 317), which reminds us that the poet has a public life that goes on as the internal life continues to mull over past passion. "An Appointment" is followed by a poem that speculates on desire, picking up the theme of "That the Night come" but presenting a vision more general and unattached to remembrance of the beloved. The vision is that of the Magi, unsatisfied by "Calvary's turbulence" ("The Magi," 139, 126; 146, 318) and desiring, apparently, a repetition of the manifestation of divinity in life: "the uncontrollable mystery on the bestial floor." The desire here is not for control or ultimate knowledge but for revelation in life. But the next poem playfully rejects the "bestial." In "The Dolls" (140, 126; 147, 319), the dollmaker's artifacts are outraged at the appearance of a real baby in his household, and the wife apologizes for the mistake. For the dolls, there has occurred not a miraculous incarnation but an outrageous affront to their artistic improvement over nature.

A number of times, we discover, the movement from poem to poem in the *Book* is marked by an image, word, or some thematic material triggering a play on it in the next. These connections sometimes emphasize the principle of playful recklessness or nonchalance itself. But this sort of movement is secondary to the passionate change that the poems, often painfully, chart. The process seems to involve endless questing, which is, it turns out for the poet, the making of a self by way of dramatic performance or the mask. It may seem surprising, therefore, that the poet ends *Responsibilities* with "A Coat" (141, 127; 148, 320), which rejects outright all clothing (and, one might think, masking) on the ground that his old coat of embroidered mythologies has been copied by fools. In disgust he vows to abandon all clothing whatever—but, it turns out, not by any means for good. The poet's development is one of passionate, vacillating growth. He has moments of high feeling when he casts everything out— only to begin again.

In the untitled epilogue to *Responsibilities* (142, 128; 149, 321), the poet is back at Coole and prepared to forgive, in that atmosphere, all those accidents, as he calls them, that have made him notorious and defiled his works. It is a moment of depression, the reasons for which have not all been made clear in the preceding poems. We do know, however, that the poet has become a public man, and perhaps defilement of his "priceless things" is the price to be paid for this.

4

The Pressure of Events and Growing Antithetical Power

The Wild Swans at Coole (1919)

Coole was a retreat once before, and it is again. But now there is a different air about the place. The older, more experienced poet witnesses the mourning of Lady Gregory over the death of her son Robert. A place of retreat, Coole is not therefore a place to escape all cares. The passing of time and the elegiac dominate the first poems of the section. Toward the end, however, these themes give way to denser ones in two dialogue poems and a poem in which one of the dialogue characters tells of an extraordinary vision. The poems suggest that the poet has undergone an important intellectual change. It seems to have been brought about in connection with marriage, although it is not directly asserted that the poet is married until the end of the following section, *Michael Robartes and the Dancer*.

It is generally acknowledged that the title poem of *The Wild Swans at Coole* (143, 131; 150, 322) is one of Yeats's greatest achievements. It is a technically accomplished work, giving that illusion of ease that the poet speaks of in "Adam's Curse." The swans floating on the "companionable" streams provide a wistful contrast to the old men admiring themselves in the water and to a later poem of this section, where the poet compares himself to a "weather-worn marble triton / Among the streams" (146, 136; 153, 329). The swans float among the stones at Coole in a real and allegorical autumn. The water does not rush by; time is their milieu even as they seem to be beyond time as the poet understands it. He has counted them here before, maybe on that earlier occasion when he had visited Coole worn out by unrequited passion. He imagines himself having trod more lightly then, but in the meantime the swans' hearts have not "grown old" like his. They are paired, lover by lover, as they were (curiously, however, the poet counts them as fifty-nine; does he for a moment wish to imagine himself one of them?). The poem has strong suggestions of Keats's great odes. Like Keats's nightingale, the swans do not age. The streams, like Keats's "cold pastoral" urn, have an oxymoronic quality, for the swans are perfectly at home on the water. Even Keats's question about whether he wakes or sleeps is called to mind when the poet characteristically ends his poem with a question and asks where the swans will be when "I awake some day / To find they have flown away" (143, 132; 150, 323). The theme of the changing nature of the hearts of men and women, as against the unchanging swans, presses even more urgently on the poet later in this section.

Other things have flown away. Major Robert Gregory's fighter plane was shot down in Italy in 1918, and the poet, living now in an "ancient tower," performs a courteous act that turns Gregory into a courtier in the elegy that follows (144, 132; 151, 323). This deliberately magnanimous poem is a sign of how seriously the poet regards those ideas that group themselves about the mask. It is a brilliant, controlled performance, with a certain naturalness of voice blended with the recognizably deliberate artifice of the traditional elegy. Readers sometimes resist the formal hyperbole of the poem, but the formality, balanced with the accomplished rhythms and movement of the sentences, helps to shape its power. The feeling expressed is connected with our awareness that the elegy is written for Lady Gregory, all of the poet's devotion to her lying behind it. If the poem seems affected, we should recognize that the gesture of high performance is one that the *Book* comes to endorse strongly. The conclusion invokes the "bitter wind" that has blown so ominously through the recent poems and confesses in its high elegiac way to the poet's inability to continue; his imagination has not, he says, been able to deal adequately with this death:

> I had thought, seeing how bitter is that wind
> That shakes the shutter, to have brought to mind
> All those that manhood tried, or childhood loved
> Or boyish intellect approved,
> With some appropriate commentary on each;
> Until imagination brought
> A fitter welcome; but a thought
> Of that late death took all my heart for speech.

> (144, 135; 151, 327–28)

And so he tries again, not in the elegiac mode but in the mode of empathetic identification. He will reach out to speak for Robert Gregory at the moment of his death. Here Gregory is said to have achieved the mask of internal purposiveness, "a lonely impulse of delight" that has nothing to do with enemy or friend, love or hatred ("An Irish Airman foresees his

Death," 145, 135; 152, 328). Neither the past nor the future but only the moment is significant. This moment the poet in his meditation on the swans and time did not achieve and can only imagine now in his reckless hero.

In the light of this and the previous poems, "Men Improve with the Years" (146, 136; 153, 329), in which the poet compares himself to a "weather-worn marble triton," takes on special significance. It is not time alone that has eroded this triton. It has been dreaming and slow time contrasted implicitly with the brief moment of Robert Gregory's life. The poet claims that his form of delight is wisdom. Yet he acknowledges that this, too, may be but a dream. The thought causes him to wish that in his "burning youth" he had met the young woman he has been observing. The poem fades out with lines repeating its beginning and acknowledging that, indeed, he does live among dreams.

"The Collar-bone of a Hare" (147, 136; 154, 330) carries the regression to dreams further, reintroducing imagery of an earlier stage of the poet's career. But the poet seems to recover from this characteristic but now only momentary lapse in "Under the Round Tower" (148, 137; 155, 331), which offers cryptic hints that a new structure of imagery is being given shape. Sun and moon remain but are now to be involved in a structure of sexual opposition, conflict, and cyclicity. The beggar Billy Byrne, asleep on his great-grandfather's grave, dreams of the sun and moon in a gyring dance in an ancient Irish round tower. He takes the dream to be an omen of good fortune, and he interprets it as advising him to move on. This may be wise (the traveling man, whether beggar, fiddler, or itinerant poet, indicates endless movement, aimless quest), and wisdom is a theme of "Solomon to Sheba" (149, 138; 156, 332). They, like sun and moon, have "gone round and round" talking on the "narrow theme of love." At the end of *The Green Helmet and Other Poems*, the poet had thought he should not hesitate any longer to begin the study of love. Now, married and in their own tower house, as the beginning of the Gregory elegy told us, the poet and his wife, under the names of Solomon and Sheba, discourse learnedly on love, discovering that "'not a thing but love can make / The world a narrow pound'" (149, 138; 156, 333).

However, despite the apparent success of this marriage, the poet does not escape the unruly behavior of his heart. The dialogue with the heart that was commenced in "The Folly of being Comforted" is resumed. This suggests the return of thoughts of the beloved, though she is not mentioned. Now the theme is that of the wiser poet giving advice to his "discontented heart" (we do not hear the heart's reply this time): Replace your discontent with the contentment to be received from contemplation of works of art:

> . . . beauty that is cast out of a mould
> In bronze, or that in dazzling marble appears,
> Appears, but when we have gone is gone again.
>
> > (150, 139; 157, 334)

The idea seems to be that the momentary apprehension of beauty makes no continuing claim on the heart. Such beauty is "indifferent to our solitude."

The poet has been attempting to cope here with a discontented heart. In the next poem, he goes further. He has treated the heart as discontented, but he has nevertheless addressed it, reasoned with it, as if he were trying to convince it that it, too, is old and that it must accept its solitude. In "A Song" (151, 139; 158, 334), he views what he has just said with a certain surprise, because he had never imagined that the heart could grow old. Played out here is the drama of his coming to terms not only with his growing age but also with what has happened in marriage: more order and a further estrangement from the dreams on which the heart has fed. One might have imagined this heart's irritation at the poet's new satisfactions, and indeed the poem expresses regret, as if in some way all of this were a betrayal.

Settled wisdom can, of course, be pompous, and the poet is somewhat so in the two poems that follow, "To a Young Beauty" (152, 139; 159, 335) and "To a Young Girl" (153, 140; 160, 336). Ostensibly of sage advice, both poems are of quite personal sentiments. For the moment successful in subduing his heart and perhaps the desire he nevertheless still possesses, the poet becomes the wise giver of advice, having earlier, in "The Folly of being Comforted," been the receiver. In the first poem, the advice appears to be the gratuitous sort a young person particularly dislikes and usually resists. It is surely an excuse to allow him to express his view that fools should not be suffered even gladly. In the second, he plays a role more like that of Lady Gregory in "The Folly of being Comforted," which more and more looks like a very important poem in the *Book*. Here he offers sympathy to his beloved's daughter, who is in love, but the sympathy is by way of the claim that he can identify the feelings of the daughter with those of her mother. He can do this because it was he who caused the mother's heart to stir. The mother cannot see this because she resisted and now denies it. It is an interesting moment of self-assertion and contains a combination of resentment, detachment, and superiority as well as sympathy. The superiority he expresses is not merely toward the young girl, where it is a superiority of experience, but also toward the beloved, where it is a superiority of memory and touch with reality—providing, of course, that this is not a wishful history that he is constructing. The resentment is expressed in lines alluding to his broken heart, and the detachment, severely qualified by this, lies in his capacity to speak about the matter at all.

"The Scholars" (154, 140; 161, 337) seems a reaction to his own just previous didacticism. He has become learned at least on the subject of love; perhaps he has become even respectable. It would be well if he did not walk the way of the scholars, however. "Tom O'Roughley" (155, 141; 162, 337) ensures against that. It picks up what began in the beggar and fool poems of *Responsibilities* and will culminate in the poems of "Words for Music Perhaps." Tom is the traditional wise or antithetical fool, superior to scholars and "logic choppers." His antithetical wisdom rejects purposiveness in favor of an "aimless joy" and "zig-zag wantonness." The poem is spoken by the poet, who quotes Tom. However, some of Tom's deliberate aimlessness creeps into the poet's own attitude, for he says of Tom, "Or something of that sort he said," refusing to "edit and annotate the lines" as the scholars do. Tom's speech becomes more cryptic as it goes along, a characteristic the poet himself develops and passes on to various later speaking characters: Crazy Jane, Old Tom, and Ribh.

Robert Gregory's death has remained in the poet's consciousness. When, at the end of the poem, he recalls Tom saying, "And if my dearest friend were dead / I'd dance a measure on his grave," the memory of that recent death comes again to expression. The poet, however, does not dance, except insofar as any poem can be said to be metaphorically connected with dancing; if that is so, "Shepherd and Goatherd" (156, 141; 163, 338) is by contrast to Tom's a stately dance, though it contrasts strongly with the formal, courtierlike gesture of "In Memory of Major Robert Gregory." It invokes the classical pastoral elegy.

Something else is happening. The goatherd offers the first serious indication that the poet has developed a myth of an afterlife. It involves the idea that the soul in death passes back through the events of its life to birth and renewed ignorance. This backward passage is described as the paths of sun and moon were described in "Under the Round Tower": It is a whirling, gyring movement. The Yeatsian term "pern" is introduced to express this: "He unpacks the loaded pern / Of all 'twas pain or joy to learn" (156, 145; 163, 342). The renewed thought of this death produces dejection. The poet is not journeying back to youth, as the goatherd has Gregory doing. Rather, he is left with the "embittered sun" ("Lines written in Dejection," 157, 145; 164, 343). He regards himself as having lost the inspiration he identifies with a mysterious, passionate life that goes on under the moon, replete with exotic leopards, witches, and centaurs. At the age of fifty, he must "endure the timid sun."

In the next poem, "The Dawn" (158, 146; 165, 344), that sun rises figuratively, and he declares for ignorance, as if he were tacitly making a distinction between wisdom and knowledge. This wisdom, already identified with Solomon in his relation to Sheba, seems to include a special wise foolhood, or so it might seem to others. It is at least "wanton," he claims, as if ignorance were a sort of purity. It is perhaps like the state the goatherd declares Gregory to be achieving in passing backward to birth. This gesture of embrace of the dawn—and thus the detested sun—indicates the poet's decision to go ahead, as poet, into a world dominated by mundane values, holding antithetically and defiantly to his own.

"On Woman" (159, 146; 166, 345) provides a return to the consideration of wisdom in this new context—a wisdom of ignorance brought out of the experience of the heart, not of knowledge. He would, he says, live it all again, if it is true that life is cyclical. The dance of King Solomon and Queen Sheba is a dance led by the woman, who seems to be the source of wisdom. (Here Sheba seems to be a conflation of the poet's beloved and his wife.) To agree to live it all over again is to declare the experience of gaining wisdom, or the wisdom of experience, more important than knowledge. Wisdom is temporal, knowledge abstract and detached. The poet opts for experience, even to the extent of saying that he will go through the whole process of finding what he has found, knowing what he has known.

A fisherman ("The Fisherman," 160, 148; 167, 347) is a solitary creature of the dawn. In declaring that he will write to please such a person, he deliberately recalls "The Fish" (45, 58; 46, 146), where he himself was the seeker. Now he imagines a much more solitary and accomplished figure, not a netter but an expert, graceful fly-caster—an ideal figure for whom he will now write. His poem will be "maybe as cold / And passionate as the dawn." He accepts the dawn and its cold light. He answers his own complaint that his heart has grown old by setting for himself a new passionate task that we might call the task of passionate intellect rather than of the heart alone. He began to think this way "in scorn" of the broad audience he had hoped to reach. It is as if the poet, thinking that he faces his later years with the old inspiration gone, must write to a new and more demanding ideal. Appropriately, and somewhat mysteriously to the poet, there appears at this point a new bird in the poet's imagistic aviary, the hawk. This bird ("The Hawk," 161, 149; 168, 349) signifies something of his new and, to him, surprising power, to the extent that he even imagined it a sort of stupidity.

We are at a point where we expect a sharp change in the poet's work. But it is never that simple. He must constantly reearn his strength, for the forces of memory are very powerful. Just as we presume to expect the hard, cold poems prophesied in "The Fisherman," we discover remembrance of the beloved flowing back to the surface once again. The short "Memory" (162, 149; 169, 350) invokes her—as memory. Seven poems dealing with that memory follow. One, "The People" (164, 150; 171, 351), is a remembrance of a conversation with her of nine years before: The poet recalls complaining about the Dublin public, only to be reproved by her. This moment, in which he responded to her with an effective argument, he now recalls abashedly, as if he were the guilty one for having complained. Here, for the first time in the *Book*, she is conceded the moral advantage, and there is no remembrance of accusation or threat on his part. The poem "His Phoenix" (165, 151; 172, 353) has a quality quite different from the other poems about the beloved. The title recognizes, I think, her power as memory to keep being reborn, as she has been in this sequence. Accusation and self-pity apparently purged, the poem is almost like a rowdy song of praise. The one that follows ("A Thought from Propertius," 166, 153; 173, 355) is a postscript, an afterthought, the poet implying, "Oh yes, and this, too." It is a passionate, high statement, poised against the somewhat rowdy style of the preceding one, which suggests a street ballad. Next, in "Broken Dreams" (167, 153; 174, 355), he turns to address the beloved in her present state, though she is not present. The poem rambles garrulously and shows that the heart, aged as it may be, remains passionate after all, even as the poet declares his poem to be "rambling talk with an image of air: / Vague memories, nothing but memories" (167, 154; 174, 357).

Nor is the bitterness entirely purged. The poet reminds her of her broken vow, which sent him to other "friends" ("A Deep-sworn Vow," 168, 154; 175, 357), yet his passionate imagining in sleep of her face overcomes the bitterness. The dream leads to another night scene in "Presences" (169, 154; 176, 358). Here there is a curious trinity of women—harlot, child, and (perhaps) queen, who seem to represent to him the readers of his love poetry:

> . . . They had read
> All I had rhymed of that monstrous thing
> Returned and yet unrequited love.
>
> (169, 155; 176, 358)

These were poems not written to the fisherman; it is implied that they were written to the beloved in some enlarged idealization. The idealization seems to lift him from specific memories, as he commands,

> Hands, do what you're bid:
> Bring the balloon of the mind

> That bellies and drags in the wind
> Into its narrow shed.
>
> ("The Balloon of the Mind," 170, 155; 177, 358)

It is the old wind, identified with his love for her and with the unworldly desire associated with the beloved, that makes it difficult to control a mind with a tendency to romantic inflation.

In the slight poem to a squirrel ("To a Squirrel at Kyle-na-no," 171, 155; 178, 359), which follows, we are reminded that the poet is at Coole. He is in a gentle mood in a quiet place, and this may account in part for the attitude expressed in "On being asked for a War Poem" (172, 155; 179, 359); but the main reason for his refusal to write the poem is that he is an Irish poet. He invokes a picture of himself as poet that his work belies:

> He has had enough of meddling who can please
> A young girl in the indolence of her youth,
> Or an old man upon a winter's night.
>
> (172, 156; 179, 359)

The female trinity, the fisherman, and the poet's role are politely, but I think ironically, diminished as the poet performs a political refusal to take England's part.

There have been deaths other than Robert Gregory's in this period. The poet plays the laureate for his Pollexfen ancestors in a stately poem, "In Memory of Alfred Pollexfen" (173, 156; 180, 360). It is a poem dedicated to someone the poet seems not to have known very well or to have particularly admired. [Yeats himself had known Alfred Pollexfen well enough.] Yet he performs a familial poetic duty with considerable grace, and this points up again the grace of the refusal to write an "English" poem. The death of a woman friend [Mabel Beardsley, the actress, sister to Aubrey] has struck the poet's imagination much more forcibly. "Upon a Dying Lady" (174–80, 157; 181–87, 362) is not an elegy but a sequence describing moments in the lady's last days or, rather, moments in the poet's observation of her at this time, which are sometimes moments of the poet's observation of himself. The cumulative expression is one of her heroism, which is characterized as possessing virtues we have seen the poet admire before—courtesy, civility, courage, and gaiety. All of these things are part of a performance and therefore a mask. Hers is a fantastic *sprezzatura*. The "wicked" tales she tells are a form of courtesy and recklessness designed to keep up the spirits of those who come to visit her in her dying. Gifts of dolls are brought to her by friends. The poet implies the inadequacy of these gifts in a sad irony: "We have given the world our passion, / We have naught for death but toys" (175, 158; 182, 363).

He also praises her refusal to succumb to piety. She gives no quarter and makes her visitors vie with her in bawdy stories; her heart does not fail her. He predicts that she will join the heroic "who have lived in joy and laughed into the face of Death" (179, 159; 186, 366). He speaks of the "predestined dancing-place," to which she will go. He acknowledges at this moment that he has for this place no language but that of the "pagan speech" of his youth. In fact, as we shall soon see, his later poetry gives to the act of dancing a particular importance as the expression of a perfect moment of freedom achieved momentarily in life by some special people. This freedom has already been implied, with strong connections to innocence, in "To a Child dancing in the Wind," and it is not a surprise that he sees the dying lady as "playing like a child." Courteously asking pardon of the "great enemy," death, he describes himself and others presenting her with a Christmas tree. He asks that death may forgive her laughing defiance:

> Give her a little grace,
> What if a laughing eye
> Have looked into your face?
> It is about to die.
>
> (180, 160; 187, 367)

The poet, not himself like the laughing dying lady whom his poems so admire, speaks beseechingly to death in a way that the dying lady would not deign to do. He reveals that he is anxious about her defiant gaiety even as he praises it.

All through the sequence, it is she who is strong, her visitors who are weak and inadequate to the roles they call on themselves to play. In the Gregory elegy, death is called a discourtesy, a sort of outrage when it is visited on one so young. Here the poet asks death for the courtesy, not given to Gregory, of "a little grace."

To this point in *The Wild Swans at Coole*, two themes have been dominant—the elegiac and, more muted and under the figures of Solomon and Sheba, the development, occasioned by marriage, of wisdom about love. The latter has not been without resistance provided by the heart's memory of the beloved, but the memory has itself been affected and tempered by the elegiac. The conclusion of *The Wild Swans at Coole* is dominated by three poems, two in dialogue, that develop the earlier suggestion that the poet's marriage and a growing body of experience have brought a new activity of intellect. These poems are watersheds in the life we are reading [though Yeats himself quite misleadingly played down their importance to the *Book*].

The title of the first, "Ego Dominus Tuus" (181, 160; 188, 367), seems to make two allusions. One is apparently to Jesus' remark to the disciples in John 13:13–14, where he refers to himself as "I your Lord and Master." A subsidiary suggestion is Jesus' revelation of himself to the two disciples on the road to Emaeus and implies visionary experience. The other allusion is clearly to Dante's *La vita nuova*, in which the "lord of terrible aspect," or love, appears to Dante and declares, "I am thy master." The first of these allusions is religious, the second secular, though with religious connotations as the result of Dante's beatification of Beatrice. For the poet, the visionary aspect of the experience, which involves the appearance of an image, is of the greatest importance. The connection with Dante's love for the distant and lost Beatrice suggests some latent connection with a desire for his own beloved that cannot quite be exorcised. But the "master" is clearly going to be the imagined "antiself" figure of the poem, and this figure is, in contrast to those suggested by the allusion, clearly secular.

The vision of Jesus and of the "lord of terrible aspect" both have to do with the search in "Ego Dominus Tuus" for an "image" rather than a "book": This is a distinction perhaps similar to the one between kinds of books discussed in the first chapter. There is nothing abstract about these visions; they are alive and particular. A distinction between the particular and the abstract has been hovering over the poet's story since early in the text. The two characters of the poem again suggest it, and they appear at first not to be equal. The image-seeker, Ille, who desires from the antiself whom he seeks a secular vision, has the upper hand and the last word in this curious debate, but Hic does have his innings, and what occurs in later poems suggests that Ille's is but a momentary victory, that indeed his complete triumph would be a disaster. The poem is closely tied to the later "Phases of the Moon" in that Ille and Hic seem to represent a division of the poet into two parts. Living in the tower near Coole, he has been burning the midnight oil over an old book left to him years before by a mysterious traveler named Michael Robartes. [This is the book familiar to us from *A Vision* as Robartes' source for much of the mysterious lore of wheels and gyres.] It is as if the descent from the tower to earth (and water) has divided the poet into these antagonistic parts. Robartes, after having disappeared for many years, turns up in "The Phases of the Moon" with his antagonistic acquaintance, Owen Aherne, walking across the bridge beneath the tower. In "The Phases of the Moon," the poet, who is split into Hic and Ille in "Ego Dominus Tuus," has returned from the scene on the riverbank to study the book once more. Either Hic has after all influenced Ille to seek a book or Robartes' book is a very special kind of book, antithetical to most books—a book of the image or at least properly so constitutable.

Beneath the tower in "Ego Dominus Tuus," Hic, as interlocutor, plays the role of rational skeptic, tending toward impatience and a feeling of superiority over the misguided Ille. At first he does not question Ille, but rather makes a statement challenging Ille's odd behavior:

> On the grey sand beside the shallow stream
> Under your old wind-beaten tower, where still
> A lamp burns on beside the open book
> That Michael Robartes left, you walk in the moon
> And though you have passed the best of life still trace,
> Enthralled by the unconquerable delusion,
> Magical shapes.
>
> (181, 160; 188, 367)

His perception of Ille's behavior identifies it slightly with the sad shepherd's searching on the seashore. He implies that Ille's search for the image in the sands has been foolish and has gone on quite long enough. His attitude is that of wondering contempt. This is not surprising if we consider that Ille's search is on a terrain quite similar to the riverside on which Dante met the lord of terrible aspect for the second time. Hic, doubtless playing the rational side of the self and doubtless suspicious of the poet's emotions, knows quite well what a toll the poet's meeting with love has taken. (The poet had no doubt read *La vita nuova* in Dante Gabriel Rossetti's Pre-Raphaelite translation, and its style was that in which the poet had unsuccessfully wooed his beloved. No wonder, then, that Hic suspects this to be but another doomed love search.)

But in spite of the Dantean suggestions, the poet is not searching for the image of the beloved, though Hic probably has good reason to think that even if Ille is not he is on some equally foolish search characteristic of his past actions.

On the defensive from the beginning, Ille attempts to explain his motives. (In the *Book* it is always the Ille figure who is called to self-defense or to confession of guilt.) By meditation on an image he would call up his own opposite. He is seeking neither love nor religious revelation but the secular other. Hic then states the issue between them in its first version: *He* seeks himself, Ille seeks the image. Ille replies that the search for the self has been mistaken and is responsible for the present sorry state of intellectual culture. Search for the self he seems to identify with an Arnoldian notion of criticism; he declares, "We are but critics," clearly dissatisfied with that state. (Arnold had declared for sweetness and light and had announced an age of criticism.) Ille sees this as indicating a loss of creative power, a power he characterizes in its appearance as "the old nonchalance of the hand." Art has become the art of analytical thought. The issue seems to be that between, say, the earnestness of an Arnold and the *sprezzatura* of a Sidney or of a Robert Gregory, eulogized earlier as "our Sidney and our perfect man."

The latter is a search for the image, the creation of a dramatic mask, which, we are to presume, would display the recklessness of a Gregory or the courtesy of a dying lady. Particularly valued here is spontaneity of action not separated from the self but reaching out from it to another being. This "nonchalance" is of the "hand" as against the reason. It is like that of the fisherman's spontaneous grace, so well learned as to seem natural.

The search for the self advocated by Hic is the search for the truth of a book. Hic is clearly a rational sort. He offers Dante as a great poet who successfully found himself, but Ille questions this, claiming that Dante chose the most difficult of searches, driving himself to fashion an image of desire. Again *La vita nuova* and the lord of terrible aspect play in the background: In Ille's view the search is the act of making the image of one's desire while inevitably remaining always short of its realization.

At this point, the second version of the difference between Hic and Ille is presented. It is treated as the opposition between the life of action and that of art. Hic has suggested that there have been poets who have made their poetry not of "tragic war" or the division that Ille sees but instead of achieved happiness. Ille denies this, claiming that those who "love the world," that is, have actually before them their desire and achieve it, may "paint or write," but it remains action rather than art. Of this sort of action there are two kinds: rhetoric and sentimentality. They are named "action" by Ille because they are definable in terms of some external purpose. Both forms are deceitful—of others and of the self, respectively, and so from Ille's point of view they are not really successful even in their own terms, being but "the struggle of the fly in marmalade."

Art, on the other hand, is a "vision of reality." Actually, Ille says art is "but a vision of reality," emphasizing art's lack of external purposiveness and thus, from Hic's point of view, its meagerness. Vision is of the image, which is apparently always what Blake called a "minute particular," as we shall see in the later "Double Vision of Michael Robartes" (188, 172; 195, 384). At this point, in a rhetorical question, Ille claims that the artist must inevitably have as his portion of the world "dissipation and despair." Two models seem to be behind this statement. The first is near to hand in the earlier treatment of the poets of the Rhymers' Club in "The Grey Rock," and the argument of Ille here turns out to support that earlier defense of their lives. The other is in another poet's poem that is never far from Yeats's consciousness and that we have had cause to mention before (A phrase of the poem was ever so slightly recalled in "In Memory of Major Robert Gregory"): Wordsworth's "Resolution and Independence." In it, the leech-gatherer is a man who, unlike Gregory, lived to wear "grey hairs." Wordsworth describes himself as thinking morosely on the lives of poets: "We poets in our youth begin in gladness, / But thereof come in the end despondency and madness" (48–49). He recovers from the threat of this state in his meeting with the leech-gatherer, a ghostly figure who in Ille's mind would surely be interpreted as Wordsworth's saving ideal image or antiself.

Ille regards the artist as having awakened from the "common dream," which appears to be the illusion of the utilitarian world of action, only to face "dissipation and despair." One notes here that the villain remains the same world castigated in the second poem of the *Book*, "The Song of the Happy Shepherd," a world that was described there, as it is here, as a world of dreams. But now the remedy is no longer to dream a different, opposed dream but to engage in search. When Wordsworth first sees the leech-gatherer, he thinks him

> Like one whom I had met with in a dream;
> Or like a man from some far region sent,
> To give me human strength, by apt admonishment.
>
> (110–12)

It is clear that Wordsworth has *not* dreamed this figure; Ille makes a claim for the reality of his search against the self-deception (or dreams) of happiness in writers of action. Ille's notion of the antiself is not, however, that it will come as an admonisher, possibly because this sounds too moralistic and externally purposive. He does not deny that it might come as a lord of terrible aspect. Even if it does, the poet does not require a moralistic antiself to admonish him, for he has already proved fully capable of self-admonishment in many previous poems, just as in a later poem he will declare that he can forgive himself rather than seek external absolution ("A Dialogue of Self and Soul," 242, 236; 250, 479).

We can imagine here that the poet might now treat some of his earlier works as examples of the very action he deplores. In old age the poet will do this (see "The Circus Animals' Desertion," 373, 346; 381, 629), for so many of his earlier poems had a clearly active design on the beloved or were employed to castigate her or himself. Many were clearly rhetorical or sentimental deceptions. [Does this mean that by Yeats's judgment, at least, they were bad poems—"the struggle of the fly in marmalade"? No, only if he treats them as part of an actual personal history outside the context of the *Book* and its story. Yeats, it appears, wanted to save his early poems from his own dissatisfaction with them. Revision and contextualization in the *Book*, including some reordering and putting them into the voice of a fictive characterization of himself, were the means he employed.]

Hic still resists Ille's argument. What about Keats? Was he not happy?
Hic harms his own challenge to Ille here, even as he offers it, by describing
Keats's happiness as "deliberate." Ille immediately counters by making a
distinction between Keats's art and his mind and paints a picture of Keats
yearning for the luxury his poems present. Hic either is silenced in defeat
or decides that further reasoning with Ille is hopeless. He offers no more
argument. Besides, it appears that Ille is now acting even more strangely,
tracing odd figures on the river sand beneath the tower. Hic returns to his
earlier manner and asks somewhat scornfully and/or with wondering
disbelief,

> Why should you leave the lamp
> Burning alone beside an open book,
> And trace these characters upon the sands?
> A style is found by sedentary toil
> And by the imitation of great masters.

> (181, 162; 188, 370)

Hic offers here, virtually as an admonition (he is an admonisher, even
perhaps what Blake called an accuser), the classical Horatian notion of the
poet as an imitator of great predecessors. Ille's notion of the poet contains
much more tension. He replaces the predecessor with the antiself figure,
who may well be of terrible aspect. The poet is a solitary quester, whose
quest is to create. Hic's tradition, Ille implies, has become shallow. Ille has
left the book up in the tower to seek an image, to trace on the sands diagrams from that book, to actualize them in the hope that he will lure the
antiself to incarnate appearance before him. This suggests the connection
of the image with a visionary moment, for the wind and water will inevitably sweep the diagrams away, and they will remain only in the memory
of the moment, or the moment of the antiself's appearance, just as the
leech-gatherer remained an image in a spot of time for Wordsworth, the
lord of terrible aspect so remained for Dante, and Jesus so remained for
the disciples.

It is clear that the idea of the book plays an ambiguous role here. For
Hic, the book is a sufficient container of, or rather pointer to, truth; for
Ille, the book is ultimately insufficient as such. Impelled by his study of
Robartes' book to further search and accompanied inevitably by his ra-
tional side, he has come down from the tower to trace characters on the
sand, hoping to call up the image, from these abstract figures, of

> . . . the mysterious one who yet
> Shall walk the wet sands by the edge of the stream
> And look most like me, being indeed my double,

And prove of all imaginable things
The most unlike.

(181, 162; 188, 371)

Hic, who believes in solitary toil, does not question the book. It is as if for Ille the characters on the sand *require* the ephemerality suggested by the threat of their imminent erasure. This is not the Platonic suspicion of writing as such but wariness of the deception of rhetoric and sentimentality. It is the sense that a book having the purposive design of rhetoric will by that power fix itself into law and become the vehicle that suppresses art. Ille's leaving the book he studies (about which we are to learn more in "The Phases of the Moon," 183, 163; 190, 372) to walk the sands in moonlight is a denial of the book in this sense, but it affirms the possibility of a book as a means toward speculation and search for the antiself. This latter book is what I called in chapter 1, using Yeats's own term, an "antithetical" book. The problem is to understand what kind of book one is reading, or perhaps it is to understand how to constitute a book *as* antithetical.

The term "antiself," offered in this poem, occurs nowhere else in Yeats's *Book*. It embodies an important paradox that needs discussion here. One might at first imagine that Hic is Ille's antiself. After all, he appears to be his opposite. But this is to misunderstand the concept. Hic and Ille are surely in opposition, but this opposition is best described by Blake's term "negation." In negation, disagreement does not allow for equal, potentially creative opposition; one side must triumph. Neither Hic nor Ille finds the other a creative "contrary," another Blakean term. What resolution there is in the poem comes only by Ille's having the last word. Ille's thought, rather than really addressing Hic as a true contrary, wanders away from him into its own imagistic language without regard for his presence. The true antiself that Ille seeks is neither only a repetition of himself nor only a figure completely different from himself. The relation of Ille to his antiself he characterizes as a "double" that is nevertheless "most unlike" him.

This curious relation needs a name, and I would like to call it "identity," in the sense that this term harbors difference and indifference *at the same time*.[1] Identity has the same form as does a metaphorical trope (under which term I include metaphor in its more restricted sense, metonymy, and synecdoche), where sameness and difference coexist in language. It is not surprising that Ille's search should be involved with metaphor, and a most strenuous metaphor at that—something that is both same and at the same time "of all things imaginable / The most unlike." It is not surprising

1. On this point see my *Philosophy of the Literary Symbolic* (Tallahassee: Florida State University Press, 1983), pp. 6–7, and "The Dizziness of Freedom; or, Why I Read William Blake," *College English* 48, no. 5 (September 1986): 433–34.

that the figure Ille seeks suggests an earlier formulation of an ideal in the poem about the fisherman, to whom the poet claimed he would now write. It will also not be surprising that when we read "The Tower" (205, 194; 212, 409) we will find the poet contemplating the triumphant end of the poet's search and there rejecting that triumph, or completion of the self in the antiself, which would end up as no different from Hic's finding of the self. Such completion the poet will regard in "The Tower" as a threat to the sanity of his readers, as the triumph of an externally purposive rhetoric: "For if I triumph I must make men mad" (205, 196; 212, 411). Thus the *Book* begins to form itself as, in part, the story of the ethical necessity of continued search.

Entering and exiting from the tower turns out to be a motif. The single poem that performs a bridge between "Ego Dominus Tuus" and "The Phases of the Moon" is like a ritual. "A Prayer on going into my House" (182, 162; 189, 371) asks for simple things such as "the great and passionate have used" and curses anyone who will spoil the view. In "The Phases of the Moon" (183, 163; 190, 372), Hic-Ille (the poet is not just Ille) seems to have returned to the tower and is once again poring over the book that Robartes had given him years before. Return to the book risks the danger of reading it only as fixed doctrine, the danger Ille has tried to escape.

With the poet apparently studying the book, Michael Robartes and Owen Aherne, figures about whom the poet had written stories years before, come across the bridge beneath the poet's window. It is a night of a "dwindling" moon, which suggests that the poet reads under domination of his Hic half. In the relation between Aherne and Robartes, Robartes is the visionary, and Aherne is the interpreter. Indeed, Robartes seems to act as Aherne's eyes: It is Aherne who, startled by a sound, asks what made it; it is Robartes who provides the answer, as if Aherne were blind. Robartes explains where they are and that the poet is reading in the tower above them. Robartes suggests that the poet "has found, after the manner of his kind, / Mere images."

In "Ego Dominus Tuus," Ille declared that he sought the image, and Robartes is correct in his characterization of the poet as an image-finder. There is irony in Robartes' use of the word "mere" to describe the images the poet has found. He implies that discovery of images has been somehow insufficient for the poet, who, as Hic-Ille and under a waning moon (where Hic dominates), has returned to study the book. He seems to take some malicious pleasure in declaring that the "mysterious wisdom" the poet seeks will not be found in a book. He seems to align himself with the spontaneity of oral performance, and what follows is such a performance. We can see, of course, that it is written by the poet; but it is written in the form of a drama of speech, which makes it part of what I have called an "antithetical book," the two major characteristics of which are drama and the creative, antirhetorical employment of tropes.[2] As such, it must be read more for its drama and gesture than for what doctrine can be extracted from it.[3] This Aherne has virtually no capacity to accomplish, and this the poet in the tower is alleged to have difficulty doing with the book before him.

Aherne, too, bears some malice toward the poet and suggests that Robartes go to the tower door and reveal just enough to frustrate him further. We learn the reason for at least part of Robartes' indignation. The poet had written about him in the style of Pater and had killed him off many years ago in a story.[4] He chooses to remain dead to the poet. But he does not choose to torment the poet further, as Aherne imagines doing. The reason for Aherne's malice is not stated, but as the poem develops, it does become clear that Aherne is the type who covets. Once thinking that he possesses Robartes' wisdom, he jealously keeps the secret. He is an interpreter, a member of what Blake saw as a "priesthood," with a strong tendency toward abstraction and moralization, and he would read Robartes' song as allegories of an abstract truth. He is a curious combination of childish follower and rational guardian of the faith. In Robartes' company he is not only blind but also like a child asking an adult to sing a song once again. He would make the event into a ritual of belief.

Robartes' song is interrupted by Aherne's interpretations, which twice lead to brief dialogues in which Robartes seems to endorse Aherne's readings or at least to tolerate them. His ego is perhaps gratified by having a disciple. [In *A Vision*, the interpreter figure is Yeats, who begins by trying to grasp the instructors' messages as a ground for doctrine, in spite of the fact that they warn him that they have come to give him "metaphors for poetry."]

The song, like everything in the *Book*, should be read as a particular act

---

2. I employ "rhetorical" in the traditional sense of the use of tropes in discourse to move, convince, or delight. My meaning is older than the recent usage made popular by Paul de Man, in which rhetoric refers to all discourse on the ground that all discourse employs tropes. De Man's usage leads to the notion that *all* language is untrustworthy and seductive. I use the term in the older pejorative sense of tropes in the pay of persuasion. My meaning distinguishes between such an externally purposeful use of tropes and the use of tropes to aid in search of an image, or, as Mazzoni says, to make an "idol." My meaning is Ille's in "Ego Dominus Tuus." Both uses are pejorative—de Man's about language in general, mine about tropes used to clothe and make agreeable bad arguments.

3. I am not aware that the former has very often happened with the poem, for critics hardly ever pay appropriate attention to its drama. The same can be said for most critics of *A Vision*, the abstractions of which are subtly hedged around and framed by comedy and dramatic performance. Yeats himself is partly to blame for this because of certain disparaging remarks he made about the poems that seem to explicate his "system" of thought. But Yeats rarely could resist drama and tended to turn everything in its direction.

4. The story is "Rosa Alchemica." Actually, in the story it is not clear that Robartes dies.

in a drama. It is not a mere explication, nor is the whole poem [no matter what Yeats said about it]. The poem expresses, among other things, Robartes' nature and mode of vision and his attitude toward Aherne and the poet. It also expresses Aherne's attitudes and, by extension, the relation of antithetical and primary personalities. Both Aherne and Robartes seem rather disreputable-looking figures, though perhaps only because they have traveled far. That Robartes is a traveler suggests a relation between him and the traveling men of earlier poems in the *Book* (and of Irish literature generally) for whom the poet seems to have affection.

In Robartes' song there are clearly occult implications. If we approach it as Aherne does, we seek the abstract idea behind the cryptic code. Much occult writing dating back to neoplatonic allegories seems to be a coded message or the interpretation of the world regarded as a code. But Robartes' language dissuades us from this even as it seems to invite it. There is reason to agree with Northrop Frye that poets' interest in the occult in the second half of the nineteenth century indicated a search for a poetic language disenfranchised and driven underground with the rise of science.[5] But there is a vast difference between occult writing that requires a key and the dramatic language of poetry, which tends to decadence and dullness when it offers itself merely as code. It is best to read Robartes' song as an obscure speech in a dramatic poem. One builds meaning *from* it rather than finding meaning behind it. There is considerable question whether or not Aherne fully grasps this when, at the end, imagining himself tormenting the poet with cryptic speech, he thinks "that what seemed so hard should be so simple."

It is not simple. That there are twenty-eight phases of the moon is simple enough. That these phases have highly imagistic descriptions is not. Robartes describes the life of man on the wheel of the moon as a summons to adventure, the birth of heroism, internal warfare, the soul becoming body at phase fifteen and then becoming the world's servant until it moves through the last crescents of "hunchback, saint, and fool." Most important to Robartes' song is phase fifteen, and it is here that it is most obscure. At this point Aherne enters and asserts the dialogical situation, as if he decides that Robartes needs an interpreter. Phase fifteen, which apparently marks the moment of greatest bodily power and the unity of body and soul or complete absence of the division, is particularly important because Robartes connects it with the pure image.

It appears from Robartes' song as a whole that the distinction between soul and body, with the body negated, dominates the early and late lunar

---

5. Northrop Frye, "Yeats and the Language of Symbolism," in *Fables of Identity: Studies in Poetic Mythology* (New York: Harcourt Brace and World, 1963), pp. 218–37.

phases, which are childhood and old age. However, in the phases near the full of the moon (phase fifteen), the body overcomes its negation. In those near the dark of the moon, thought dominates, and in those near the full, imagistic beauty. At either extreme—phases one and fifteen—there can be no life, for these phases are perfect of their kind. Thought in its perfection is pure abstraction, complete bodily annihilation, soul dominating fully. Image in its perfection is complete union of body and soul, to the extent that body as body and soul as soul are "cast away beyond the visible world," and only the beautiful image *as* image remains. This can be seen as the apotheosis of body, but only in that it is spiritualized into a bodily image, a *purely* sensuous abstraction, a concrete universal or universal concretion, what Blake called the "spiritual body."

At this point, Aherne interrupts the song with an interpretation: "All dreams of the soul / End in a beautiful man's or woman's body" (183, 165; 190, 374). Aherne recognizes that to *imagine* the soul is to give it an image. Robartes endorses this view with a rhetorical question ("Have you not always known it?"), which indicates that Aherne's statement is so obviously, instinctively true that one should not need the song to know it. On the other hand, maybe Aherne does, for he then goes on to a further interpretation. He imagines as the object of love the figures whose bodies have been denigrated, wounded, self-flagellated. For him, the image—an image still dominated by the type of personality he represents—remains transfixed by the ascetic ideal. One supposes that this sort of image is the nearest that Aherne, captured by abstract thought, can come to admission of the sensuous. It suggests a certain masochism in Aherne, who is attracted to the bodily passions but really desires to purge them.

Robartes answers with the observation that "the lover's heart" knows what Aherne has just said, indicating again that this knowledge is directly available to the feelings. Aherne, who has heard this song before, nevertheless produces what seems to be a new reading of or speculation on it: The terror in the eyes of lovers is, he imagines, the "memory or foreknowledge" of the annihilation occurring at phase one. Robartes does not comment on this. It was certainly again spoken from the point of view of the soul, which resists giving itself to the complete sensuosity of the image. Continuing his song, Robartes treats of contemplation of the pure image. It is a condition in which the perceiver and the perceived no longer are merely a subject to an object but are, though separate, fully involved with one another. They maintain their identities while remaining identical. The relation is that of imagistic contemplation and empathy as opposed to abstracting, distancing, and self-destroying thought.

The song proceeds, punctuated by Aherne's malicious laughter at the thought of the poet in the tower. Robartes describes the waning phases, the reemergence of the external world and its domination of the soul. Aherne provides a neat interpretation: "Before the full / It sought itself and afterwards the world" (183, 166; 190, 376). Robartes' answer to this again seems to endorse Aherne's reading, but it is an odd compliment: "Because you are forgotten, half out of life, / And never wrote a book, your thought is clear" (183, 166; 190, 376). Robartes implies that Aherne's thought, identified with the dominating soul, gains its power from its distance from life, in the sense of abstract contemplation of it. Clarity is identified with this abstraction and requires the purging of the image, as in Plato's valorization of mathematics. Absent here would be the capacity to identify the self with the image—the aim of Ille and of the artist. Robartes' remark that Aherne's thought is clear because he has not written a book is a sarcastic comment on the poet, who is a writer of books. It implies a suspicion, similar to Plato's, that writing dulls the mind by abstracting one from one's thought.

Aherne seems gratified by this, and he is now content to punctuate the song with questions that encourage Robartes to proceed. Without these comments, Robartes would lapse into silence. Aherne plays the role of disciple or communicator of the word. He looks beyond himself for truth and is inevitably a follower. Indeed, his tendency to want to make a book of Robartes' vision—the book as book of revelatory law—not only makes us somewhat wary of him but ought to make us wary of Robartes because of Robartes' power over him. This power, which is the antithetical power of the pied piper or the magician, can be used perversely. As Blake remarked of people like Aherne, "Those who restrain desire do so because their desire is weak enough to be restrained."

The song completed, or, at least, the last lunar phases mentioned, Aherne maliciously imagines himself tormenting the poet with his occult knowledge, concealed in Robartes' language, regarded as an allegorical code:

> I'd stand and mutter there until he caught
> "Hunchback and Saint and Fool," and that they came
> Under the last three crescents of the moon,
> And then I'd stagger out. He'd crack his wits
> Day after day, yet never find the meaning.
>
> (183, 167; 190, 377)

Is the poet in the tower a poet who is but a critic, as Ille accused poets of his age of being? Is this the reason that the poet seems to pore endlessly over the book that Robartes gave to him years before? Or is it only that no one in actual life can reach perfect identification with the image of phase fifteen, that indeed no one in life can reach either perfect abstraction or perfect artifice? The reader, it appears, is always caught in this situation. Hic is always present to Ille and Ille to Hic. It is then a question of how best to write and to read. Ille has said something about writing. Reading may be just as difficult. [In *A Vision*, Robartes seems never to have solved the problem of reading the book that he has discovered, and eventually, after rejecting order and reason, he is orally instructed in its crucial missing pages by an old Arab.] Reading is inevitably and to a considerable degree Ahernean—the question may be only to what degree—and the writer of even the most antithetical of books may have to take deliberate measures to limit the success of a reader who would by interpretation turn the book into some set of generalizations.

Blake wrote of this problem in his letter to Dr. Trusler, advocating texts that "rouse the faculties to act" and distinguishing between "allegory addressed to the intellectual powers" and that addressed to the "corporeal understanding," by which latter he meant a mind committed to a concept of language that would purge it of tropes and drama and would reduce its conveyance to abstractions thought to imitate or accurately signify an external, "real" world or some ideal one. One notices that in "The Phases of the Moon" at each extreme there is no life, only the ideal. At one extreme is the ideal of perfect nothingness, which is also perfect submission to God. At the other extreme is the ideal of the perfect image, the perfect *somethingness*. The poet has not had Robartes present us with a situation in which spirit is at the idealist end and matter at the materialist one. The reason for this is that materialism is identified not with the sensual, as one might suppose, but with the ascetic. The poetic is identified with the sensual and sensuous. Why? For this *Book*, materialism spiritualizes reality. Materialism finds reality in the Lockean primary qualities of experience, devoid of the unmeasurable sensuous secondary qualities, which Locke located in the subjectivity of the mind. If one takes away the secondary qualities, what remains are the primary qualities, but one has no way to apprehend them. The only way to conceive of them is in a mathematical symbolism, which is purely abstract (having no imagistic quality) and therefore pure spirit. The world of the materialist is thus the world of pure spirit. The scientist, who studies matter, and the saint, who would denigrate the body, have this in common. The former studies spirit; the latter practices asceticism.

On the other hand, the poet, always tied to the ideal of the image, must have sensuosity. He insists on investing externality with the secondary qualities, opposing the subject-object distinction. He is a sensualist but not a materialist. The materialist, as we have seen, has much more in common with the saint. Both think a form of the subject-object distinction. It is fair, therefore, to call Aherne "primary," connecting him with the

Lockean valorization of the primary qualities [as Yeats actually does in *A Vision*], and Robartes "antithetical," that is, antithetical to the dominant or primary tendency in the culture, which is to valorize the primary. The term "antithetical" escapes the denigration of "secondary." Robartes is associated with a resistant tradition that has had to go underground and has risked decadence in its flirtation with and occasional embrace of occultism. He is disreputable and sensual. If, as Blake says, one is what one beholds, it should be no surprise that, as readers, we should have a clearer *image* of Robartes than of Aherne. Robartes beholds the image, Aherne the abstraction.

We must remember, of course, that the poet casts himself in his poem as a silent third person, thus playing two roles—author and offstage performer. This indicates that Robartes and Aherne are two aspects of himself but also that they are projections of these aspects, invented by him and taking on their own life as dramatis personae. They are both antithetical projections and thus—even Aherne—images, not merely concepts. One advantage of the antithetical vision is that it can include its contrary as an equal, whereas primary thought cannot *imagine* the contrary except as secondary to it. From this point forward it is clear to the poet that his role is to be antithetical to the prevailing primary phases of history in which he lives. He had already begun to act instinctively on this insight; now he has a myth to justify and enhance his role.

The poems that follow "The Phases of the Moon" develop aspects of Robartes' song. "The Cat and the Moon" (184, 167; 191, 378) involves the idea of the cat as a lunar animal that moves in mysterious concert with the moon. This identity is treated in the image of a courtly dance, which recalls previous dancing figures whom we can now identify with Robartes' phase fifteen, the dance being the supreme image of sensual art, embodying the ideal of antithetical freedom. The dancer's self-absorption is one that the wind, as the poet uses it, has used it, and has feared it, cannot touch, as it failed to touch the dancing child in an earlier poem.

The antithetical image of dancing suggests a close connection between the antithetical and performance. It would seem, then, that a performing art—dancing or acting—is superior in this respect to the making of paintings, sculptures, musical works, or poems and that a free form of such activity is superior to a role accepted from without. The drama of the making of the *Book*, can, of course, be seen in the larger context of real history as an effort by the author W. B. Yeats to project himself into a role, to act antithetically. However, it is important, and the whole point of this study, to think first of the whole of the text or its authority as simply a performing, antithetical acting, not necessarily that of a historical W. B. Yeats, not the kind of "action" opposed by Ille in "Ego Dominus Tuus." The poet who acts in the text, soon to name himself William Yeats, must himself create a role, and it is the drama of such creation that we are reading. But we see also here the possibility of an infinite regress of actors and of more and more expansive readings or contexts for readings, each one of which has its own set of critical problems. [The notion of infinite regress in the image is one not foreign to the Yeats of *A Vision*, who employs there the figure of a room full of mirrors, the image itself being both one and many at the same time.] The authority of the *Book* is an arrangement made by someone, who is invented by someone in a larger arrangement, who may well be invented, and so on.

"The Saint and the Hunchback" (185, 168; 192, 379) follows. It is an elaboration of part of Robartes' story, being a dialogue between figures representing two of the last three lunar phases mentioned in "The Phases of the Moon." The hunchback, who resents his hump, suggests growth of hatred of the body that culminates in the saint's asceticism. But the hunchback is still a sensualist; he hates not all bodies, only his. Though the saint would "thrash" Alexander, Caesar, and Alcibiades from his flesh, the hunchback gives thanks to all these and especially to Alcibiades, the most disreputable of the trio, whom he glorifies here in defiance of the saint. Robartes had spoken obscurely of the saint:

> The burning bow that once could shoot an arrow
> Out of the up and down, the wagon-wheel
> Of beauty's cruelty and wisdom's chatter—
> Out of that raving tide—is drawn betwixt
> Deformity of body and of mind.
>
> (183, 166–67; 190, 377)

The fool, the last phase, is utter deformity of mind, as the hunchback is deformity of body. Between them, between these two phases, the saint draws the "burning bow," but the lines indicate that he can no longer shoot the arrow "out of the up and down" and is destined for foolhood.

The term "deformity of mind" to describe the fool is ironic. The fool no longer controls his body or his mind. He is "out" of both; they are not so much deformed as absent to his consciousness. "Deformity" is thus a word that takes the point of view of an observer who does not grasp this and sees only something grotesque. The fool does not hate his body, as the saint does, but has lost his sense of relation to it. It is now irrelevant to his sense of being, if we can say he has such a sense; the body is still present, though he cannot control it.

The songs in "Two Songs of a Fool" (186, 169; 193, 380) are ironic, too. They are spoken by the poet as, in a sense, a fool. The first seems to be an allegory of a domestic scene. The poet speaks of the burden of what we

might call external responsibilities and fears for his ability always to remember them. His mind threatens, foollike, to wander off. Indeed, the
poet-fool does fall asleep, and one of his charges does wander off. "Another Song of a Fool" (187, 170; 194, 381) is more recognizably in the
tradition of fools' voices. The poet contemplates a butterfly he has captured, reading into it an earlier life as a schoolmaster. This reincarnation
of the butterfly seems to indicate a process of opposition from one life to
the next.

After these moments, where parts of Robartes' vision seem to play in
the poet's life, we are returned to Michael Robartes, who remembers a
night alone on the Rock of Cashel in the moon's dark. "The Double Vision
of Michael Robartes" (188, 170; 195, 382) may continue the play with the
idea of the fool. Robartes is no fool, and there is no reason to think he has
entered that phase of life, but it is possible to say that Robartes' visions
appear foolish to primary types not subject to the hypnotism of his song.

Once again, as in all three of the important longer poems at the end of
The Wild Swans at Coole, the scene is carefully set. It is a place conducive to
the raising of spirits. Robartes apparently went there to summon up a vision. It is interesting that he attempts to create a vision of the ultimate
primary by antithetical means, that is to say, by imagistic and dramatic
means. How else could there be a *vision* of the primary? It is the *eye* of the
mind that calls up the spirits of phase one at the dark of the moon. Of
course, strictly speaking, a visionary image of the primary is impossible or
at least a false copy, as Plato would say, but this does not deter the antithetical Robartes, who, in good antithetical fashion, wills its appearance.
The figures that he produces are puppets, totally externally controlled,
symbols of submission of the body to outer authority (whether God or
nature it is not said; rather, the force is described as "some hidden magical
breath"). Because antithetical vision is empathetic, Robartes declares himself to be like them in the moment of the vision: He has lost his own will.
They are the ideal image of the primary. One may think of them in contrast to the dolls of "The Dolls," who take on more of a life of their own.
These

> . . . do not even feel, so abstract are they,
> So dead beyond our death,
> Triumph that we obey.

(188, 171; 195, 382)

Suddenly, however, in part 2 of the poem, the vision changes. Whether
this represents a second visit to the rock on the night of a full moon or the
willing of an antithetical vision of ideal antitheticality is undecidable. The
dancer, who is ideal and pure image, is positioned between Sphinx and

Buddha, which are declared to represent intellect and love, respectively. All three of these images, being antithetically ideal, have solitude and indifference about them. In recalling this moment, Robartes asks a rhetorical question: "For what but eye and ear silence the mind / With the minute particulars of mankind?" (188, 172; 195, 384). The answer must be that nothing but sensuous representations such as these silence the mind, which is here identified with primary abstract thought. The minute particulars, the indubitably indifferent, independent self-being and beauty of objects, are the products of antithetical vision. This constitution of their being is the ultimate form of empathetic identification, in which one both is and is not the *same* as the object, and the object is let be. Robartes calls such objects both alive and dead, temporal and atemporal.

The vision is described as gone in part 3, and Robartes attempts in memory to understand it. He believes that he saw the ideal woman of his dreams, the image of sensual desire in contrast to the *image* of ascetic desire for annihilation conjured in part 1. In memory, this experience leaves him feeling as if he had been "undone" by Helen of Troy, whose beauty was indifferent and thoughtless (like that of the poet's beloved, the poet once claimed, when he identified her with Helen). Caught, then, between the two visions, he now imagines that he was made a fool. The poet thus connects this vision to his own preceding poems, where he was the fool figure. Admission of foolhood does not cause Robartes to repudiate his double vision. He has made a song of it and gives thanks for it, playing the role of fool as prophet.

Michael Robartes and the Dancer (1921)

The dancer to whom Michael Robartes talks in the title poem of this section (189, 175; 196, 385) is not the ideal dancer conjured up in "The Double Vision of Michael Robartes." Rather, she is a real young woman. The motives of Robartes, who encourages her to emulate that ideal, are not so ideal. His argument is an attempt at seduction parallel to that of "The Mask." It is perhaps impossible for the antithetical Robartes to converse with her on this kind of subject and not attempt seduction. The scene is apparently an art gallery; Robartes, observing an altarpiece depicting Saint George dispatching the dragon, interprets the scene as the man's rescue of the woman from her thought. The ideal dancer of the previous poem, we recall, has "outdanced thought." In this more mundane situation, thought, according to Robartes, is abstract "opinion," which must be dispatched. The woman being addressed has her wits and at once interprets the painting as a domestic quarrel. The painting becomes a means to speculative conversation and verbal play. Robartes identifies wisdom with beauty and the work of becoming beautiful that we remember being mentioned by one of the women in "Adam's Curse." He proceeds to argue, very much as does the casuist of "The Mask," that it is this achieved beauty that her lover will identify with her true being. He will be irritated at all else.

The woman sees at once that this may imply that she should not seek education, for the argument implies that education is training in abstraction.

> Go pluck Athena by the hair;
> For what mere book can grant a knowledge
> With an impassioned gravity
> Appropriate to that beating breast,
> That vigorous thigh, that dreaming eye?
> And may the devil take the rest.
>
>   (189, 175; 196, 386)

The book is denigrated more decisively here than in Ille's distinction between book and image.

The dancer's response implies that Robartes has relegated women to a secondary role. This is true from one point of view; it is certainly true that Robartes' argument is at least part seduction and that he employs "thought" against her. But at the same time Robartes' argument is consistent with his antithetical position, opposing the negation that privileges soul over body, primary abstraction over the thinking of the body. In school, she has already learned this negation as doctrine. Robartes' rhetorical question involving the Incarnation and the Eucharist implies that God gave human beings not merely souls but also bodies. The question unsettles the young woman.

At this point, Robartes calls on a book for support—apparently the same thing that he earlier claimed cannot provide an adequate knowledge. But *this* book is an antithetical book, for it opposes the opposition of soul and body: "Blest souls are not composite." We suspect that Robartes may have written this book himself, though he claims it to be a Latin text: "all beautiful women may / Live in uncomposite blessedness," providing that they "banish every thought." There is one qualification: If the body thinks the thought, it is all right. The oxymoronic expression "thinking body" is antithetically opposed to the body/soul division. The young woman's response leaves unclear whether or not the seduction has worked. The poem as a whole shows Robartes equivocating on the nature of the book. It appears that book/image may no longer be the right opposition and that two kinds of books oppose each other.

The three poems that follow move from the Robartes-dancer fiction through another Solomon-Sheba poem and a dialogue of He and She to a significantly dated poem in which the poet for the first time directly addresses his wife. The first, "Solomon and the Witch" (190, 176; 197, 387), involves the connection the poet has earlier made between his marriage and acquisition of wisdom. It treats a serious matter comically. The witch is Sheba, who is a sort of medium. Her wisdom is, therefore, not that derided by Robartes under the term "opinion." It is connected with her sexuality; the moment of possession by a "strange tongue" comes in sexual embrace.

Solomon responds wittily with a complex, learned discourse to Sheba's recounting of the previous night's event. He imagines that the crowing of a cockerel signaled the creation of the world and that with their love-making it had crowed again to end time. In spite of the fact that lovers bring imagined images of their beloveds to the bridal bed and there find real images, the joining of lovers, Solomon remarks, does end the world. But Sheba observes that the world remains. Solomon's response is that the image brought to the bed was either too strong or too weak, that is, not equal to the real. But he goes on amusingly to remark that whatever it was, the cockerel thought it "worth a crow," and Sheba implores him to try again.

Like all moments of antithetical intensity in the *Book*, it cannot be sustained. Remembrance of it becomes confused with the passage of time and the resurgence of primary force in the external life. Wise Solomon knows this. He knows also that

> . . . love has a spider's eye
> To find out some appropriate pain—
> Aye, though all passion's in the glance—
> For every nerve, and tests a lover
> With cruelties of Choice and Chance.
>
>   (190, 177; 197, 388)

The ensuing dialogue, "An Image from a Past Life" (191, 178; 198, 389), is so titled to suggest that the image called up by the lovers is now alien to the poet's present life, that a new life has begun. The scene is the tower. There are two characters, He and She, clearly the poet and his wife. He hears a bird's or beast's cry, and it is quite the opposite of the cockerel's crowing. It is an image of "poignant recollection," and She declares it "an image of my heart that is smitten through." Like a witch or medium, She conjures up the sound's source in the ghost of his "sweetheart from another life," employing in her description a figure the poet had used years before in "He wishes his Beloved were Dead" (73, 72; 74, 175).

There is a sense in which the beloved *is* dead, but it is the ghost that frightens her:

> A sweetheart from another life floats there
> As though she had been forced to linger
> From vague distress
> Or arrogant loveliness,
> Merely to loosen out a tress
> Among the starry eddies of her hair.
>
> (191, 178–79; 198, 390)

This vision, which frightens her, moves He to respond directly to her fear: How could She imagine that any image She calls up could do anything but make him fonder of her? It is her capacity to bring wisdom through the antithetical thinking of her body—the witch's cry in a "strange tongue," for example—that has strengthened the bond between them. This has not been enough. The ghost remains.

At this point, the poet throws off all allegorical reticence and speaks directly to his wife in "Under Saturn" (192, 179; 199, 390). "In Memory of Major Robert Gregory" was addressed to her at the beginning, but the gesture was ritualistic. Here, for the first time, it is direct and passionate. He would attempt to calm her anxiety:

> Do not because this day I have grown saturnine
> Imagine that lost love, inseparable from my thought
> Because I have no other youth, can make me pine;
> For how should I forget the wisdom that you brought,
> The comfort that you made?
>
> (192, 179; 199, 390–91)

The remaining lines of the poem recall other aspects of his youth, including the beloved, who is part of a larger cast of characters from his past and is thus made to seem relatively less important. The others are all ancestors, and the poet is claiming that it is the whole past that he must have "inseparable from [his] thought," not just the beloved's memory, which is but part of it and cannot be separately obliterated. The poem is an effort to deal honestly with both his wife and his memory of his "lost love," which surged back to occupy him in several poems of *The Wild Swans at Coole*. It is, nevertheless, a sort of purgation, for the beloved's ghost never again dominates the poems, though she does appear. This is the reason, I think, that the poet dates this poem. It is dated "November 1919."

He then sets a precedent by printing a poem dated earlier, "September 25, 1916," and later another, dated "June 1919." Other deliberate shifts in the fictive chronological order of the poems will occur in *The Tower* and *The*

Winding Stair and Other Poems. The datings mark in the poet's stance toward his work a change that seems to have been generated by the relationship established with his wife and symbolized as having achieved a strong grounding in "Under Saturn."

To be able to shape the poems not entirely (fictively) chronologically opens up new possibilities of self-expression for the poet. These new possibilities have been generated, he obviously believes, by the "wisdom" that has come to him through his wife. Hence, his poems are not to his mind so much responses to external forces as shapings of those forces into a personally constituted vision. It should be remarked here that as the *Book* proceeds from this point, the proportion of poems that directly express moments of whatever kind in the poet's life is smaller, and the poet begins to produce sequences that, though having their places in the chronology of his creative life, are themselves internally organized as fictions. These may be strictly chronological, partially so, or ordered on some other principle. Finally, that the poet will actually name himself "William Yeats" at the end of *Michael Robartes and the Dancer* indicates willingness that the text be identified as an autobiographical fiction. This, coming near the beginning of the dating of several poems, may well indicate a deliberate emphasis on the tension in an autobiographical fiction between life and art.

Until "Under Saturn" was written and dated, the poet was apparently unable to discover a place for "Easter 1916," dated September 25, 1916. Presumably it could have appeared in *The Wild Swans at Coole.* Reticence is apparent not only in the way the poem develops dramatically and in the fact that the stated date of composition is approximately six months after the Easter Rising took place but also in the deliberate delay in its appearance once it was written.

"Easter 1916" (193, 180; 200, 391) begins and proceeds in a curious way for a poem celebrating a great national event and written by a major national poet. The Rising took the poet by surprise. He has trouble thinking of the people he is supposed to eulogize as heroes. He is concerned, perhaps, about what the event might mean to his conception of character and human action. Indeed, it is difficult to think of any great celebrative poem in which the poet seems initially so reluctant to perform his task or in which the poet turns the poem so drastically and for so long to his quite personal response to the event. At the end of "In Memory of Major Robert Gregory," the poet declared that he could not continue; there, the declaration was part of an elaborate formal gesture. In "Easter 1916," there is nothing of that. It is true, of course, that as the poem proceeds the poet drives himself to play a conventional laureate role. But he has to convince himself that he can do it, less by rational means than by coming to accept that his view of things had been, if not downright wrong, at least simplis-

tic and excessively personal. These are great concessions for a poet to make
in such a situation, but he has previously made confessions of misunderstanding at critical moments. They have been part of his growth. Indeed,
the talk of newly attained wisdom and the great dialogue poems of *The
Wild Swans at Coole* suggest that there have been changes making possible
the sort of self-revelation "Easter 1916" contains.

The poet does not like to imagine as heroes the people he must celebrate. Two of them, Pearse and MacDonagh, were poets; and in "Ego
Dominus Tuus" he has spent some time justifying the behavior of poets as
opposed to people of action. Here are two who have turned out to have
acted. They seem to be a refutation of the oppositions that the poet has
elaborately developed and in which he seems to have invested so much.
He does not dismiss their work as either rhetoric or sentimentalism—the
forms of pseudopoetry that Ille attacked. MacDonagh is praised as a poet
of great promise, a person of sensitive nature and daring and sweet
thought. Our poet must recognize his own difference from them, and to
do so is not easy.

The one woman of the group later appears in the sequence in "On a
Political Prisoner" (196, 183; 203, 397) and still later is ironically eulogized. The poet admits to extreme distaste for her political activity and her
shrillness, certainly the opposite of what Robartes and Solomon had
praised or made into a feminine ideal.

Finally, there is MacBride, who, to the poet's shock, married the beloved and from whom she separated. This is perhaps the most difficult
transformation to heroism for him to accept. He does so with deliberate
reluctance. It is interesting how obliquely the reason for his distaste is
introduced. The beloved and her daughter are discreetly referred to as
"some who are near my heart," and it is MacBride who is mentioned last.
The term "resigned" is used to describe them all, but it is offered specifically in connection with reference to MacBride and is identified with the
act of leaving one role—a comic one—to take on another.

All of these people have previously presented themselves in one way to
the poet's imagination. Now, admitting to a willful, subjective illusion because of personal resentment or distaste, he must recognize that there is
something entirely different about them. With MacBride he even admits
that he had "dreamed" what he had thought him to be. The poet is also
suspicious of the kind of commitment the martyrs have made. But he is
also critical of his own blindness about these people with "vivid faces,"
whom he and others were willing to mock behind their backs. Moreover,
he implies a misunderstanding on his part of the truth about life in Dublin,
which he had identified, from a self-assumed position of superiority, with
"motley" and "comedy." All of this he must in this poem admit was wrong.

At the beginning of the third stanza, the poet is compelled, in the process of explaining to himself what has happened, to consider the question of commitment itself. This is done antithetically, that is, imagistically, in a meditation of great beauty that does not refer directly to any of the heroes. Play on the imagery of stone and water in earlier poems is recalled, but with a difference. Now the stone in the stream of time is a figure of the heroes' singleness of purpose, which even in death troubles that "living stream." The connection is to the "vivid faces" that provide such contrast to the stream of Dublin workers. Their vividness generated mockery, derision that was perhaps caused by the observers' discomfort. Everything the poet imagines in this stanza belongs to time and change—except the stone.

As the fourth stanza begins, the meditation turns sharply and turns, and turns again, in an expression of troubled and competing thoughts threatened by both wishful thinking and discouragement. It begins: "Too long a sacrifice / Can make a stone of the heart" (193, 181; 200, 394). This brilliant imagistic thought has brought him to deep doubt about what such sacrifice can mean. Perhaps it is not just these people's hearts that have been turned to stone—perhaps it is also Ireland's heart after centuries of fruitless sacrifice. What does this do to a people? The question ("O when may it suffice?") has probably been imminent since the bitter "Red Hanrahan's Song about Ireland," which very nearly asks it.

Having worked through the problem as he has, he is able to concede only that the question is for heaven. It is the duty of the celebrative poets and those still alive to murmur the heroes' names as if they were sleeping children. But, turning again, he refuses to accept the elegiac convention of rebirth that he has just suggested. Indeed, he treats it as childish and sentimental. These were not children sent to bed only to waken in the morning. But having done this, he nevertheless hopes that the deaths were not needless. The poet puts forth the faint hope that England will keep faith. And there is yet another turn that takes us back to the imagery of stone. The opposite is imagined: Perhaps it was not a heart of stone that brought fanaticism but an excess of love that brought bewilderment. The turn identifies these heroes with the earlier ones treated as delirious in "September 1913," a title that no doubt helped to engender this one. Solomon, speaking to the witch, had suggested that an image can be too strong or too weak, and the poet for a moment tentatively offers a related thought: An excess of love perhaps bewildered them. Love always is of an image. If they were bewildered, he perhaps suggests, they had the wisdom of foolhood. Whatever the case, it seems now not to matter. The poet has worked his way through his own resistances in a dramatic ordeal and can now properly eulogize them. His duty in this sort of situation is to keep their names alive, to "write it out in verse," which he does.

After this tour de force, one might think that the poet would have felt either his job completed or his powers to write on this subject exhausted. This is far from the case, though from the date it appears that some considerable time elapses before the sequence is taken up again. "Easter 1916" and the elapsed time seem to have performed a purgation of feelings and cleared the mind for far less equivocal thought on the subject. As we have seen before, this poet does not usually approach a subject, treat it, and leave it. Instead, he allows time to pass, walks around his own attitude, and charts changes in it.

Time has passed. In "Sixteen Dead Men" (194, 182; 201, 395), the poet addresses the English, who have delayed Home Rule. The resistances dramatized in "Easter 1916" have not returned. There is, perhaps, a certain relief in being able to write an unequivocally revolutionary poem, for the poet is able to proceed at once to another in the same vein, "The Rose Tree" (195, 183; 202, 396). The issue has been settled; the poetic logic of the martyrs outweighs any other logic or diplomacy. It is Pearse's terrible logic of blood sacrifice that in its beauty dominates. The poem gains much from a balladic form, which, with its formal inevitability, shapes the argument as inevitable.

These two poems have probably expressed more of what the poet thinks the public expects from him, yet in their way they, too, are terrible. One can certainly read fanaticism into the words the poet makes Pearse speak, and something distasteful to the poet can be read in his remark that "words are lightly spoken." This cannot be the poet's view, though sometimes it may be his suspicion, as in earlier poems where he remarked that he might have "thrown poor words away and been content to live." This takes us back to the poet's struggle between his commitment to poetry and his acknowledgment that the life of a poet is antithetical to the life of action. We shall see more of this in *The Tower*.

These poems having been written and his laureate responsibility, to some extent at least, having been discharged, the old reservations return in "On a Political Prisoner" (196, 183; 203, 397), which is about Constance Markievicz in prison after the Rising (her death sentence was commuted). The poet is bitter about the change that politics worked in her. The grey gull that comes to her prison windowsill and eats from her hand suggests a momentary return to the antitheticality he thought her to have possessed when young, before "her mind / Became a bitter, an abstract thing." Her moment with the bird he imagines as a moment of identity with it, with all the suggestion of antithetical individualism, radical freedom, and the power of empathy that the bird has come to suggest through repeated use.

But this is only a moment in her life, and the poem is but a moment in his. The bitterness, however, takes control, and in this state he produces "The Leaders of the Crowd" (197, 184; 204, 398), which brings the sequence to a close with an attack on the political leadership that arises after the Easter deaths. These new leaders are described as having lost not just truth but the way to seek it. The student's lamp is declared to be "from the tomb," identifying truth with the dead in opposition to the language of politicians and at the same time accusing the politicians of not understanding the student's life.

In these poems, the martyrs speak impolitic words that the poet has tended to identify with the antithetical. Yet there is an apparent contradiction because these have been antithetical people of action and now in death they have the power to incite more action. The equation of antithetical with inaction and primary with action wavers.

What events will occur as a result of this incitation are not clear as yet, but surely the poet's state of mind (and the state of his country) must be one of anxious anticipation. The section ends in a series of poems that express this mood personally in dreams and visions, some arising out of his domestic life. "Towards Break of Day" (198, 185; 205, 398) describes, with characteristic questioning, two dreams—one his, one his wife's. They may, he thinks, have actually been one dream. The sense of closeness suggested here is not unlike the treatment of his relation to the beloved as he recalled it in "O do not Love Too Long," which suggests waning of the beloved's power as his wife's has grown:

> Neither could have known
> Their own thought from the other's,
> We were so much at one.
>
> (88, 84; 91, 211–12)

In this poem, he speaks of a memory that had "magnified / So many times childish delight." In the next, "Demon and Beast" (199, 185; 206, 399), there is a similar attitude. The poem describes what in memory seems a moment of visionary freedom; but once it has passed, the poet is unsure of its truth. It is characterized by the disappearance of "that crafty demon and that loud beast / That plague me day and night" (199, 185; 206, 399). They are described as hatred and desire, and the poet characterizes himself as having whirled ("perned") back and forth between them. Now he recalls a moment of spiritual understanding and identity with thoughts of others, a moment of joy. It occurred in an art gallery and extends to a moment outside it where the poet observes (what else?) birds in a park. The experience is important particularly because it roused his "whole nature." He describes himself as having ceased in this moment to be demonical, by which he means searching for the mask or antiself, and as having become *purely* antithetical, unifying body and soul. But, reflecting on the experience, the poet must ask whether or not it was illusion, and he concludes that it was. This may be the price of *thinking* too fondly on the matter. Thought must *explain*, and explanation must be abstract. Such thinking stands in opposition to the Wordsworth of the preface to the second edition of *Lyrical Ballads* (1800), who imagines a discipline of recollection that in "tranquility" brings the past actually before the mind (but not necessarily to the Wordsworth of *The Prelude* [1805], who in at least one place questions his memory). Here the center of the poem tends to be displaced from the vision to dramatization of conflict between the moment and the thought it generates. [This is typical of Yeats's skepticism. One recalls that he had to resign from the esoteric section of the Theosophical Society because of his insistence on proof.]

The moment of apparent freedom generates skeptical thought, and then questioning speculation, in the last stanza of "Demon and Beast." The excitement of such a moment seems to engender the subsequent vision of "The Second Coming" (200, 187; 207, 401). The poet is living in his tower in the West of Ireland. This retreat is reminiscent of the medieval Irish monks who made a remote monastic life partly to escape the violence of their times. The poet's retreat is, of course, a secular, domestic one. There is violence in Ireland, obliquely predicted (perhaps to some extent abetted) by "Sixteen Dead Men" and "The Rose Tree." There has been a terrible war in Europe, which claimed the life of his great friend's son. There is cause to fear the destruction everywhere of high culture. These anxieties are intensified by the poet's still relatively new perspective as a family man and his concern for the future of his recently born daughter, which is expressed in the next poem, "A Prayer for my Daughter" (201, 188; 208, 403). Anxiety is often the possession of those who have much to lose; "The Second Coming" is engendered by the state of mind of the previous poem, but it is also a product of the anxiety that invades the very freedom of the vision itself. The poem begins as if the vision were present in the act of writing, yet it ends in a question; there is no interposition of memory.

The "ceremony of innocence" that somehow the solitary Constance Markievicz momentarily recaptures in "On a Political Prisoner," the world of antithetical tradition and reckless grace, is drowned not just in Ireland but everywhere. The "leaders of the crowd" are in control, full of the passion that Ille called "action"—rhetoric and sentiment. Among the best people "conviction" has disappeared. [In the conclusion of *A Vision*, Yeats describes his own convictions as having "melted" at an age when they should have hardened, but there this actually saves his imagination and enables him to be free of what Blake called "fixities and definites." There Yeats is seeking to build a new kind of antithetical stance based on created fictions rather than received primary truths, so "convictions" are finally treated as potentially dangerous or at least stultifying.] Reference to the loss of conviction among the "best" indicates a period of radical disorientation and transition in which belief itself must be rethought. The movement of the falcon in ever-widening circles is the opposite of the dancer tightly wound in the dance of "The Double Vision of Michael Robartes" and of the poet, whom we shall see meditating antithetically in "All Souls' Night" at the end of *The Tower* less than a year hence.

Yet this is but the first stage of the vision. The violence that the poet sees suggests the coming of a whole new historical era. In this tense moment he expects a prophetic revelation, but when it comes it is strongly ambiguous. It is not yet born. As a sphinx it is both human being and beast, not God and man, so that it does not in its prenatal state indicate it is Jesus come again. The desert birds, hardly typical of previous birds in the *Book*, torment it as if they represent the last spasms of a dying era. They are carrion scavengers, or what Blake called "devourers," the opposite of the "prolifics."

The sphinx in its earlier, classical incarnation brought a riddle that Oedipus alone was able to answer. The riddle asked what creature walked on four legs in the morning, two at noon, and three at night; Oedipus correctly answered, "Man." This sphinx is itself a riddle to the poet. He is able to answer only partially the question it represents. He knows that a cycle of two thousand years is coming to its end, but he cannot completely identify the beast. The vision fades, and he must ask what it is.

It is this vision that provides an appropriate context for "A Prayer for my Daughter," which in the *Book*'s fiction [and in actuality] was written in June 1919 earlier than "Under Saturn" and "The Second Coming," and which is prophetic of the "future years" feared in it. The poet therefore places it where the prophecy endorses its anxiety. "A Prayer for my Daughter" seems a secular prayer in that it is not explicitly directed toward God, perhaps because this new age itself appears secular and "conviction" is disappearing. The sphinx is certainly a creature of the "bestial floor" mentioned in "The Magi," and it may be an "uncontrollable mystery," but its appearance would not be of the sort to satisfy the Magi. The center of Christian civilization has disappeared, and with it have gone received notions of social and spiritual order. In an ordered society it is possible to act innocently (without "thought") because the forms of culture are there as protective guides. This is not to say that the "ceremony of innocence" is Christian or even religious, though it has belonged to that era. It is expressed in its highest antithetical forms in art, reckless courtesy, and so forth. The career of Constance Markievicz and certainly that of the beloved as he now sees it mark the disappearance of all of this as well. What is the proper response? The deliberate *making* of the image of freedom by an aloof but dignified and gracious defiance. The gesture may be futile, but it is a tacitly declared heroic search. It is valuable in itself no matter what the end.

"A Prayer for my Daughter" expresses the desire that she become the sort of person who maintains antithetical ideals in the sun-dominated primary phases of the dying and new cycles of history. The scene appears to be constructed in deliberate contrast to the calm before the storm of Coleridge's "Dejection: An Ode" or the calm that "vexes" Coleridge's meditation on his child in "Frost at Midnight." The wind that once murmured among the reeds and perhaps prophesied terror and disaster, could it have been correctly read, is now in full storm, reflecting the condition in which the poet finds all life. He is in a "great gloom," and even the imagery of dancing is now depressingly identified with the anticipated years of continuing violence. The poet therefore prays that his daughter will have all of the antithetical virtues, including a certain beauty and courtesy. He hopes that she will be free of intellectual hatred—that "opinion" derided by Robartes. Disdainful reference to "an old bellows full of angry wind" recalls the poet's remarks about the politics of Constance Markievicz and his own beloved. The principal images are the tree of life and the cornucopia, which are identified with "custom and ceremony" in the sense of actions so a part of the actor that they seem natural and artificial at the same time.

The poem that follows, "A Meditation in Time of War" (202, 190; 209, 406), refers to the troubles in Ireland (World War I has ended). Here is yet another remembrance of a moment of mysterious freedom. The poet has wished that his daughter become symbolically a tree of custom, but the terrible wind has broken the old tree under which the poet sits. Nevertheless, he says, for a moment "I knew that One is animate, / Mankind inanimate phantasy" (202, 190; 209, 406). To animate the abstract, primary One of Platonic thought is to force the antitheticality of the image on it, or it on the image. This is surely the poet's desire, but the price seems to be the reduction of the human being to a sort of dream. The division remains, but the image is on both sides of it.

At this point the poet makes a declaration. He names himself for the first time in the *Book,* as if he were engaged in a ceremony that accomplishes identity. He names himself and offers the gift of his restored tower to his wife, also named. He declares a domestic identity in the face of time and the terror to come. He hopes that the words he has carved on a stone at Thoor Ballylee (203, 190; 210, 406) will survive the material restoration and subsequent ruin.

5

Views from the Tower

The Tower (1928): First Return

The assertion of his name and the declaration of restoration and ownership in "To be carved on a Stone at Thoor Ballylee" extend the change in the poet's stance toward his own work that we noticed occurring in *Michael Robartes and the Dancer*. To this point, the poems have told a dramatic-mimetic story; they have been arranged, with the exceptions recently mentioned, chronologically as (fictively) written. The dated poems in *Michael Robartes and the Dancer* indicated special moments of the fictive life. In *The Tower*, however, dated poems appear, for the most part, in reverse chronological order. In addition to the first four ("Sailing to Byzantium" [1927], "The Tower" [1926], "Meditations in Time of Civil War" [1923], and "Nineteen Hundred and Nineteen" [1919]), four other poems are so dated ("Youth and Age" [1924], "Leda and the Swan" [1923], "The Gift of Harun Al-Rashid" [1923], and "All Souls' Night" [1920]).

There appear to be two deliberate chronological reversals here. The first four poems move backward through tumultuous events to the time of "A Prayer for my Daughter" (dated 1919) of the previous section. The other dated poems, undated ones interposed, seem to have a thematic arrangement that also reverses chronology so that the whole of *The Tower* culminates in "The Gift of Harun Al-Rashid" and "All Souls' Night" of 1923 and 1920, treating in separate ways the poet's earlier achievement of a certain occult knowledge. *The Tower* as a whole, then, enacts two reverse movements of memory. The precedent for this can be discovered, without recourse to *A Vision* (where it is discussed in detail), in the earlier "Shepherd and Goatherd," where the goatherd describes Robert Gregory in death:

> Jaunting, journeying
> To his own dayspring,

He unpacks the loaded pern
Of all 'twas pain or joy to learn,
....
Knowledge he shall unwind
Through victories of the mind.

(156, 145; 163, 342–43)

In the first movement, from "Sailing to Byzantium" backward through "Nineteen Hundred and Nineteen," there is a willful "dreaming back" and "return" through events from a position of achievement.[1] It is as if the meditations that took place between 1919 and 1923 had to be worked through yet again in order for the vantage of Byzantium to have its meaning.

While Ireland was in upheaval, the poet was undergoing a remarkable intellectual experience that would change his thought or, if not change it, shape it. The second movement to which I have referred takes us back to the intellectual or visionary events that made possible the prophetic poems "Among School Children," "Leda and the Swan," and others that followed them. The poems constituting this movement are presented in *The Tower* in the revised form of a "dreaming back" and "return" to 1920. Appropriation in life of the "dreaming back" and "return" is itself a bold antithetical gesture. Both are supposed to occur after death as a mithridatic purgation, under solar and primary domination, of the most intense experiences of life. The purgation is a preparation for rebirth. In *The Tower*, the poet, as when later in *The Winding Stair* he forgives himself by an act of antithetical will, performs an act that would normally be imposed on him in death by external primary force. This force he here defies in order to insist on the reversal as a free choice. Further, the aim is not purgation and forgetting but the charting of his own growth of antithetical power, a retention of the process, as if the process were as important as the end. This itself is the assertion of an antithetical principle.

It is "Sailing to Byzantium" (1927) that signals the poet's will to dream back. Of course, one cannot *know* one is dreaming while dreaming; if one

---

1. John Holloway, "Style and World in 'The Tower,'" in *An Honoured Guest*, ed. D. Donoghue and J. R. Mulryne (London: Edward Arnold, 1965), p. 93, identifies part of "The Tower" (the poem) as a rehearsal in meditation during this life of the stages of the dreaming back (pt. 2, sts. 1–3) and the return (closing stanzas) in *A Vision*. Daniel A. Harris, *Yeats: Coole Park and Ballylee* (Baltimore: Johns Hopkins University Press, 1974), p. 213, n. 14, claims that there is no relation technically between these stanzas and the dreaming back but some relation to the return. He goes on to say that the stanzas are "too generalized to be given precise labels from *A Vision*." In my view, the dreaming back and return are generally characteristic of the whole set of poems. The precedent in the *Book*, as I have claimed, is "Shepherd and Goatherd."

does know then one is awake, and so it is a willed "dreaming." "All Souls' Night" (1920) at the end of *The Tower* declares the beginning of the poet's movement toward new strength, a new "dayspring," as the goatherd put it with respect to Robert Gregory.

I shall discuss the poems in the order in which they appear in the text— the reverse fictive chronological order, but the proper order of the willful "dreaming back" and "return." Of course, one can recognize three possible shapes for Yeats's poems. The first of these, which does not concern us here, would print the poems according to their actual dates of composition to the extent to which these can be known (the dates Yeats put on his poems were not always the actual dates, whatever "actual" might mean here). The second would arrange the poems according to the recorded dates (some fictive) and would place "Nineteen Hundred and Nineteen" at the beginning and "Sailing to Byzantium" at the end of *The Tower*. This is the implied fictive chronology that remains alluded to by the datings in the text. It is not foregrounded, however, for there is the third ordering made in 1928 by the fictive poet, now named William Yeats, upon completion of "Sailing to Byzantium" as a gesture antithetically willing a double "return" at that fictive moment of a fictive life. This is a radical departure for the poet. It implies a new form of control and a willingness to shape his expression according to the principles of his recent intellectual experiences. A new tone of self-assertion has already presented itself in "To be carved on a Stone at Thoor Ballylee"; there seems to have been no turning back from that. Nor is there a lessening of tension or struggle, for what the poet has learned has not diminished his sense of strife. Rather, it has confirmed its inevitability and indicated a possible pattern for it.

"Sailing to Byzantium" is, then, both the first and the last poem of *The Tower*. It is first in that it is the first poem we read. It is last in that it represents the momentary stopping point from which the poet recapitulates his development over almost a decade by means of the willed "dreaming back" and "return" that constitute the order of the poems that follow.

The assertiveness that characterizes "Sailing to Byzantium" (204, 193; 211, 407) belongs to a situation about which the poet may appear to protest too much. By this I mean that the initial tone of the poem suggests (especially in the light of the depressed beginning of "The Tower," which precedes [follows] it) a deliberate effort by the poet to convince himself that what he says is true and proper and that he has worked out a solution to a problem. This is to be made all the more poignant by our subsequent reading of the "dreaming back" and "return" and the internal strengths that have made the stance offered in "Sailing to Byzantium" even possible. The exceedingly emphatic assertions suggest some doubt that the poet may yet be trying to overcome.

The poet dramatizes himself as an old man who rejects the world of teeming generation and youth, not really because he has wished to leave it but because he believes he can no longer belong to it. He complains loudly that in such a country the young "neglect / Monuments of unageing intellect." The treatment is such that at first one cannot easily be certain whether the poem is of visionary ecstasy or deliberate self-encouragement. The images of generation are dismissed, but they are still appealing enough that throughout he refuses to oppose them with images of asceticism or a Platonic realm of the pure idea made to seem preferable to them. These would be the usual modes by which to oppose generation, but they are not employed. This makes the poem and the one that follows (precedes) it full of conflict. The poet imagines a situation of forced asceticism and rejects that as well. [This attitude, is, of course, one of antithetical opposition to the primary that is developed in *A Vision* and treated without these specific terms in "The Phases of the Moon."] The poet now holds on to sense and image, taking a position that seems opposite that of the early quasi-Platonic searches of his youth. (We shall see that the "dreaming back" and "return" chart a dismissal of the Platonic.)

The reason given for rejection of the youthful world is not that the poet disapproves of what goes on in it but that he now sees clearly what is neglected there. He does not claim eternality for the "monuments of unageing intellect" that are neglected in the realm of generation. Rather, these monuments seem to him a Blakean contrary to the negating oppositions of youth/age and life/death. They are works that demonstrate the continual liveliness of intellect as it is embodied in their making. They become for the poet a proof that intellect—and, of course, his intellect—does not have to grow old in a generative sense. What it does is what it is. But, then, why "monuments," with its suggestion of death and memorialization? Because such images are antithetical to the customary negation of life/death by containing, in a confounding of primary logic, both and neither at the same time.

In the poem's second stanza, the possible roles of an old man are explored. The first, which is the role one plays if one does not resist the drift into primary abstraction, is that of a "paltry thing" likened to a scarecrow. The soul of antithetical man (the soul, if anything, would remain strong and active in old age) must now strenuously assume the role of the whole man and sing in behalf of the body and senses, even though that body—and because that body—is but "tatters" after all. There is nowhere to go to learn such a song; there must be recourse to a study of the monuments with their implicit celebration of antitheticality.

It is apparent that such study is radically personal and solitary. It is a tower study, and in old age it is actively opposed to the natural movement of generation. In the natural movement, as it was envisioned by Michael Robartes in "The Phases of the Moon," the declension past phase fifteen is toward the soul's domination of a fading body. The poet accepts this as a fact, but he declares that his soul will oppose it nevertheless. In the later phases, proper behavior for the soul as it divests itself of the body is to purge the image, but for the poet this is to declare an end to his activity. So he states that the soul must sing *for* every bit of what remains of his body and that in coming to see the need to do this he has sailed not across the traditional Platonic sea to the world of a shady afterlife but to Byzantium, which is no longer a place but a condition of mind. There *is* no Byzantium (it is now Istanbul); Byzantium must be made in the poet's imagination.

Byzantium was once a special sort of holy city. True, it was the seat of the Eastern church, but in choosing its name for his holy city, which is really an antithetical holy city and therefore secular, the poet has not become religiously orthodox, desiring annihilation in God or even submitting reluctantly to spiritual authority. The mental journey has been taken in order to meet and converse with certain images. It is a renewal of the search for the antiself declared by Ille in "Ego Dominus Tuus," but now the antiself of old age must be differently characterized. This new characterization implies the poet's movement into the later primary phases of life even as the search remains insistently antithetical to the natural declension of these phases. The images are those of sages *as if* they were figures in a golden Byzantine mosaic. The fact that the poet offers this description in the form of a simile is important. On the strength of what is only a simile, not an assertion of identity, the poet yet insists, as the poem proceeds, on an identity between the sages he calls on and art. There is something of stress and crisis here when, recognizing his bodily form as that of a "dying animal," the poet rouses his poetic faculty to insist on the sages as an image of art even as the simile admits only an "as if."

It is potentially a dark moment; to profess less would be to abandon the antithetical position entirely (and thus his laboriously created identity) in favor of the abstract primary and to lose claim to the name of poet that he has only recently believed he has earned. The new antiself cannot be wisdom in any abstract spiritual formlessness of the pure idea. It must be those imagistic sages who have survived in image the fiery furnace that normally dispatches body and image to ashes. Yet to be proper antiselves to the aged poet, these sages must be, like the poet, wasted in body. The new singing masters are the spirits of the great imaginative works of the past, intellect and imagination being the same thing, as in Blake's identification of the term "intellect" with his principle of imagination. These images, by synecdoche the sages in their mosaical forms, are asked to come forth and lead him in yet another song. In the situation of old age, the poet asks not to be taught a new dance but to sing, though he would have the sages "pern in a gyre." If all this were to happen, he would survive the fiery furnace not in a generated body but in pure artifice or pure image, as if the furnace were transformed into an artisan's forge like that, say, of Blake's heroic figure Los.

Here the poet reaches a second crisis, expressed in the phrase "artifice of eternity." This crisis can be understood as a moment in which the poet tries to persuade himself that eternity has the form of artifice. But is "eternity" only a word signifying a wishful illusion? The poet has attempted to extend the "as if" from its original state of simile into a metaphorical identity. The act appears to be part of his self-persuasion and defiance. The eternity imagined is not that posited by theologians but only that created by poets, who have traditionally peopled it with images, thus drawing it back into the realm of the antithetical. In the last stanza, having appeared to persuade himself, the poet declares that *his* afterlife out of nature will be in neither the world of generated bodies nor the world of pure spirit but the world contrary to this negation—the world of a Byzantium that is neither here nor there or is both here and there. This form is offered in the shape of "as if" ("But such a form as Grecian goldsmiths make"), the violent assertion of rejection being somewhat muted by simile as the poet imagines an ahistorical Byzantium that nevertheless inhabits time. Here the golden bird can continue to sing of events. I have already suggested that the gesture of the poem is a strenuous one of deliberate excess because it is made *against* what the poet now imagines as overwhelming primary force. The image of an artificial golden bird is itself antithetically excessive, a bauble "to keep a drowsy emperor awake," and the whole gesture is deliberately hyperbolic, celebrating energy over fact and the inevitable.

From very early in the *Book*, certain birds have seemed to be images of fulfilled desire. Early on, this desire was vague and uncertain, as if the poet were not yet able to posit successfully the notion of an antiself. Desire was associated with flight to some other place, though that other place was often viewed with suspicion or ambivalence. But now the desire is to move toward death without succumbing to annihilation of the poetic intellect. The last stanza hovers close to the assertion that the poet would actually like to be gathered into art, that is, become his poems in *this* world, the golden artifice suggesting not so much flight elsewhere as continued singing here. The "artifice of eternity" seems to turn into the hopeful antithetical notion of the eternity of artifice. This idea, quite tentative because part of the "as if," is combined with a nostalgia that the figure of Byzantium, lifted from time, cannot entirely evade. The nostalgia is for an age that the poet can imagine providing his song with aristocratic listeners. The ideal moment is that of the apotheosis of Byzantine culture. This nostalgia replaces the earlier nostalgia for ancient Ireland and is generated, no doubt, out of events in Ireland and Europe about which the later (previous) poems express anxiety.

There are, then, several states contemplated by the poet: first, the world of generation, which the poet knows he must abandon and which he protests against because it does not give enough attention to the intellect; second, the world of death and both bodily and imagistic annihilation, which, as a poet, he gestures against; and third, the condition of artifice, which the poet attempts to imagine as a contrary to the negating opposition of the first two. This third state is imagined with considerable tension, including a tendency to posit an idealized past moment. One might think of this tendency as the nostalgic or sentimental side of the antithetical, indulged by the poet in old age as he contemplates the death of friends and early hope. It is balanced by the temper of defiance and energy, the history of the development of which is reviewed in the rest of *The Tower.* Though we can think, perhaps, of Byzantium and the golden bird as figures of art and of the poet as his poems, it would be wrong to think "Sailing to Byzantium" a triumphant conclusion. It is instead an antithetical conclusion, which means that it is also a going-on, a process that never yields the contentment of triumph, which is always a primary condition gained by negation. From the antithetical point of view triumph yields stasis and is self-defeating. It is all the more tentative because it is a *willed* antitheticality, which is held to deliberately in the face of primary force.

The potential heroism of "Sailing to Byzantium" is strenuous and the gesture one of high oratory, of which the poet has become a master. The achievement, even though it cannot be a stopping place (indeed, because it is not and virtually declares that it is not), is impressive. The vision of Byzantium as a condition of mind from which to speak—tentative as it has to be—must have been won through powerful experience, and possibly in spite of it. From that vantage, which, as I have suggested, is a willed antitheticality opposed to the negating opposition of youth/age, the poet wills his own "dreaming back" and "return" *in* life. Thus he continues his defiant antithetical gesturing, preempting primary activity and transforming it into something positive. His tower is the embattlement from which he has observed with bitterness the Irish Civil War and, before that, the period of the Black and Tans. Not a "learned school," it has been at least the school of experience. In the poems that follow (precede) we plunge back into those events as he relives them in willed memory.

In the poem called "The Tower" (205, 194; 212, 409), the poet engages once again in the familiar dialogue with the heart; but here, in contrast to its behavior in "The Folly of being Comforted," the heart does not reply, or perhaps all of part 1 after the question is the heart's answer. If so, it is a heart grown old but now intent on preserving the "unageing intellect" that is the pride of antithetical personalities. The description that the poet offers of his situation seems to be a deliberate refutation of the path that Wordsworth took in his great "Ode: Intimations of Immortality," where, as the poet reads Wordsworth's poem, the imagination is declared to have grown old and given way to a wisdom of acceptance. If not a refutation, "The Tower" is a defiance that claims no difference of imaginative power between himself now and when, as a boy, he sought to emulate an earlier antiself, the fisherman. The world seems to tell him to become a Wordsworthian sage and seek primary transcendence, accept the loss of antithetical poetic vitality, and choose a Platonic antiself. The only other possibility would be to accept humiliation in the form of the irrelevant, decrepit body. One sees that "Sailing to Byzantium" is an answer to the negative alternatives that the poet has articulated and worked through in the previous year and is now recalling as part of his accomplishment.

The poet paces on the battlements; he looks outward to the tower's environs, and then by imagination he looks beyond in time and by memory backward, as if once again to call on an antiself that would renew poetic power. (It is, of course, the act of search, not the achievement of the goal, that renews.) Yet it must be remembered that this seeking outward is also a shoring up and a defense against not only the condition of old age but also the external world of the poet's own time. The two poems that follow (precede) this one dwell bitterly on that time. The tower is a fort, and the poet walks there in a doubly embattled state. For him to "send imagination forth" is also to make a defense. The defense is made in a place with a history, now lost, of such defenses. The search seems now to be less self-assured, as if a single image called up might not suffice to yield the antiself. It is as if the poet would call up any ghost available to help him. The gesture suggests both desperation and slightly garrulous senility. In his sight are the "foundations of a house," a ruin that must call up in his mind the ruin of his own body and the future ruin of his tower, which is explicitly a matter of concern in the following (earlier) poems and takes us back to the lines of "To be carved on a Stone at Thoor Ballylee." This is balanced by the reference to a tree, referred to as "Tree," as if it possessed a proper name. Tree thrusts itself up from the earth with the sooty appearance of having survived a fiery cataclysm. Virtually addressed, this tree is recognized as if it were some mysterious antiself that has survived fire, like the sages of "Sailing to Byzantium." "Tree" slightly suggests some primordial act of worship or communication as ancient as the Druids or some Irish hero buried upright and now being reborn finger first through the soil. This tree, other "ancient trees," and the ruined house are the environment from which the poet would call up "images and memories."

The figures called form a curious group: Mrs. French; Mary Hynes; a fictive character named Hanrahan, whom the poet himself has created and whose song about Ireland we have read; and the nameless, last owner-inhabitant of the tower, who vacated it long before the poet restored it. The purpose is to ask a question of these dead. They are collected under the theme of enchantment, for reasons having to do with the question. Mrs. French's butler is enchanted and driven to act on her slightest expression of desire, confusing the literal with the figurative. The power of her word surrounded by the aura of her position triumphs, but with dire results. Mary Hynes was the subject of a poem by the blind itinerant poet Raftery, and his poem was so triumphant that it enchanted certain men to madness, one being drowned because he could no longer distinguish night (the moon) from day (the sun). To this point, the meditation has been growing in garrulousness, as if it were about to wander totally into free association.

When it does pull back, it is not because the poet is aware of his garrulousness but because he becomes concerned that he himself may exert the same kind of poetic power inducing madness in others. Behind this concern is his awareness that his own poetic theme has been similar to Raftery's: the beauty of a woman. "Triumph," that is, complete poetic success, in this matter would be disastrous. Fear of it elicits a cryptic prayer: "O may the moon and sunlight seem / One inextricable beam" (205, 196; 212, 411). It is a curious moment, in which the poet, who earlier in his work has identified poetry and bodily beauty with the moonlight, now recognizes the danger of drowning others or being drowned in moonlight as was the crazed man in the "great bog of Cloone." We remember that Michael Robartes identified phase fifteen with the absence of life. In actual life antitheticality as powerful as that which the poet recalls is dangerous. We can conclude that the poet's earlier difficulty in coming to terms with the Easter heroes had something to do with this reticence about antithetical purity. So he prays for an infusion of sunlight, seeking to bring in the opposite. The primary cannot generate its opposite; it can only objectify and distance it. The antithetical can contain the primary because its principle is empathetic identification. Tied not to fact but to fiction, it can include the former in the latter. This is convenient for the poet because he must accept his movement into the primary phases of life even as he asserts his continuing antitheticality. Here his prayer asks for antithetical and primary to become "one inextricable beam." Is he asking for an interweaving or a oneness, an opposition or a cessation of conflict? I think that indecision about this is the reason that the question is not pursued and another example of enchantment is introduced. By now, the meditation has become much more personal (though still garrulous), and the figure called up is one actually invented by the poet—Red Hanrahan. (At this point the *Book* reaches out to include *Stories of Red Hanrahan* as one of the poet's creations.)

The poet has a certain attitude toward this character's fictiveness. He describes Hanrahan as having been driven by him "through the dawn," suggesting that he has treated Hanrahan as a maneuvered puppet for some personal purpose. (The very late "Circus Animals' Desertion" confesses that he so used his inventions.) But if Hanrahan is a puppet, he is oddly unruly, with a tendency toward a life of his own, because he must be "driven," forced to act as he does. This idea is developed in the stanza that describes Hanrahan's actions and treats them as if poor Hanrahan were the victim of the poet's thoughts and as if the poet were a bit ashamed:

> And I myself created Hanrahan
> And drove him drunk or sober through the dawn
> From somewhere in the neighbouring cottages.
> Caught by an old man's juggleries
> He stumbled, tumbled, fumbled to and fro
> And had but broken knees for hire
> And horrible splendour of desire;
> I thought it all out twenty years ago.

> (205, 196; 212, 411)

That Hanrahan is the poet's creation, yet with a certain life (and death) of his own, may make him the best person to query, being both in and out of life or neither and thus purely antithetical; but there is a delay. The poet's mind wanders into reminiscence and finally forgetfulness until he again gains control of his thoughts and recalls the last owner of the tower. (This struggle against primary senility is part of the poem's drama, enforcing the very situation it addresses.) All but Hanrahan are real, but all are also products now of fable, the last of them being completely unknown. The question he would ask them he now enunciates:

> Did all old men and women, rich and poor,
> Who trod upon these rocks or passed this door,
> Whether in public or in secret rage
> As I do now against old age?

> (205, 197; 212, 413)

But they are "impatient to be gone." Why? Because in death the question no longer interests them? It merely impinges on their solitude.

The poet dismisses them but asks that Hanrahan remain. Hanrahan, a purely fictive being declared killed off by his author but always alive in the stories, has a curious status antithetical to life/death. He should be fully experienced and perhaps wise. Presumably a possible antiself, he may answer. It is as if the first question had been merely a displacement. The second seems the one that really occupies the poet, and Hanrahan, a lover of women, is a likely person to know its answer: "Does the imagination dwell the most / Upon a woman won or woman lost?" (205, 197; 212, 413). The answer is indirect, and we are uncertain whether the voice is Hanrahan's or the poet's. Perhaps it does not matter; perhaps in this confrontation the poet meets only his own conscience calling on him to face the consequences of an answer he has known all along:

> If on the lost, admit you turned aside
> From a great labyrinth out of pride,
> Cowardice, some silly over-subtle thought
> Or anything called conscience once.
>
> (205, 197; 212, 413)

He must admit failure and responsibility. The admission is far different from his behavior in the early poems, where responsibility is placed on the beloved or on circumstance and where there is little probing of his own role.

Perhaps, though, it is egotistical of the poet to imagine that he had ever been able to control the situation with the beloved. Despite this, it is fair to say that his willingness to assume responsibility, neglected earlier even when responsibilities became the theme of his work, is an important step. He recognizes, in a telling assertion, that if the memory of these matters recurs, reason (the sun) is blotted out and the moon reigns. This state he has already declared dangerous; it is like the possibility of complete poetical triumph that frightened him earlier. Such an event would return him to a condition of enchantment like the conditions of those he has just mused on. He would be victimized, or would imagine himself victimized, once again.

At this point, the meditation stops abruptly, and the poet declares that he should now carry out a responsibility: He should write his will. This is a recognition of age, if not also of the impending death of imagination. It seems a response to his own garrulousness, but it is also a defiance. To write one's will is also to assert one's will, which is, after all, the antithetical act, especially when it is in the form of a poem, the life of which can survive the author. Yet it is as an antithetical will drifting toward the primary phases that he speaks. The heir of the will is the figure for whom he had earlier declared that he wrote his poems—the antithetical fisherman. His legacy, he declares, is "pride," and this pride is connected with a

certain faith, which he also would pass on. Pride is, for him, an antithetical virtue, and the legacy is not merely to fishermen already possessing
this quality; it is an encouragement to a new generation to enact antithetical values.

What is meant by "pride," and why is it antithetical? It is not defined in
the poem but is treated figuratively. It involves a certain kind of freedom
implied earlier by the apparently self-absorbed, indifferent dancer of "The
Double Vision of Michael Robartes." This idea, identified with artistic
performance, is transferred in "The Tower" to the notion of political and
doctrinal independence from mob attitudes and from identification with
either masters or slaves (those caught in the negating cyclicity Blake
dramatized in the conflict of Urizen and Orc). True pride seems to require
a state of mind that can give in a disinterested way, "disinterest" here
meaning the absence of self-interest. Without this absence, the gesture of
giving is ethically tainted. The formulation seems related to Kant's aesthetic notion of internal purposiveness or, as Kant also called it, purposiveness without purpose, which Schiller transformed into the realm of ethics
with his concept of the play drive, mediator between the sensuous drive
and the formal drive. But here the poet emphasizes a matter to which neither Kant nor Schiller paid attention. The mode of activity that represents
pride is lonely and aloof by virtue of its disinterest and stubborn independence.

There follow in the poem five examples of this pride. The first identifies
the poet with a certain generation in Ireland that he thinks exemplified it:
"The people of Burke and of Grattan / That gave, though free to refuse"
(205, 198; 212, 414). The identity is with Anglo-Irish figures of the late
eighteenth century. The poet offers here not a mere simile but a direct
declaration. From a restricted point of view, never current among the
Catholic Irish, perhaps it is possible to identify the Anglo-Irish politicians
of the period as neither the master (English) nor the slave (the principally
Catholic Irish). The point of view would be an Anglo-Irish one itself. To
locate that people with Grattan in particular would identify pride not only
with eighteenth-century Anglo-Irish literature but also, specifically, with
the freedom of the old Dublin parliament bartered away in the Act of
Union. This identification from the point of view of Irish politics in Yeats's
time, however, has struck many as, at best, self-delusory and, not even at
worst, fatuous. The achievement of identity sought here is a troubled one
because the poet can hardly avoid recognizing that identification of antitheticality with the Anglo-Irish is tenuous. Furthermore, the Anglo-Irish
line, with which the poet would identify himself, has, as he sees, nearly
disappeared as a political force. But that may be just what enables him to
declare his identity with it. The poet nostalgically and, I think, defiantly,

forces the old Ascendancy to become an image of antitheticality contrary, though (indeed because) dying or dead, to the negating oppositions he has recently seen in Irish life: Irish against Irish (discussed in "Meditations in Time of Civil War"), Irish against English (discussed in "Nineteen Hundred and Nineteen").

It is worthwhile recalling the following lines from "The Fisherman": "A man who does not exist, / A man who is but a dream" (160, 149; 167, 348). In that earlier poem, he imagined writing "for my own race," but he there defined the race in much larger terms and found he could not tolerate what one might call its "politics." It was then that he began to imagine writing for the fisherman antiself. In "The Tower," that figure has become persuasively identified through the idea of pride with a now lost Ascendancy culture. In an odd way, it is because that culture did not *belong* that the poet seems now to value it, for belonging would seem to involve a politics of self-interest, no matter on which side one took a position. If the poet deludes himself, perhaps deliberately, about the "people of Burke and Grattan" and must quarrel with much history in order to characterize that people as he would wish them to have been, there is perhaps enough in the mythical aura surrounding Burke and Grattan to make them into the lonely, aloof, independent figures that here he seeks as models. But the important thing is the struggle and the inner drama. The difficulty of making the myth good enforces the tension of the situation of trying to discover and assert antitheticality in a primary situation.

The four similes that follow continue the attempt to make good an ideal that the historical referent cannot entirely live up to. Pride is identified with the heroic condition of antithetical bravery in the face of an overwhelming force. The morning, which is identified with the growing preeminence of the sun and primary life, symbolizes the condition under which antithetical man needs to express oppositional pride and bravery. The horn of plenty is a symbol of opulent creativity. The "sudden shower" of summer and daylight provides momentary refreshening, but apparently no more than that, in a parched land. The swan sings its own death. All of these similes build to the notion of antitheticality in the face of sure defeat. They therefore imply disinterest as opposition, even a deliberate refusal to join the public, the masters, the slaves, or the mob. The poet's will, as legacy, is an assertion of antithetical will(fulness).

The faith declared is outrageously contrary to the primary facts. The poet directly defies the force that would make him accept a Platonic notion of the reality of the pure idea, and for good measure he rejects Plotinus, insisting that both life and death are human creations and declaring that the primary realms of external force are themselves projections of human thought. The point here is the *gesture* of defiance, admittedly bitter, the assertion that antithetical thought can include primary abstraction as one of its own projected fictions. As the assertions pile up, they become more insistent and more difficult for us to accept. The gesture increases in intensity as if the poet were possessed, but this possession, unlike the divine madness that Plato attributed to poets, is not from without; it is generated from within by a strenuous act of will. Yet even if what the poet asserts is so, he tacitly recognizes that he must make the journey into death that this hyperbolic mythical projection requires. The important matter, as always, is the way this is done, and so the "learned school" of "Sailing to Byzantium" is anticipated as the source for the discipline of the final antithetical effort to enact freedom. The tension present in all of this is well exemplified by two possible readings of "I have prepared my peace *with*. . . . " Does the poet reach a peace with "learned Italian things," his imaginings, "memories of love," and "memories of the words of women"? Or *by means* of them? Both, I should say, for the journey of the poet seems to work both through and against his experience, which is the antithetical way.

The poems as such—as objects—are not what he leaves to those he encourages to live by antithetical principles. Rather, he would leave behind the model of their gesture, which teaches the lonely pride capable of making one's own free, aloof, hopeless gesture. That it has taken him this long to achieve the capacity to make such a gesture is part of the lesson bequeathed. It is acknowledged freely that the world antithetically created is a dream, but everything is in this sense a dream. This is not the dream of escape of the early poems; it is, rather, the expression of a rigorous, oppositional discipline. The assertion is a radical expression of faith in a fiction that he believes is culturally and ethically necessary. Human beings in some part of themselves declare their capacity to control their own destinies even though their primary selves hold that this is not possible. The statements against Plato are therefore violent, the assertions about radical creativity insistent and exaggerated, as befits deliberate resistance to growing primary power. The dream is said to resemble a mirror, but it is not a copying of some external original world, not a mirror held up to nature, but an image imposed on the world. It seems a mirror because of its particularity of imagistic projection.

Dream making is natural and instinctive in the sense of being a fundamental act of preservation and protection of the species. It is like the acts of a mother bird building and then resting on her nest. The comparison to the bird occurs as the poet recalls his imagination to the battlements, where he paces and notices the daws making their nests. This return to the particular arrests the meditation; the poet reiterates the substance of his will and turns to unfinished business—his soul. We recognize suddenly that he is declaring his intention to pursue the project already described as in progess in "Sailing to Byzantium." In some strange way—via the willed "dreaming back" and "return"—time is being reversed. The poet is not dead; he defies death and wills this activity in life. "The Tower" ends in a moment that obliquely recalls yet again, and again by opposition, the conclusion of Wordsworth's "Ode." The poet will cling to the body and study the image, enduring the worst of losses, as these things recede from his consciousness but never actually disappear as long as his consciousness exists. The poet's sense of a necessary action that he must will himself to perform is the ground for complaint against Wordsworth: One advances to a certain age; one becomes famous; one becomes religious, abstract, primary. Not this poet. He recognizes decay but not the philosophy that accepts and rationalizes it. There is continued antithetical commitment; it is therefore not a surprise after all to find in the description of the distanced horizon not "other races run" but the same race and, in the midst of acknowledged fading strength, the poet's favorite antithetical image itself fading away, it is true, but nevertheless still audible: "a bird's sleepy cry / Among the deepening shades" (205, 200; 212, 416).

The next step back in time is to live through the events of the Civil War. "Meditations in Time of Civil War" (1923) (206–12, 200; 213–19, 417) is a sequence of seven poems, moving from emphasis on the past through the present to a horrified anticipation of the future. At the same time, it moves from a meditation on outward things inward to personal circumstance and thence outward again, traversing the route of the Yeatsian gyre. Despite its stately movement, the sequence is a work of bitterness and anxiety. The very first word, "surely," indicates the possibility of wishful thinking, as if the poet were trying to convince himself of the truth of his musing:

> Surely among a rich man's flowering lawns,
> Amid the rustle of his planted hills,
> Life overflows without ambitious pains;
> And rains down life until the basin spills,
> And mounts more dizzy high the more it rains
> As though to choose whatever shape it wills
> And never stoop to a mechanical
> Or servile shape, at others' beck and call.
>
> (206, 200; 213, 417)

These images would describe a life that has reached the condition of art. The notion of internalized perfection devoid of external purposiveness is combined with the romantic image of constant creation and overflow. All of this embodies freedom. The fountain, with its capacity to change yet remain a single form, is contrasted to a shaping imposed by some external, mechanical force. The opposition is that of antithetical to primary.

Yet the stanza expresses what is immediately acknowledged to be but a momentary and reckless thought: identification of the great house and its life with the antithetical. Nevertheless, the poet does not want to abandon the idea:

> Mere dreams, mere dreams! Yet Homer had not sung
> Had he not found it certain beyond dreams
> That out of life's own self-delight had sprung
> The abounding glittering jet; though now it seems
> As if some marvellous empty sea-shell flung
> Out of the obscure dark of the rich streams,
> And not a fountain, were the symbol which
> Shadows the inherited glory of the rich.
>
> (206, 200; 213, 417–18)

Even though it rejects the idea of the first stanza, the second is an attempt to rebuild a faith. It is a new self-encouragement to retain the very notion at which the poet has just scoffed. (Though there is only one voice here, one can almost imagine the poem as a dialogue.) Surely, the poet answers himself: Homer was produced from a cultural situation that can be identified with self-delight, symbolized by the fountain of the great house and identifiable with the antithetical phases of Michael Robartes' lunar wheel.

But the "surelys" and "yets" cannot prevail over a darker suspicion that finally captures the poet. This is first signaled by the appearance of a familiar image, the seashell, which is as hollow of life as the poet suspects these houses may now be. He imagines that a violent desire for the mask brought about the flowering of the culture, but he fears that the sweetness he identifies as both object and eventual product of that desire cannot be maintained without the very same violence that engendered it. The antithetical situation, though earlier symbolized in its ideal and impossible perfection as the self-delighting dancer absorbed in her dance and freed from external purposiveness, seems in the real world to be always characterized by violent desire. As violence of desire ebbs, so does greatness. What then? Is the historical pattern a repeated cycle of antithetical desire and decadence? As the stately but anxious "Ancestral Houses" ends, the poet fears that this is so.

We have already noticed the tendency toward internal dialogue in "Ancestral Houses." "My House" (207, 201; 214, 419) carries on the suggestion of drama by appearing at the outset to be almost a stage direction. The poet has turned toward his own possessions. Familiar images appear once again: the rose and the winding stair, the latter suggesting a gyre; the poet has surrounded himself with actual embodiments of his favorite symbols. The view he offers of his tower suggests embattlement and isolation. There is some connection, I think, to the fountain of the previous poem. The tower, with its winding stair, suggests the possibility of climbing and the solitary life. Is there perhaps a saving difference here from the stately ancestral house? Well, in the first place the tower is no longer an ancestral house, though it may again become one. The poet is a new founder. What is the history of these old Norman towers? They antedate the great eighteenth-century houses by centuries. Ballylee was mentioned as early as 1585 and may have been in existence for some time before that. The first inhabitant probably had a grant from the king of England to build and fortify Ballylee against "the King's Irish enemies," as the Celts were called at the time. The tower garrison, its owner, and a small entourage must have been isolated and sometimes under attack. Not a rich man, the first founder was probably a pioneer or a mercenary.

The poet identifies himself, as a second founder, with this man. He calls the place "tumultuous," this word being the first allusion in the sequence to the Civil War, unless one wishes to see in the image of the sea-shell a burnt-out great house, a common sight at the time. It is not just that the original founder experienced tumult here. The poet solidifies his relation to the first founder by describing him as eventually "forgetting and forgot." This must refer to the pioneer colonist's eventual sense of difference from those who sent him and prepares the poet to see a connection between himself and the Anglo-Irish tradition. In both cases, the poet imagines a people who represent an antithetical neither-nor or both-and. This idea of being in the condition of neither-nor or both-and gives the poet some very bothersome moments before the poem ends, as does his sense of cyclicity and repetition. These states he must come to accept for himself and history, as he finally begins to in "Sailing to Byzantium." But the acceptance must be a defiant one. In "My House," the poet perhaps imagines himself forgotten in this isolated spot or, if not forgotten, rendered inactive. That theme, and the torment of apartness (in this case fighting on neither the Free-State nor the Republican side and yet being Irish, like both sides), comes up later in "The Road at My Door." The poet would hope, in any case, that his own descendants not go the way of sweetness and declares that he will leave behind "emblems of adversity"— this tower, this stair—for meditation and the maintenance of antithetical desire.

The sequence moves even further inward with "My Table" (208, 202; 215, 421), where the poet meditates on another physical symbol, Sato's ceremonial sword lying before him. The poet speaks of his own present aimlessness. At this point, we do not know what compels him to describe his activity in this way. If we recall "Ego Dominus Tuus," where Hic defends the active life, we may obtain a clue; as we read further in this sequence we learn that the poet feels abashed in the face of the active, committed lives being lived by the combatants on both sides in the Civil War. The connection with "Ego Dominus Tuus" has to do with our awareness that there Ille is quite sensitive to Hic's criticism.

The poet's meditation on the sword has important connections with the earlier (later) "Sailing to Byzantium." Here the poet meditates on the symbol of a unified culture that embodied simplicity, ritual, and a tradition of artistry passed on from father to son. It seems in his mind to be the antithesis of an ascetic primary discipline. Imagining the culture that produced the sword, he sees the sword itself as a symbol of antithetical transcendence (an impossibility, of course, because in life the antithetical can never be that). This artistic accomplishment must have been achieved by someone whose heart ached with desire, a parallel in that culture with the bitter creator of the great house. The unchanging sword expresses in a single symbol violence, beauty, sexuality, and the always changing moon. It stands contrary to the traditional opposition permanence/change by embodying both or neither. The poet muses that the tradition of artisanship, which suggests the "learned school" that the poet will come to mention in "Sailing to Byzantium," "seemed" unchanging to those who belonged to it; this must have made a great difference to them because they could imagine the beautiful and the unchanging together. In such a tradition, the poet muses further, the inheritor would not go the way of "Ancestral Houses" but instead would continue to possess the aching heart of antithetical desire. Dwelling on this, the poet imagines a momentary apocalypse. It would have to be, from his point of view, miraculous, because it defies the cyclical reality. The peacock and the statue of Juno from the earlier section are now recalled, the poet imagining the scream of Juno's peacock as if the culture that produced the sword were a moment of absolute miraculous completeness figured forth as this bird's sudden call breaking in upon cyclical time and stretching out the moment. But the poet is careful to say only that it *seemed* as if this had occurred. He cannot say that it did, but that it *seemed* may be enough or all that can possibly be garnered from time.

It is the center of the sequence, the imagining of a completion that is also not a completion, of a moment that is also not a moment. It is the embodiment of perfected desire in the activity of the artificer. That the figure for this moment is a sword gathers together both violence and desire and also the marvelous illusion of unchanging metal.

But the moment in which the moment is contemplated passes, and anxiety floods back in, picking up the theme of decline. Again the emphasis is on seeming, as the poet imagines life as a flowering family tree in spring:

> . . . and yet it seems
> Life scarce can cast a fragrance on the wind,
> Scarce spread a glory to the morning beams,
> But the torn petals strew the garden plot;
> And there's but common greenness after that.
>
> ("My Descendants," 209, 203; 216, 422)

"Common greenness" suggests what he now regards as a threatened decline in the quality of Irish culture. But the poem more specifically expresses his fears about his own children and theirs. The poem turns into a
secular prayer or poetic casting of a spell reminiscent of "To be carved on
a Stone at Thoor Ballylee," where the poet wills that his carved words
remain "when all is ruin once again." Here the prayer is more threatening,
for the poet would have the tower return to ruin if his descendants fail to
live up to the criterion of antithetical desire. Once this threatening prayer
is uttered, however, the poet seems relatively content with having established in the tower a monument to his friend Lady Gregory, his wife, and
himself. This will suffice, for he is beginning to find some bitter solace in
the thought that the world moves in cycles. The imagery of gardens, foun-
tains, and new growth has not served up the optimistic vision that would
have mitigated his anxiety. We may contrast these images with the sooty
tree of "The Tower" and see that the preceding (later) poem has left behind
certain hopes (and, as a result, fears), having begun to work through a
bleaker, but in the end more satisfactory, treaty with cyclicity and ruin.

In this poem, the poet describes himself as prosperous, but he is not
content, and in "The Road at My Door" (210, 204; 217, 423) his meeting
with both Republican and Free-State soldiers raises once again the whole
question of the opposition of active and contemplative lives, renewing his
inner disquiet. He has spoken of his role as the "nourisher of dreams," but
now he turns from his door in envy of the active life. His own dreams
seem cold and confining. He broods and once again threatens to turn his
back on the world. This renewal and reworking of old problems is not
uncharacteristic of the poet—or of most of us. Some problems have to be
confronted more than once.

In these last sections the troubled poet seems to be wandering through
his house, peering out of windows, in a state of mind that seizes on things
irrationally and in an associative way. At his window he observes the bees
building and the birds nesting, and he calls on the bees, makers of sweetness, to "build in the empty house of the stare" ("The Stare's Nest by My
Window," 211, 204; 218, 424). It is a prayer for creativity and peace,
a return to what might be regarded as a benevolent, natural cyclicity op-

posed to the destructive war going on in the countryside around the tower. He identifies himself with the tower ("My wall is loosening") in a way that anticipates the concerns of "Sailing to Byzantium" and includes himself in the cycle of decline. The last lines epitomize the situation of the Civil War for the poet and give rise to the vision of cyclicity of the last section. One feels that here the poet has made an epitome of Irish history since the Normans came and of the brutalization of Irish imagination. For centuries England had been the enemy. Freedom had come, and the Irish proceeded to make enemies of each other, perhaps to fill the void.

> We had fed the heart on fantasies,
> The heart's grown brutal from the fare;
> More substance in our enmities
> Than in our love.
>
>   (211, 205; 218, 425)

The refrain calling on the bees to "come build in the empty house of the stare" is most poignant in its last repetition after these lines. The bitter comment that precedes it certainly has a relation to the earlier "Easter 1916," where the poet muses, more tentatively, "Too long a sacrifice can make a stone of the heart." The events brooded on are related, and the poet sees a growing brutality since that time.

The "cold snows of a dream," in which the poet finds himself caught in "The Road at My Door," are recalled in the last poem of the sequence, when the poet, having climbed to the tower's top, looks out over the terrain and sees a "mist that is like blown snow" ("I see Phantoms of Hatred and of the Heart's Fullness and of the Coming Emptiness," 212, 205; 219, 425). However, the two images actually provide a contrast. The phrase "cold snows of a dream" expressed self-deprecation, but now the poet is looking outward again, and the images that come to his mind are to be accorded the respect due a vision. The moon, "a glittering sword," shines in the sky, so the situation is one for antithetical vision, but the moon is only a sliver, so we can assume that in the larger picture the solar world dominates, as it has seemed to do throughout the poems of *The Tower* and now in the poet's life. The poet's reverie is bewildering, but it is not the dream of "The Road at My Door," which was born of a sudden feeling of worthlessness. Indeed, it is the opposite. Though it is horrible and greatly disturbing to the visionary, it rapidly gives rise to two contrary visions that allow the poet to move toward acceptance of his own nature and activity in a way that makes it possible to return in "The Tower" to this same place, more forcefully declare for his role, and make his will. The fresh image is that of violence and revenge, which has a compelling quality very nearly inducing the poet to embrace it, but it is effectively blotted out by an image representing perfect antitheticality. This gives way, in its turn, to the primary opposite. Retreating from the whole visionary scene and descending the winding stair, the poet accepts his antithetical role and recognizes that primary accomplishments could not have satisfied him, for such accomplishments, like those of the rich inheritor of "My Table," would have "but made us pine the more."

And so the poet accepts the "daemonic" imagery, which is always only "half-read." He accepts search and incompletion as antithetical necessities. He recognizes here, even, that the antithetical quest yields an "abstract joy"—a joy separate from the life of action of the "brown lieutenant" and "affable irregular." The use of "abstract," employed so negatively in Yeats's writing, reasserts lightly, with a certain wistfulness, the poet's reticence about embracing his antitheticality fully, seeing it, as he already has seen it in the sequence, from the other point of view. But now he seems to be better prepared for the struggle with Plato and Plotinus (and Wordsworth) with which "The Tower" begins.

When we press back further in time to "Nineteen Hundred and Nineteen" (213, 206; 220, 428), we discover that the thoughts of "Meditations in Time of Civil War" have arisen from and responded to an even darker vision. The poem is a lamentation culminating in a vision of mindless horror not balanced by the opposite. Addressing at first the fact of endless destruction in history, it speaks bitterly of the collapse of the illusions of his own generation. The tone is self-castigating: "O what fine thought we had because we thought / That the worst rogues and rascals had died out" (213, 207; 220, 428). The Black and Tan violence is powerfully evoked in the description of a drunken, murderous soldiery. What is to be done?

> He who can read the signs nor sink unmanned
> Into the half-deceit of some intoxicant
> From shallow wits; who knows no work can stand,
> Whether health, wealth or peace of mind were spent
> On master-work of intellect or hand,
> No honour leave its mighty monument,
> Has but one comfort left: all triumph would
> But break upon his ghostly solitude.
>
> (213, 207–8; 220, 429)

This stanza provides the source for the notion of triumph, already discussed, in "The Tower." "He" is, of course, the antithetical man who maintains his wits in crisis. In this earlier poem little comfort is found. Indeed, "comfort" is the wrong term for what is eventually found in "The

Tower"; "resolve" is a better term. What comfort there might be is to know that triumph would be no comfort at all. Establishment of the total victory of antithetical values would be hollow. All strife and therefore life would cease. Triumph would break on the rock of an indifference, similar to the response of the ghosts called up in "The Tower," who are impatient to be gone when confronted with questions about love and growing old. The poet would have effected for himself a complete isolation, one more intense than even the "cold snows of a dream" in which he finds himself in "Meditations."

Therefore, man can find some comfort, he implies, in the fact that such triumph has not occurred. But unlike "The Tower," where this notion has been more fully accepted and enunciated, the poet's mind is not settled by it. In his dejection, the poet finds no comfort from it after all, and he really does seek comfort here, in contrast to his later behavior, when he moves beyond the depression of the times while at the same moment expecting comfort no longer. But he is not capable of finding much: "Man is in love and loves what vanishes, / What more is there to say?" (213, 208; 220, 429–30). This assertion, an attempt at ironic self-solace, leads eventually to both of the questions later asked in "The Tower." Both have to do with impermanence and loss and with the love of those lost things—lost youth, lost beloveds—that must be given up. In "The Tower" the questions are expressed in a condition of greater maturity than the tormented statements of "Nineteen Hundred and Nineteen" can achieve in the immediacy of contemporary events.

Part 2 is particularly depressed. The poet goes so far as to employ one of his favorite antithetical images in a context where it appears to express bondage and enclosure rather then anything approaching self-delight. (The reader's lesson here is that we cannot read the poet's images as fixed or his poetry as systematic; the poetry is passionate and dramatic, with imagistic values shifting under the domination of feelings and events. The poet himself told his beloved this in "Reconciliation," where he spoke of his earlier, half-hearted imagistic machinery.) The world is cyclical, and "All men are dancers and their tread / Goes to the barbarous clangour of a gong" (213, 208; 220, 430). The cyclicity observed here has little of the curious satisfaction that it gives the poet later, after the crisis of these poems is worked through. Here he responds to cyclicity by trying to imagine the individual human soul heroically opposed to cyclicity in pride, the word "pride" meaning something simpler than it means in "The Tower." Here it signifies lonely defiance, whereas later it comes to signify not only that but also aesthetic freedom and absorption in an intellectual tradition. The image of the swan here turns out to be insufficient, for it brings

> . . . a rage
> To end all things, to end
> What my laborious life imagined, even
> The half-imagined, the half-written page.
>
> (213, 209; 220, 431)

The section ends in his despair and self-contempt for having been deceived by history. In the process, "triumph" is again invoked, but in an even more depressed context. The poet refers to a Platonist who

> . . . affirms that in the station
> Where we should cast off body and trade
> The ancient habit sticks
> And that if our works could
> But vanish with our breath
> That were a lucky death,
> For triumph can but mar our solitude.
>
> (213, 209; 220, 431)

The Platonist is said here to regard triumph as a nuisance and a distraction to the perfect solitude of death, as an encumbrance to be "cast off" along with "body and trade." The poet in depression is tempted to the Platonic solution, but there is something that prevents him from it, though he has no other at the moment, being in bitter despair at the naiveté of his and his generation's illusions. The meaning of "triumph" implied by the Platonist is different from that in its earlier usage in the poem. The Platonic solution contemplated by the poet would be, in truth, a rejection of the concept of the antithetical contrary that has developed in the poet's thought from at least "Ego Dominus Tuus." The Platonist identifies "triumph" with earthly accomplishment in the realm of appearances; such things would be distracting and would have to be purged away in death. To reject pure antithetical triumph, as the poet does in "The Tower," is not to reject appearances as distracting unrealities best transcended. It is to accept a world of particulars as real and recognize the need to maintain the strife of opposition between image and idea, antithetical and primary.

The rejection of the Platonic and the return to life under extreme difficulty occurs in sections 5 and 6, after the poet reaches the nadir of his despair in section 4. The return begins sarcastically in the call to mockery of everything, but it ends in ironically turning the call inside out. After calling for mockery of the great, the wise, and the good, who are all made to seem foolish, the poet would

> Mock mockers after that
> That would not lift a hand maybe

To help good, wise or great
To bar that foul storm out, for we
Traffic in mockery.

(213, 210; 220, 432)

To stand aside finally in a mocking stance of superiority to commitment is rejected. The poet reaches far down into himself and finds there something—an ethic—deeper than doctrine and belief which prevents him from abandoning life. He finds his antitheticality. This willed "dreaming back" and "return" is not part of a process of purgation, such as is supposed to happen after death. It is rather a working back to a discovery of something, a bringing to birth of his fundamental nature. The mockery turns into antithetical commitment.

This makes possible a vision. It is not a pretty one, but it marks a return to life. It is a vision of mindless violence and desire, the foul incubus of Lady Kyteler, the executed witch of medieval Kilkenny. Violence and desire are later implicated in the creative opposition of primary and antithetical. Both are held back from triumph by that opposition. The poet's fears are not abated by any of this; all but the horror seems blotted out, but the way is opened for the fuller cyclical vision that ends "Meditations in Time of Civil War." Here the poet sees as yet only the impending triumph of mindless insolence. The experience of "All Souls' Night" had not yet occurred in 1919.

The Tower (1928): Second Return

We have traveled back in time from the moment of the poet's voyage toward Byzantium through the bequeathing of pride and faith to the future, through the meditation on violence and the first steps toward positive acceptance of the antithetical role in old age, and finally to the nadir of despair over "violence on the roads," indeed, to the discovery of violence and conflict at the source, so to speak. This is a discovery not to be forgotten in *The Winding Stair* and later works, where violence is explicitly identified with the antithetical.

There is now a turning and then a working back again, but in this second movement the subject is not the poet's troubled relation to external events but his concurrent intellectual experience during those years. There comes from this a quite personal historical vision.

"The Wheel" (214, 211; 221, 434) and "Youth and Age" (215, 211; 222, 434) mark the turn. "The Wheel" sums up momentarily in a gesture of philosophical disinterest the situation of antithetical desire by treating it as part of the cycle of nature. The poem is apparently an adaptation of a theme from Leonardo da Vinci, who wrote:

> Now you see that the hope and desire of returning to the first chaos is like the moth to the light, and that the man who with constant longing awaits with joy each new springtime, each new summer, each new month and each new year—dreaming that the things he longs for are too late in coming—does not perceive that he is longing for his own destruction.[2]

Leonardo's statement and the poet's adaptation explain desire and require, if things were really this simple, no more tormenting personal analysis. For the poet, this poem signals at least a moment of security and understanding. The passage back that begins with "Youth and Age," dated 1924, sends the poet to the event dramatized in "All Souls' Night" of 1920, which seems to have been made possible by the vision of Robartes and Aherne in "The Phases of the Moon" in the previous section of the *Book*.

The result is the production of poems of prophecy and wisdom. This movement is characteristically punctuated with troubled moments, however, even as it contains some of the poet's most remarkable achievements. "Youth and Age" implies that his sense of oppression by the world has diminished and that now the world flatters him as it "speeds the parting guest." In "The New Faces" (216, 211; 223, 435), while addressing his old friend Lady Gregory [the poem was written in 1912 but finds its place here in part by virtue of its tone], he imagines their ghosts haunting the gardens where they walked in life, the antithetical triumphing over the primary. These ghosts slightly recall the roving shades of "The Indian to his Love," but there is a difference in that their forms seem to be those of their accomplishments. There is a modicum of comfort here that the poet of "Nineteen Hundred and Nineteen" despaired of finding.

"A Prayer for my Son" (217, 212; 224, 435) signals the more personal nature of the poems to follow (precede). It seems to be connected with the experience of ghostly visitants and perhaps expresses some fear that his conversing with the curious voices that will be allegorically mentioned in "The Gift of Harun Al-Rashid" (1923) has generated vengeful evil spirits as well as friendly instructors. The poem is followed (preceded) by three important prophetic works. When I speak of prophecy, I mean not prediction of future events but visionary assertion about the shape of history. The poet has already worried about the future and has suffered visions of a rough, sphinxlike beast, the incubus Robert Artisson, and a vengeful

---

2. *The Literary Works of Leonardo Da Vinci*, ed. J. P. Richter (Oxford University Press, 1939), 2: 242.

mob, the last being an external counterpart to the evil forces that he imagines murdering his son.

"Two Songs from a Play" (218, 213; 225, 437), "Fragments" (219, 214; 226, 439), and "Leda and the Swan" (220, 214; 228, 441) have been much discussed and require no detailed explication here. It is important to see them in the *Book* as part of a significant development of the poet's historical vision, which in turn is important not so much for its sagacity or its capacity to offer a detailed scholarly analysis of the relation among events as for its establishment of a way of taking in and assimilating, without despair and with even a sort of magnanimity, a mass of often dreadful, apparently irrational movements and seeing them in antithetical perspective.

"Two Songs from a Play" presents a cyclical vision that has been well discussed by Richard Ellmann.[3] It emphasizes a cyclicity in which the return not of the same but of the opposite in the same occurs. The conclusions to be drawn not only from its first three stanzas but also from "Fragments" and "Leda and the Swan" are unexpected. The historical moment of Jesus' life and death canceled yet carried on, in a pattern of sameness and difference at the same time, an earlier movement from Dionysiac irrationality to "Platonic tolerance." A new irrational moment occurs, but it is primary to the previously antithetical. The conclusion is one mirrored in the movement the poet makes from "Nineteen Hundred and Nineteen" to "The Tower," for it allows him to come to terms with terror. "Two Songs from a Play" begins to establish a sense of form in the movement from order to irrational disorder thence to order again:

> Everything that man esteems
> Endures a moment or a day.
> Love's pleasure drives his love away.
> The painter's brush consumes his dreams;
> The herald's cry, the soldier's tread
> Exhaust his glory and his might:
> Whatever flames upon the night
> Man's own resinous heart has fed.

> (218, 213–14; 225, 438)

The vision is in two ways antithetical. First, it employs in its joining of the same and the different the antithetical logic exemplified by the metaphor. Second, as the last two lines above indicate, it is humanly centered.

In establishing an antithetical history, the poet has had two momentary visions. One ("Fragments," 219, 214; 226, 439) is of John Locke as Adam

---

3. Richard Ellmann, *The Identity of Yeats* (New York: Oxford University Press, 1954), pp. 260–63.

and the spinning jenny as Eve and marks the symbolic beginning of a cycle within a larger cycle—the development of the modern theory of the mechanical universe that the poet so dislikes. The other vision is, of course, that of Leda's rape by Zeus in the form of a swan ("Leda and the Swan," 220, 214; 228, 441), before which in time the poet does not pretend to see. The imagery of the swan throughout the poet's work is given a special meaning by the invocation of this myth. By choosing the swan as the vehicle of his act, Zeus gives to it a special, superhuman significance. The children of this violence have something of the swan in their being. In the version of the myth that the poet employs these children are Castor and Pollux and Helen of Troy, who represent the two fundamental poles of metaphorical sameness and opposition in the poet's thought—strife and love. This historical vision of beginnings implicitly endorses the poet's earlier metaphorical identification of the beloved with Helen in "No Second Troy" and elsewhere as well as his identification of the swan with antithetical pride.

Just before this, in a moment of meditation on a painting, the poet asserts his readiness to make the prophecies we have heard him utter. The centaur of "On a Picture of a Black Centaur by Edmund Dulac" (221, 215; 229, 442) has been variously interpreted as the poet's special Pegasus and as Ireland as he has known it. The centaur remains mysterious in many ways, but perhaps it can be more generally thought of as those things that command his allegiance and that symbolize values worth protecting. He reasserts his allegiances and his capacity, grown over time and in travail, to "keep a watch" against "those horrible green birds," which suggest the Irish chatterers whose shallow, shortsighted patriotism has held back the enactment of antithetical values. There seems to be a bitter connection here with the fearfully anticipated "common greenness" of "Meditations in Time of Civil War." In "On a Picture" he describes allegorically his poetic and intellectual history:

> . . . I, being driven half insane
> Because of some green wing, gathered old mummy wheat
> In the mad abstract dark and ground it grain by grain
> And after baked it slowly in an oven; but now
> I bring full-flavoured wine out of a barrel found
> Where seven Ephesian topers slept and never knew
> When Alexander's empire passed, they slept so sound.
>
> (221, 215; 229, 442)

The suggestion is that his early poetry was a poetry of psychological crisis and repetition that he has now passed through. The poems that surround this assertion are his proof: "Leda and the Swan" comes before it, "Among

School Children" after. [Both are generally regarded as among Yeats's finest achievements.]

In "Among School Children" (222, 215; 230, 443), the poet, now a public man, visits a progressive school, calls up the memory of a story told to him years ago by his beloved, and then imagines her as she must have been as a child. Comparing that child to her present appearance calls him back to his own present, and he meditates on Platonic forms, nature, Pythagoreanism, and music. In this stately, passionate poem, the poet attempts to imagine a condition of creative life where the soul/body relation is not what Blake would have called a negation, that is, where one is privileged over the other. In such a condition, beauty would not have to be born of ungratified desire, wisdom would not have to be paid for by "midnight oil"; the actor and the act would be one. Conjuring up a great chestnut tree—roots in the earth, blossoms in the air—he raises the question of its essential being, which in time seems broken up into root, blossom, and bole. He asks the same question about dancer and dance and, by implication, about child and old woman.

The questions remain questions. They have been interpreted as implying the answer "yes," as implying anxiety that the answer may be "yes" or may be "no," and so forth. However, it is best, I think, to see the poem as a dramatic working through of a problem to the answer that actually precedes these questions:

> Labour is blossoming or dancing where
> The body is not bruised to pleasure soul,
> Nor beauty born out of its own despair,
> Nor blear-eyed wisdom out of midnight oil.

> > (222, 217; 230, 445–46)

The key word is "labour," with its two meanings of giving birth and toil. This word, which joins the ideas of natural creativity and the toil of artistry that the poet describes as early as "Adam's Curse," goes on, according to the poem, in a place or condition—a spiritual space, one might say—where negations are successfully opposed. That would be an antithetical condition. In such a pure condition of creation the questions that follow would not have to be asked. It is in moments such as these, which, as Blake said, Satan's watch-fiends cannot find, that the poet's work is done—moments not subject to the analytical process, which must have its either-or and its linear time. The questions rouse the faculties to act:

> O chestnut tree, great rooted blossomer,
> Are you the leaf, the blossom or the bole?
> O body swayed to music, O brightening glance,
> How can we know the dancer from the dance?

> > (222, 217; 230, 446)

From the antithetical point of view already expressed, the answer to the first question must be in the form both-and. The answer to the second question, antithetically formulated, is that we can properly know the dancer from the dance by also knowing the dancer as the dance. Primary formulation of these questions would have to be imagined as occurring under the antithetical pressure of the preceding assertion. The primary formulation would indicate confusion, anxiety, and a failure to understand that the antithetical stance does not require one to embrace only one side of an opposition and privilege it; rather, one has one's sameness *and* one's difference.

We note that "Leda and the Swan" also ends in a question answerable by either "yes" or "no"—"yes," perhaps, if knowledge and desire were not regarded as negations of each other, "no" if they were and if the human beings produced from the union were regarded in purely naturalistic terms. The latter view is particularly dominant in an age that imagines woman as the spinning jenny. The antithetical view identifies knowledge with desire and both with power.

In "Colonus' Praise" (223, 218; 231, 446), an adaptation of a chorus from *Oedipus at Colonus* turns Colonus into the environment of the antithetical, shaded from the primary sun, site of dancing ladies and perfected bodies. The connections to the imagery of "Among School Children" are many, the poem being a vision of an idealized antithetical life that gives rise, I think, to carrying the antithetical vision into the poet's classroom musings.

We continue to study the second "dreaming back" and "return" by observing poems that show the early signs of self-confident assertion of gnomic wisdom: "Wisdom," "The Fool by the Roadside" and the sequence called "A Man Young and Old." In the midst of these, "Owen Aherne and his Dancers" strikes another note, which we shall consider. These poems begin to presage *The Winding Stair and Other Poems*, with its sequences and aphoristic prophecies arranged deliberately without respect to "chronology," as the dated poems show.

"Wisdom" (224, 219; 227, 440) seems deliberately cryptic, as if the poet had adopted an oracular mode that leaves the reader to puzzle between opposed possibilities (much as do the previous [later] "Among School Children" and "Leda and the Swan"). Does art "amend" and thus correct myth and legend, producing the true faith by means of the aestheticization of the tale? Or does it distort some original vision? Is wisdom the product of the marriage of abundance and innocence, a coupling that suggests sameness/difference with/from Leda and Zeus? To whom did the cognomen "wisdom" seem best? The church? Philosophers? History? The culture that had to interpret Jesus' life? What does it mean to consider "what wild infancy / Drove horror from His Mother's breast"? Is the mother's horror that of being involved in a miracle? Something unnatural? Is the child's "wild infancy," being natural, a sign of wisdom, having calmed the mother? The tone indicates to us complete confidence.

In "The Fool by the Roadside" (225, 219; 232, 449), another form of the oracular appears with a new persona who is actually a traditional figure: the prophetic or wise fool. The poet now seems to step behind an irrational voice possessed with cryptic truth. These kinds of voices, and others, will continue to appear, speaking as if both inside and outside of time and events, speaking in image and particularity but projecting an aura of universality. All move toward the later sequences in which are heard the voices of Crazy Jane, Old Tom, and Ribh.

It has always been typical of the poet that personal anxieties and remorse flow back in just as we confidently assume that they have finally been put aside. "The Gift of Harun Al-Rashid" (1923) will seem to say once and for all that the poet's wife can feel secure in his need for her, but vestiges of concern over earlier events remain. As we follow the "dreaming back" and "return" to "The Gift of Harun Al-Rashid," we must traverse a poem of concern and torment that one might have thought would not now be written. As we shall see, the last (first) poem of the "dreaming back" and "return," "All Souls' Night," will speak of achieved antithetical knowledge. The knowledge would, if put in earlier terms, be identified with Michael Robartes. But his primary opposite, Owen Aherne, is never negated; to negate him would be uncharacteristic of the antithetical stance. So at this moment, in the appropriate role of Owen Aherne, the poet recalls events that antedate the poet's marriage and the achievement of the knowledge that we are going to learn his wife has brought him; he plunges back in memory into the confusions and remorse of an earlier affair.

"Owen Aherne and his Dancers" (226, 220; 233, 449) tells of yet another dialogue with the heart. But this heart is older and, if not more cautious, at least more knowing. He remembers that the heart had advocated that he turn away at fifty from a young woman. It had done this in the name of natural propriety and the desire not to see the young woman put in a "cage" when still "wild." So the heart remains an advocate of passion after all and accuses Aherne of an unnatural desire. For his part, Aherne speaks passionately enough, accuses the heart of madness, murder, and lies, and declares that the woman at his side now (presumably the poet's wife) is not someone he found in a cage. She too is a young woman. But the heart has triumphed and maliciously reminds the poet that his earlier passion is over. Aherne can rail against the heart as much as he wants to, for he can no longer persuade "the child till she mistake / Her childish gratitude for love." This is a troubling reminiscence that floods in after the poet has completed a sequence of eleven poems called "A Man Young and

Old," which is an effort to deal wisely with male sexual passion from youth
to age and is presumably definitive, but it has its opposition in Aherne's
compulsive, dialogical confession.

"A Man Young and Old" (227–37, 221; 234–44, 451) is a complicated
manipulation of voice. The poet imagines a man speaking the passionate
moments of his life from youth to age, yet the whole sequence seems to
add up to more than this voice can utter. It is as if he, like the fool by the
roadside, is an unknowing oracle who has somehow managed to say more
in the whole than in the parts. The oracular source is, of course, the poet.
Ending with an adaptation of the great chorus from *Oedipus at Colonus*, the
sequence takes the man from first love to a final comment on life that is a
preparation for death. It introduces for the first time an important theme
of the poet's subsequent work, the idea of "tragic gaiety":

> Never to have lived is best, ancient writers say;
> Never to have drawn the breath of life, never to have looked into
>   the eye of day;
> The second best's a gay goodnight and quickly turn away.
>
> (237, 227; 244, 459)

Suggestions of the poet's own life of passion, refined to a sort of essence
and offered in a spare lyric style, are present, as if now brought into mature focus and included as a synecdoche of the larger story that is the *Book*.
I say "as if" because there are some elaborations and opposites to be
brought in, including "A Woman Young and Old," that the poet has yet to
accomplish.

"A Man Young and Old" is the first sequence the poet attempts that is
detached from personal chronology. Appearing where it does, it is an effort to sum up in a fiction the life of male human desire; its suggestions of
personal experience may be what generates the poet's revival of the Aherne
character to express a troubling memory that doesn't find its natural representation in the sequence. This itself endorses the heart's view as expressed in "Owen Aherne and his Dancers."

Following (just before) "A Man Young and Old" and just before (following) "The Gift of Harun Al-Rashid," a short poem called "The Three
Monuments" (238, 227; 245, 460) reminds us of the poet's continued concern with the local political scene. The experience treated in "The Gift of
Harun Al-Rashid" seems to have provided the poet with a greater sense of
ironic detachment. Conflict and impurity he accepts as necessary to human life, and he imagines the statues of Parnell, O'Connell, and Nelson
(all "old rascals") laughing at the behavior of popular statesmen who claim
that "purity built up the State" and that pride and intellect would "bring
in impurity."

That the poet divulges only in an obscure allegory the role of his wife as the medium who has supplied most of his new thought indicates some reticence. As "The Gift of Harun Al-Rashid" (382, 445; 246, 460) proceeds, we become certain that the poem is written obliquely to her, as an earlier long poem, "The Old Age of Queen Maeve," was written obliquely to the beloved. Kusta ben Luka, poet and scholar in the court of Harun Al-Rashid, is the poet himself, an older man presented with a young wife who not only shares the poet's interest in occult philosophy but also turns out to be an unwitting spirit medium through whom the desert djinns speak a cryptic wisdom. Kusta has "accepted the Byzantine faith" (a reference to "Sailing to Byzantium") and declares that, having chosen a wife, he has chosen forever. There is a special reason for this assertion, but before we learn it we must hear that he is uncertain whether his wife loves him or only the mysteries that interest both. For his part, he worries that she might imagine, did she realize she was a medium, that his interest in her is only for the sake of her mediumship:

> Were she to lose her love, because she had lost
> Her confidence in mine, or even lose
> Its first simplicity, love, voice and all,
> All my fine feathers would be plucked away
> And I left shivering.
>
>   (382, 450; 246, 469)

The assertion made by Kusta to Harun Al-Rashid that he had married by faith once and for good is part of the poet's address to his wife and further assurance of his love. Moreover, he now asserts, as the poem ends, that what he has learned from her, "all those gyres and cubes and midnight things / Are but a new expression of her body." Thus he connects his new antithetical wisdom with her as a sexual being who has brought into relation desire and conflict.

> A woman's beauty is a storm-tossed banner;
> Under it wisdom stands, and I alone—
> Of all Arabia's lovers I alone—
> Nor dazzled by the embroidery, nor lost
> In the confusion of its night-dark folds,
> Can hear the armed man speak.
>
>   (382, 450; 246, 469–70)

It is she who one night under a full moon played the role of the antiself anticipated in "Ego Dominus Tuus" and who in a trance drew those curious emblems on the sands and murmured the antithetical wisdom of the desert djinns. He is convinced, and tries to convince her, that the mysterious voice speaking through her has

> . . . drawn
> A quality of wisdom from her love's
> Particular quality.

(382, 450; 246, 469)

When we consider that we have passed through a sequence of poems on a man's love in which the love affair seems to allude covertly to the earlier beloved, and when we consider "Owen Aherne and his Dancers," not a remembrance of his wife, we see "The Gift of Harun Al-Rashid" as a necessary reassurance to her. The poet indicates his love, but he has not forgotten earlier ones and their meaning, or rather he continues to make meaning from them.

"All Souls' Night" (1920) (239, 227; 247, 470), subtitled "Epilogue to 'A Vision,'" takes us back to the poet's earliest expression of discovery of the strength that his wife's mediumship (carefully unmentioned) has brought. The poet and his wife are living at Oxford. The bell of Christ Church College rings at midnight on All Souls' Night as they sit before two glasses of wine, and the poet contemplates the calling up of ghosts of past friends. He does call them—Horton, Florence Emory, and Mathers—all occultists, but they do not appear except to memory. He meditates on each and finally declares that it makes no difference what ghost comes, only that the ghost be capable of drinking from the fume of the wine before them. Indeed, it turns out that it does not even matter whether a ghost comes at all. He called on ghosts because he thought they would be respectful and understanding listeners to thoughts that the living would mock. These thoughts he does not here divulge. Rather, he declares their absolute sufficiency for him. They are the product of the symbolic thought that Michael Robartes cryptically expressed and that the wife of Kusta ben Luka drew in figures on the sand. They make up a vision of love, desire, conflict, and cyclicity that enables him to survive the crises of terror and, in "The Tower," to declare his pride and faith and then to travel toward the symbolic city of Byzantium. We notice that in "The Tower" the poet calls up ghosts once again, but there from the beginning he does not really expect them to appear; the act of calling is really a sending forth of imagination, which is now in itself sufficient. The ghosts are propulsions of that imagination; one, his own fictive creation, he commands to stay and engage in colloquy with him. Kusta ben Luka had said that his new wisdom was from his young wife's body, not from beyond. It is that which has spurred his imagination. It is an antithetical inspiration in which "body is not bruised to pleasure soul," intellect expressing itself as body, body as intellect.

What we have observed in this second "return" is a deliberate working back through a period of unexpected intellectual and sexual excitement in the poet's life, a period that coincided with a period of historical crisis in Ireland, the subject of the first "return." *The Tower* is a strange combination of bitterness and sometimes ecstatic prophecy. The poet's work would never again be the same.

6

Antithetical Oscillation

"The Winding Stair" (1933)

There is no single poem entitled "The Winding Stair." *The Winding Stair and Other Poems* suggests that all of the poems under that title up to the sequence "Words for Music Perhaps" constitute a collection. The reference is, of course, to the spiral stone stairway of the tower and seems to imply both ascent/descent and a gyring oscillation from one side to another. These movements become themata that dominate the way the poems are ordered. In *The Tower*, as we have seen, there has already been a shift from what had been a (fictive) chronological arrangement of the poems to one that implies a double "dreaming back" and "return." In *The Tower*, the fictive poet, finally named William Yeats in "To be carved on a Stone at Thoor Ballylee," whom W. B. Yeats created or in a sense became, dated several of his poems to deepen the idea that these poems are immersed in historical moments and to display the willed "dreaming back" and "return." Also in *The Tower* we noticed the appearance of a sequence, "A Man Young and Old," in which the poet created a set of poems with fictive characters (the poet's fiction within a fiction) that turns on certain themata and has its own chronology.

Now, in "The Winding Stair," we see the poet take liberty with materials belonging to his own life and (while maintaining a loose chronology) form a collection (not quite a sequence) that emphasizes relations of opposition between poems or groups of poems. The oppositions often take the form of personal vacillation. Themata emanating from *The Tower* vie with personal chronology. The poet not only is shaped by events but shapes his thought. The great stirring events of the poet's life have by now taken place. An authoritative voice is heard, though it is a voice acknowledging vacillation as its theme.

Ten of the twenty-eight poems of "The Winding Stair" are dated; the presence of these dates in the text is enough to emphasize the poet's deliberate disruption of a strictly (fictive) chronological arrangement. The dated poems, in order and with their dates, are:

"In Memory of Eva Gore-Booth and Con Markievicz" (October
    1927)
"Coole Park, 1929"
"Coole and Ballylee, 1931"
"At Algeciras—A Meditation upon Death" (November 1928)
"Mohini Chatterjee" (1928)
"Byzantium" (1930)
"Vacillation" (1930)
"The Results of Thought" (August 1931)
"Remorse for Intemperate Speech" (August 28, 1931)
"Stream and Sun at Glendalough" (June 1932)

Replacing strict chronology is the drama of conflict and personal vacillation, now emphasized by the appearance of these dates. Oppositions are everywhere—between poems and groups of poems as well as in poems. Some of these oppositions are the dying historical cycle/the anticipated one, ascent/cyclicity, soul/self, soul/heart, religious/secular, day/night, wisdom/power, love/terror, remorse/joy, and, of course, the implied primary/antithetical.

"The Winding Stair" begins with elegy and ends by celebrating a life mystery, and it many times passes back and forth between this and other oppositions as it proceeds on its gyring way. The oscillations occur late in the poet's life under conditions that naturally favor the primary. There are temptations, like those in "The Tower," to abandon the antithetical stance. Consequently, there is a need for more vigorous expression of antithetical values, even as there is acknowledgment of a newly perceived dark side of antithetical desire. Finally, there is a movement to encompass an even larger scene of opposition. The opposition of Hic and Ille in *The Wild Swans at Coole* emphasized the life of action against that of the imagination. The opposition of primary and antithetical forces dominated *The Tower*, but this opposition was entirely within life. (This opposition is different from that of Hic and Ille in that there can be antithetical action and primary passivity.) In "The Winding Stair," the whole domain of death, regarded as primary, is ranged against life, regarded as antithetical. [This movement is the same as that which occurs in *A Vision* as it proceeds into the chapter called "The Soul in Judgment."]

"In Memory of Eva Gore-Booth and Con Markievicz" (240, 233; 248, 475), the first poem of "The Winding Stair," is in two parts, the first written before the deaths of the two women as an elegy on their youth and, by extension, the culture to which they belonged when young. (Eva died in

1926, Constance in 1927.) The time of part 1 is that of "The Tower" (1926) or slightly before. That marks it as roughly contemporary with the poet's decision in "The Tower" to "make" his soul so that the death of friends or beautiful women will seem

> . . . but the clouds of the sky
> When the horizon fades;
> Or a bird's sleepy cry
> Among the deepening shades.

(205, 200; 212, 416)

The poem begins characteristically as if the poet were setting an actual scene, but it is instead a remembrance full of nostalgia for something lost. It is also a criticism of the two women for abandoning the tradition that in their youth they and the great house Lissadell represented to him. There will be more discussion of this tradition and its demise through the early poems of "The Winding Stair."

Part 2 is written in October 1927, after their deaths and presumably after or around the time of "Sailing to Byzantium." In that poem, the poet addressed "sages standing in God's holy fire" and asked for their help. Here he addresses the two women as ghosts. He has called on ghosts before, in "All Souls' Night," but they have not accepted the invitation to converse. We do not know whether they come or not, but it matters little because the poet confidently states to them, present or not, what he believes they already know in death. Thus they become a lesson to the living not to behave as they did. He imagines them, with special attention to Constance, as now wisely beyond "the folly of a fight / with a common wrong or right." It is not the rightness or wrongness of their causes that is at stake; it is the foolish commitment to commonness, which is also a commitment to abstraction, whether political, as in the case of Constance, or spiritually Utopian, as in the case of Eva. Such commitments and the activities surrounding them the poet names "politics."

"Politics" is an extremely important word in the *Book*. In addition to its connection with abstraction (it is a primary word), it is identified with the headlong involvement in the externalities of things that, to the poet's mind, creates a harshness of imagination and loss of capacity for heroic disinterest. The poet had already observed as early as "On a Political Prisoner" that Con Markievicz's mind had become "a bitter, an abstract thing." At that time, one imagined the poet, under pressure of frustrated love for a woman of political action, resenting Constance's political life. Here the situation is more complicated, though it probably includes that earlier irritation. There is distaste for "politics," but the poet deliberately refuses to blame politics directly. Rather, he claims that time—only time—is the enemy. But there is an ambiguity about this: If time is the only enemy, then it must be time and not "politics" that Eva, "withered old and skeleton gaunt," must image, contrary to the statement tentatively set forth in part 1. Seen in this way, part 2 seems forgiving. But it is not entirely forgiving after all, because it remains an admonition, even perhaps an expression of a slightly malicious satisfaction: These two foolish women know in death the truth that he has come to know in life.

It is significant that the poet indicates in part 1 that he has often thought of seeking "one or the other out" to talk of the old days, but he has never actually done so. This is perhaps because they, being no longer what they were, would not have responded as he would have wished. When he addresses them in part 2, he willfully treats them as if they have somehow returned in death to the true antithetical natures he has willed for them. As such they become symbolic of something now irretrievably lost, and he becomes a belated survivor. He imagines that he, they, their generation, and the traditions the end of which they mark have been repudiated by the new politics of commonality (the same politics he accuses them of imagining). It is only his act of will that separates them in death from that politics. [One is fairly certain what Constance Markievicz would have thought of this manipulation of her ghost.]

It is important to note the difference from the bitter, depressed second stanza of "Nineteen Hundred and Nineteen," where the poet castigates his generation for naive, satisfied delusion:

> We too had many pretty toys when young;
> A law indifferent to blame or praise,
> To bribe or threat; habits that made old wrong
> Melt down, as it were wax in the sun's rays;
> Public opinion ripening for so long
> We thought it would outlive all future days.
> O what fine thought we had because we thought
> That the worst rogues and rascals had died out.
>
> (213, 207; 220, 428)

Now, by contrast, he is proudly willing to be convicted along with his old friends (forcibly enlisted in the tradition of dying antithetically):

> We the great gazebo built,
> They convicted us of guilt;
> Bid me strike a match and blow.
>
> (240, 234; 248, 476)

Has he forgotten that in an earlier mood he had been one of "them," convicting his generation of creating a great gazebo of Victorian complacency? Here the stance is different. There has intervened, first, a strong sense of

cyclicity and inevitability and, second, a renewed commitment to antithetical values in spite of, even because of, their waning power. At the end
of the poem, he arrogantly (and antithetically) tells the imagined ghosts
what they should tell him to do: Welcome the coming conflagration as a
hastening of the historical nadir of the age and the cyclical turn. It would
be the ultimate, reckless, disinterested, heroical act. The conclusion is a
curious blend of the earlier bitterness and a new violent gaiety.

The whole of part 2 has been a gesture of will. The poet wills the two
sisters to be what he wishes them to have been. There is a certain vacillation in this, a strenuous test of his own desire, but there is also confidence
in the reckless gesturing. This confidence is not unusual in "The Winding
Stair," where several poems seem to be assertions no longer of the moment
of passion but of prophetic certainty. This does not mean that there will
be no further vacillation, but it is to say that the vacillation becomes the
form in action that this sort of antithetical certainty often takes. Still, the
poem is a troubled and troubling one, as later poems will be. We remember that "Sailing to Byzantium" at its outset was a defiant poem, and we
see that the poet now more fully comprehends that he must build his position on a base of antithetical defiance in the face of overwhelming primary force. It is in this context that we read his refusal to accept the "politics" of the Gore-Booth sisters, his willful insistence on claiming another
nature for them, and his reckless willingness to strike the match.

"Death" (241, 234; 249, 476), which follows, carries the recklessness
that we earlier identified with Castiglione's *sprezzatura* (remembering it always as a *willed* recklessness) well beyond anything Castiglione would
have imagined. Contrasting human hope and fear of death with their absence in animals, the poet declares, "Man has created death." Again, the
antithetical gesture is foremost. Antithetical pride "casts derision upon /
Supersession of Breath." Death is identified as part of cyclicity. We are to
learn in the next poem that the dread overcome is not merely that of punishment in the afterlife or of the unknown but that of repetition of life.

However, this short poem, though full of strong assertion, as so many
of the poems now are, does not fully explore the matters about which it
makes its assertions. Furthermore, its powerful gesture of antithetical certainty, like that at the end of the previous poem, seems to suppress any
possible opposition. As we have already learned in *The Tower*, such
"triumph" is dangerous. A deeper treatment is needed, and "A Dialogue
of Self and Soul" (242, 234; 250, 477) provides it. But the poem is hardly
a dialogue. In "Ego Dominus Tuus," Hic was at least able to engage Ille so
that Ille responded to him. In "A Dialogue of Self and Soul," Soul does
not have this success, though Soul does establish the terms in which Self
seems compelled to speak, thus implying primary dominance.

Soul begins not as a questioner but as a summoner, as if in charge.

I summon to the winding ancient stair;
Set all your mind upon the steep ascent,
Upon the broken, crumbling battlement,
Upon the breathless starlit air,
Upon the star that marks the hidden pole;
Fix every wandering thought upon
That quarter where all thought is done:
Who can distinguish darkness from the soul?

(242, 234; 250, 477)

Soul introduces the notion of a pole or center around which all moves, an image that will come up again in connection with primary belief in a fixed, external point of reference to which allegiance must and can conveniently be given. Soul characterizes Self's thought as "wandering," as the poet characterized his own thought in "All Souls' Night," but Soul does so pejoratively, presuming that all thought ought to be fixed upon or revolving about a spiritual object. Therefore, for Soul, the stairway, though winding, represents a discipline of ascent. This ascent, it is implied, is toward annihilation in God.

Self seems not to hear or refuses to acknowledge hearing Soul and meditates on Sato's sword, which is bound and adorned by the tattered embroidery of some "court-lady's dress." The connection between desire and violence, which was queried in *The Tower*, is reintroduced here and will become even more intensely considered, with troubled conclusions, in "Blood and the Moon" and beyond. Something like the scarecrow of "Sailing to Byzantium" is present here, but with violence as well as sexual desire clearly alive in the sword that the tatters sheathe.

Soul either is perplexed at Self's musing or admonishes Self with a rhetorical question:

Why should the imagination of a man
Long past his prime remember things that are
Emblematical of love and war?

(242, 235; 250, 477)

The question seems all the more appropriate given the tatters that desire wears and Soul's emphasis on ultimate deliverance from the cycle of "death and birth." Intellect is again castigated as "wandering," and the whole cycle is characterized as "crime," suggesting original sin.

But once again Self ignores Soul, though there are more signs in its use of Soul's terms that it has heard or cannot help using Soul's language. Self deliberately chooses an antithetical position, symbolized by the tower, and has meditated on the sword as a symbol of continued vigorous antitheticality despite the tattered, faded embroidery that clothes it. Soul, beginning to lose interest in Self, as is appropriate for its spiritual path, proceeds to a meditation of its own, describing the ascension as if it were the path of annihilation:

> Such fullness in that quarter overflows
> And falls into the basin of the mind
> That man is stricken deaf and dumb and blind,
> For intellect no longer knows
> *Is* from the *Ought*, or *Knower* from the *Known*—
> That is to say, ascends to Heaven.
>
> (242, 235; 250, 478)

This said, Soul lapses into silence. From Self's point of view, it is as if Soul has wandered off. But that is not Soul's point of view, for Soul has said all that it feels need be said. Life and death are a crime, and forgiveness is given in heaven. Part 2 is Self's soliloquy expressing the choice of rebirth. Indeed, Self has already claimed "as by a soldier's right / A charter to commit the crime once more." Here are recalled, perhaps, the soldiers of "Meditations in Time of Civil War," so troubling to the poet; Self declares for his own kind of soldierly discipline and commitment, which as far back as "Adam's Curse" the poet has thought to be misunderstood. Soul, meanwhile, has implied that absolution is the proper aim and only the dead can be forgiven. Therefore, study death, make one's soul.

The poet indicated in "The Tower" that he would "make [his] soul," but Soul's emphasis is not the poet's as it is expressed in that poem. There the poet spoke of the making of his soul as the study of art, poets' imaginings, and memories of love and the words of women. These represented antithetical values; the change that has occurred since then is not a turning against a soul to be "made" in that way. It is a continued resistance to Soul as Soul defines its ascent to annihilation. And yet there is a difference from "Sailing to Byzantium." In that poem, the effort was to imagine a role antithetical to youth, on the one hand, and to typical old age, on the other. It was opposed to youth because the poet recognized that his youth was behind him. It was opposed to old age because of the continued need to persist in active defense of antithetical values. Youth/age was seen as a negation created by primary thought.

In the closing meditation of "A Dialogue of Self and Soul," the poet moves the whole conflictive drama to a new level or larger circumference. It is a question no longer of youth against age in life but of a cyclicity that absorbs both life and death against an opposition in which death negates life. The poet is not just defending life against death, for that would be merely a reversal of the negation; he is also embracing renewal against annihilation. The movement from "In Memory of Eva Gore-Booth and Con Markievicz" through "Death" to Self's meditation has eventuated in an identification of antithetical stance with cyclicity. This is the reason that reincarnation is embraced so often in "The Winding Stair" and later. It is the image of antitheticality in the broadest possible sense. Antitheticality is not interested in belief and fact; it is interested in opposition and gesture. Under these more dire conditions of old age, gestural force must be greater than ever before. In the *Book*, the meditation contains the first of several statements declaring "What matter if . . . ," as the poet attempts to embrace a more cosmic antithetical position. He declares not a fear of death—that fear was dispatched in "Death"—but a willingness to endure the fear of facing life again.

> What matter if I live it all once more?
> Endure that toil of growing up;
> The ignominy of boyhood; the distress
> Of boyhood changing into man;
> The unfinished man and his pain
> Brought face to face with his own clumsiness.
>
> (242, 236; 250, 478–79)

This catalog continues for two more stanzas. He is not so much reliving as anticipating what he and, he has asserted, the dead Gore-Booth sisters now know. He forces himself to anticipate even the fear that in renewal he will have to risk again imagining himself as his enemies have seen him. He will even have to become once again a completed, honored old man, the very self his present gesture is designed to oppose:

> How in the name of Heaven can he escape
> That defiling and disfigured shape
> The mirror of malicious eyes
> Casts upon his eyes until at last
> He thinks that shape must be his shape?
> And what's the good of an escape
> If honour find him in the wintry blast?
>
> (242, 236; 250, 479)

That the Self here invokes primary "Heaven," which he has rejected, shows the considerable tension generated by his choice. The primary world dominates to the extent that he cannot rid his language of its authority.

The last aspect of reliving that he mentions will be to suffer what continued to torment him in "The Tower" and what torments him yet:

The folly that man does
Or must suffer, if he woos
A proud woman not kindred of his soul.

(242, 236; 250, 479)

This surely indicates the depth of his commitment. But he goes further. He will not merely relive all the ignominy of life; he will perform the ritual act of absolution upon himself. This, like willing a "dreaming back" and "return" in life, is a supreme antithetical gesture:

I am content to follow to its source
Every event in action or in thought;
Measure the lot; forgive myself the lot!

(242, 236; 250, 479)

To do this is to cause a powerful shock generating sweetness, the object of desire of bitter men in "Meditations in Time of Civil War," which now flows into his consciousness. A moment of blessedness ensues:

When such as I cast out remorse
So great a sweetness flows into the breast
We must laugh and we must sing,
We are blest by everything,
Everything we look upon is blest.

(242, 236; 250, 479)

This kind of blessing would seem to have to come from beyond, as if some primary force were intervening; but as we move to "Blood and the Moon" (243, 237; 251, 480), we see that the poet has not merely forgiven himself; he is now performing a ritual of blessing for his tower and the ground around it. The suggestion that everyone is determined or fated ("We must laugh and we must sing, / We are blest by everything") is immediately opposed by antithetical will.

The ritual of blessing is very quickly performed in "Blood and the Moon." Only the first two lines of the poem are devoted to it. After that there are troubling thoughts in what is one of the most troubled expressions, a new turning point, in the *Book*. Perhaps the beginning ritual itself predicts this. The effort to sanctify by antithetical means is bound to fail—as ritual blessing. It remains successful, however, as a gesture opposing the primary form of the same act. The stanza that includes the blessing proceeds to a description enforcing the gesture in a curious, cryptic, and troubling way:

Blessed be this place,
More blessed still this tower;
A bloody, arrogant power
Rose out of the race
Uttering, mastering it,
Rose like these walls from these
Storm-beaten cottages—
In mockery I have set
A powerful emblem up,
And sing it rhyme upon rhyme
In mockery of a time
Half dead at the top.

(243, 237; 251, 480)

The troubling part, and the new turning, is the implied identification of value with violence, an extension into assertion of the questioning suggestion in "Meditations in Time of Civil War" that antithetical power is violent in its moments of greatest creativity. The "bloody, arrogant power" is not specifically named here, but if we identify it a little more closely than the simile requires with the medieval Anglo-Norman invasion of Ireland and the building of fortresses, of which the tower is one, we have a picture of that power gaining political domination by violence. The poet values the intellectual and artistic tradition he thinks this power generated and identifies the flowering of it with the Anglo-Irish Ascendancy of the eighteenth century. The tower itself is first seen as a relic of that great, now fading tradition. Unfinished at the top, it symbolically mocks the "half-dead" present culture. The tower is an image of antithetical power in its late stages of decline preparatory to a new cycle.

The towers that the poet evokes in part 2 of the poem are there to be contrasted to his own. His tower is much more involved with life and earth and is specifically identified with the great Anglo-Irish figures whom he wildly imagines having trod its winding stair—Goldsmith, Berkeley, Burke, and Swift. None, of course, had ever been there; they are violently appropriated and are described as walking a "winding, gyring, spiring treadmill of a stair" that the poet now claims as his "ancestral stair." The literal untruth of both these claims is patent. They must be taken as *willed* antithetical assertions. Furthermore, the winding stair is not Soul's stairway of ascent but Self's image of cyclicity, and this, along with the tower's suggestion of arrogant opposition and possible embattlement, separates it from the towers previously mentioned. It is not that Swift, first to be mentioned, rejected life but that he hated "mankind," or, more specifically, mankind's commonness. It is this, the poet willfully claims, that caused

his violent madness. Like Swift, the others all expressed arrogant intellectual power and discontent with "mankind," "mathematical equality"
(Burke), and the "pragmatical, preposterous pig of a world" (Berkeley). In
each case what is rejected is primary, unheroic, and lacking in intellectual
distinction. In each case the person glorified is made to be dissatisfied with
the world as commonly seen and invents a powerful metaphor through the
vision of which the world is changed: "everything that is not God consumed with intellectual fire." This fire is the antithetical parallel-opposite
of the primary fire of annihilation; it is the fire of the forge of creation. It
is connected with the smithy fires of "Byzantium."

But, of course, that great culture is now "half dead at the top," the fire
nearly out. Because that is so, the excitement of part 2 in which the poet
seems transported by his meditation on those great men, ebbs. In parts 3
and 4 the tone changes as the poet in his tower meditates on the moon and
imagines the moonlight as an arrow. Like some virgin goddess, the moon
is pure, yet in that moonlight the "blood of innocence" has frequently been
shed. The moon's arrow suggests the wounding of the world with desire,
yet the moon remains always pure, that desire never achieved. In earlier
times, the poet muses, this desire was expressed in violent acts of blood-
shed. Today the culture wanes, and desire is weak: "And we that have
shed none must gather there / And clamour in drunken frenzy for the
moon" (243, 238; 251, 482). This behavior is like that of the moths and
butterflies caught in the tower top's unfurnished room, clinging to the
windows in the moonlight.

The poet questions whether the situation imaged here is not universal:
"Is every modern nation like the tower, / Half dead at the top?" (243, 238–
39; 251, 482). But the question is recklessly dismissed: "No matter what I
said." The poet declares that his musings can come to nothing because
wisdom belongs to the dead, but the gesture is also connected with the
"what matter" of "A Dialogue of Self and Soul," which is an acceptance
not just of cultural decline but even of violence itself—the whole of cyclicity.

> . . . No matter what I said,
> For wisdom is the property of the dead,
> A something incompatible with life; and power,
> Like everything that has the stain of blood,
> A property of the living.
>
> (243, 239; 251, 482)

First, he recklessly gives over wisdom to death, the opposite of life, and he
accepts power and violence in life. The fearful question asked in "Meditations in Time of Civil War" is answered affirmatively. Second, the affir-

mation contains a savage irony: The pure light of antitheticality does not purify the ground. Nor does the ground stain the light with the "blood of innocence." Antitheticality in life is impure though washed in moonlight, which produces only a frustrating desire, now fully identified with a violence actively produced by the moon's aloof purity. The poet has picked up the notion of lunar aloofness from the voice of "A Man Young and Old," where the moon in its purity generates madness and plays no favorites. Yet, as the poem ends, the poet, for all this, expresses his wondering devotion to the moon because of the very purity that generates violent desire:

> . . . but no stain
> Can come upon the visage of the moon
> When it has looked in glory from a cloud.

>   (243, 239; 251, 482)

This is a critical poem in the *Book*. In it the poet has expanded his vision of the opposition of antithetical and primary movements in life to one in which life, now regarded as antithetical, opposes the primary world of the dead. But the cost of this expansion is identification of the antithetical with violence. The poet does not shrink from this vision. In "A Dialogue of Self and Soul" he agreed to "follow to its source / Every event in action or in thought," and here he has allowed himself to remain a lover of the moon even as he concludes that such desire, at its best, is violent and, at its worst (when the violence has abated), causes a drunken clamor no more effective than the efforts of the butterflies against the glass. The poet is tested to affirm his allegiance to antitheticality under ever more difficult circumstances.

A series of short, often gnomic poems follows, extending the implications of "Blood and the Moon." In "Oil and Blood" (244, 239; 252, 483) and "Veronica's Napkin" (245, 239; 253, 483), there are parallel oppositions. In the latter, miraculous transformation in death is opposed to the violence of rebirth treated in terms of vampires' nocturnal desire for blood. In the former, sky imagery is associated with a primary cosmic center or pole that controls all; opposed to this is the violent pole of crucifixion and Veronica's "napkin dipped in blood." The tower and sword reappear in contexts of resistance, blindness, and foolhood; the fool, representing the late phases of a culture, carries a sword ("Symbols," 246, 239; 254, 484). Certain poems are dedicated to observance of the waning of a historical cycle, one, "The Nineteenth Century and After" (248, 240; 256, 485), clearly recalling Matthew Arnold's "Dover Beach."

An interesting oscillation ensues. In "The Seven Sages" (251, 241; 259, 486), the sages arrogantly insist on a vision of Burke, Swift, Berkeley, and Goldsmith that conforms to their own nostalgic and anachronistic desire.

All these men are declared to have been opposed to Whiggery, which is persuasively defined as

> A levelling, rancorous, rational sort of mind
> That never looked out of the eye of a saint
> Or out of drunkard's eye.
>
> (251, 241; 259, 486)

In this poem, wisdom, which in an earlier low moment was consigned to the dead, is returned to life but assigned to a bygone age. These oscillations are of attitude. None marks a fixed position. In "Blood and the Moon" the moon is steadfast, unchanging, and pure, but in "The Crazed Moon" (252, 242; 260, 487) what would have been attributed to the results of sublunary desire is attributed directly to the moon, sexualized and crazed by "much child-bearing." Whether the moon is pure object of desire or maddened mother of events, the poet is faced with a vision of historical exhaustion. It is displayed here in the behavior of the living, who reflect the moon's madness and blindly seek out her children, as the poet apparently has done in constituting his eighteenth-century antithetical heroes. There is ecstatic, wondering remembrance of the moon's fullness, and the imagery of dancing is invoked. But now "we" are skeletal and perhaps batlike creatures participating in a last frenzy of destruction as antithetical desire fades out. This frenzy seems beyond even the "drunken frenzy" of "Blood and the Moon"; the skeletons seem an extension toward the deathlike mechanism of the moths and butterflies of that poem. "We" are now creatures of mindless destruction: "[Our hands] are spread wide that each / May rend what comes in reach" (252, 242; 260, 488). The generalized "we" of these poems clothes a deeply personal sense of impending loss.

The next three poems are devoted to Coole, Lady Gregory, and her family and are meant to be seen in the context of the preceding vision. The initial movement is backward from contemplation of present and anticipated confusion to concentration on past accomplishments and values now in jeopardy. This continues an oscillation between eulogy for those values and comments on decline. In "Coole Park, 1929" (253, 242; 261, 488), Lady Gregory and her house play the role of an antithetical center which, appropriately in life (according to "Blood and the Moon"), is characterized by "power." This is not heaven's polestar or great axis but a human center, made only by antithetical will and, of course, for that reason transient but also the more to be admired. It was strong enough to be the catalyst for the men who visited her at Coole, and it actually generated the "sweetness" that the poet, in "Meditations in Time of Civil War," imagined to be the desire of the builders of the great houses:

> . . . a woman's powerful character
> Could keep a swallow to its first intent;
> And half a dozen in formation there,
> That seemed to whirl upon a compass-point,
> Found certainty upon the dreaming air,
> The intellectual sweetness of those lines
> That cut through time or cross it withershins.
>
> (253, 243; 261, 489)

The certainty gained here cannot be of some primary center external to the imagination, perhaps to be associated with fixity and the wisdom of the dead. Rather, it is found "upon the dreaming air."

Imagining the eventual destruction of the house at Coole, the poet directs traveler, scholar, and poet—those who would actually visit the place—to do more than visit. They should take their "stand" there, that is, stand in the future for what it has represented. Upon their visit, they should for a moment do homage. This homage would be to antithetical values, which are identified with earth and life and are opposed to the old negating opposition of sun and shade, where there is no moon at all.

Both "Coole Park, 1929," and "Coole and Ballylee, 1931" (254, 243; 262, 490), seem to be set at the tower, with the poet's imagination traversing the space to Coole. In the latter poem the mind follows the underground river from Ballylee to Coole Park and imagines the water's path as an allegory of the soul's movement through life. This apparently idle thought generates the memory of a winter's day when the poet stood at the lake's edge. The memory is so vivid that for a moment he lapses in the telling into the present tense. Suddenly a swan mounts the air, and the poet finds yet another emblem, this time for the soul. The swan is here one day and gone the next; it is beautiful in a way that makes knowledge irrelevant. Its purity of whiteness is "arrogant," and its arrogance is its otherness. Curiously, the swan, as the soul, is identified in its purity with the antithetical moon of "Blood and the Moon." The poet has willfully imposed antitheticality on the usually primary soul. We recall a similar act of will in "Nineteen Hundred and Nineteen" and the association of the beloved with the swan in "Among School Children." As antithetical beauty, the swan is left to the soul's charge, in much the same way as the body is given over to the soul for keeping in "Sailing to Byzantium."

The whole image reminds the poet of a dying Lady Gregory, who epitomizes for him what had been great in the dying culture: "Sound of a stick upon the floor, a sound / From somebody that toils from chair to chair" (254, 244; 262, 491). The poet projects himself into Coole House as it is now:

> Beloved books that famous hands have bound,
> Old marble heads, old pictures everywhere;
> Great rooms where travelled men and children found
> Content or joy; a last inheritor
> Where none has reigned that lacked a name and fame
> Or out of folly into folly came.
>
> (254, 244; 262, 491)

Another stanza extends the description, setting the house against the centerlessness of contemporary life. It is to be noticed that imagined in these poems are two forms of center contrary to each other. The first is primary and described variously in the first stanza of "Veronica's Napkin" (245, 239; 253, 483). It is identified with heaven and the heavens. The second is antithetical, created by human power in the historical moment, and subject to dissolution. Apart from these, where fashion and fantasy decree, "Man shifts about—all that great glory spent—/ Like some poor Arab tribesman and his tent"—the fate of man at the end of an era.

The poem's last stanza is a bitter requiem for the waning antithetical center of intellectual sweetness that Lady Gregory represents. The poet gives special meanings to the words "romantic" and "sanctity":

> We were the last romantics—chose for theme
> Traditional sanctity and loveliness;
> Whatever's written in what poets name
> The book of the people; whatever most can bless
> The mind of man or elevate a rhyme.
>
> (254, 245; 262, 491–92)

The poet refers not to romanticism as we usually think of it—a cultural movement that began in the late eighteenth century. He thinks of "romantic" as a term connecting him, Lady Gregory, and, to some extent, his whole generation in Ireland with a tradition of antithetical desire. It is related specifically to Lady Gregory's work collecting folklore, which is the "book of the people," and to the wisdom of the great eighteenth-century figures who

> . . . walked the roads
> Mimicking what they heard, as children mimic;
> They understood that wisdom comes of beggary.
>
> ("The Seven Sages," 251, 242; 259, 487)

This is a very personal conflation. The poet employs Coole itself as the catalytic center that brings together eighteenth-century Anglo-Irish culture and ancient Irish folklore and myth. One finds it difficult, however, to imagine Burke walking the roads of Ireland to gain wisdom or any considerable relation between the poet's other eighteenth-century sages and the folklore Lady Gregory collected. The connecting link among these apparently disparate elements is, in the poet's view, a common antitheticality. The "traditional sanctity and loveliness" mentioned is really the sanctity of the tradition he imagines Coole and Lady Gregory representing, not a religious sanctity. The poet gives to it the power to bless usually identified with primary authority.

The phrase "all is changed" in the poem's conclusion echoes words in "Easter 1916," but the significance is different. There the event troubled the poet, but he saw it as a stunning, even miraculous transfiguration. Here there is no surprise, only regret. The "high horse," which is both the Pegasus of poetry and the mount of the Irish horseman, is riderless, though it still wears the saddle of Homer. The swan has not yet flown, but the water darkens, recalling the "blood-dimmed tide" of "The Second Coming."

The next poem, "For Anne Gregory" (255, 245; 263, 492), brings in the opposite for a moment, for it turns to the living, young granddaughter of Lady Gregory. An older speaker attempts to bring wisdom about love, which she resists by an innocent argument. Wisdom has the last word, but the poem indicates that another generation comes to replace the old and carries with it a new, lively naiveté. This poem ends the Coole series and is in turn opposed by "Swift's Epitaph" (256, 245; 264, 493), as if the idea of Swift has been latent in the poet's mind since "The Seven Sages." Swift's image is pressed forward by the translation of his famous epitaph and by the commentary:

> Imitate him if you dare,
> World-besotted traveller; he
> Served human liberty.
>
> (256, 246; 264, 493)

The poet scornfully addresses a listener he regards as typical of this age.

There appears now an earlier poem deliberately placed here to extend to the personal the theme of death and to provide a text that the poem following it can be seen to answer. "At Algeciras—A Meditation upon Death" (257, 246; 265, 493), dated November 1928, raises the question of what fitting answer there is to "the Great Questioner," indeed, what question He will ask. "The Choice" (258, 246; 266, 495) tells us what question the speaker anticipates (as well as his answer): What excuse is to be given for the refusal of a "heavenly mansion"? It is the question that hovers around Soul's discourse in "A Dialogue of Self and Soul." The poet gives the antithetical answer, not defending his choice but indicating what the costs of this choice must be in life:

> The intellect of man is forced to choose
> Perfection of the life or of the work,
> And if it take the second must refuse
> A heavenly mansion, raging in the dark.
> When all that story's finished, what's the news?
> In luck or out the toil has left its mark:
> That old perplexity an empty purse,
> Or the day's vanity, the night's remorse.

> (258, 246–47; 266, 495)

This is followed by another poem removed from the fictive chronological order—a remembrance of antithetical wisdom imparted to the poet by Mohini Chatterjee years before ("Mohini Chatterjee," 259, 247; 267, 495). The advice is to pray, but to "pray for nothing" and to accept reincarnation. To that advice the poet attaches an addendum that expresses not fear of return but hope that it might eventually include what has yet been denied to him:

> "Old lovers yet may have
> All that time denied—
> Grave is heaped on grave
> That they be satisfied."

> (259, 247; 267, 496)

The winding stair, it is momentarily hoped, is not a treadmill but a spiral toward fulfillment in life. It appears that the dancing referred to at the end of this poem ("Men dance on deathless feet") stands in contrast to the depressed vision of the dance to a metronomic "barbarous clangour" in "Nineteen Hundred and Nineteen." A question arises here as to whether the poet has embraced something verging on primary vision by extending Mohini Chatterjee's remarks and introducing external purposiveness into the dance. That is not the same as the idea of living it all again and again, which gives to the antithetical gesture its heroism.

This must be the reason that a hasty return to the true antithetical occurs in the next poem, "Byzantium." The poet now seems to inhabit that mental place. There are strong echoes of "All Souls' Night": It is midnight; a cathedral gong parallels the bell of Christ Church College; mummy-cloth is again mentioned; the scene is one of evocation. But the poet does not call on a ghost; something more image than shade appears. After the poet hails it as "death-in-life" and "life-in-death," it takes shape as the golden bird that the poet wishes to become in "Sailing to Byzantium." In an earlier poem, it might have been called the antiself, and it still is the antiself, but now it exists in a context that includes both life and death, being the contrary to that negation.

There is some confusion before the image becomes clear:

> Before me floats an image, man or shade,
> Shade more than man, more image than a shade;
> For Hades' bobbin bound in mummy-cloth
> May unwind the winding path;
> A mouth that has no moisture and no breath
> Breathless mouths may summon;
> I hail the superhuman;
> I call it death-in-life and life-in-death.

>   (260, 248; 268, 497)

The lines are cryptic. For example, what is Hades' bobbin? It suggests the "loaded pern," which in death Robert Gregory was said to "unpack," in "Shepherd and Goatherd." Here it seems to represent the opposite of the gyre of life, imagined as a packing or winding up. As life winds up, death unwinds, forming two opposing bobbins or gyres. Does the "may" of the fourth line above mean "can" or "might"? If "can," the poet thinks of the bobbin as capable of conveying knowledge. If "might," the poet hopes that the knowledge will actually be conveyed to him. In either case, he imagines the appearance to be from the realm of death and capable or possibly capable of summoning yet another spirit from there. The poet then hails the superhuman, which is described in the next stanza. It is superhuman because it is antithetical to the opposition of death and life. The poet addresses it as

> Miracle, bird or golden handiwork,
> More miracle than bird or handiwork,
> Planted on the starlit golden bough.

>   (260, 248; 268, 497)

A miracle we usually imagine as something that breaks in on the order of life and nature from elsewhere, suspending for a moment its laws. On the cosmic scene that opposes life to death, miracle antithetically opposes that opposition. It does so by containing it. The miracle bird can crow like Hades' cocks, or it can sing in the world of life.

At this point, however, the poet for a moment reveals yet again his own position, which reminds us of the condition under which "Sailing to Byzantium" was written. He is an old man *in* life and so he continues to emphasize, indeed, to be obsessed with, discovering a position from which he can "scorn . . . common bird or petal" as he rejected the country of generation in the earlier poem. Live it all again? Yes, but live it with the same desire to establish the antithetical stance. This stance is now more strongly than ever identified with the inevitable bitterness of antithetical life and occasional scornfulness (we have seen it in earlier poems). The poet has asserted willingness to return to the impurities of life, but only to readopt the scornful antithetical role that the miraculous bird before him—his ultimate antiself—perfectly embodies.

The miracle here is not of the usual sort. It is a miracle of imagination, which produces the heroic contrary to death/life. In the last two stanzas, the poet imagines a whole artistic world of like contraries. Contemplating in imagination a Byzantine mosaic, he sees it embodying both life and death, attributing this miracle not to some god but to the "golden smithies of the Emperor," which "break the flood" that sends the spirits depicted in the mosaic traveling on dolphins to the realm of death. The world of generation is broken by being fixed in art. As a result, the spirits do not ever get to the realm of death, nor do they remain among the complexities of life, where they would "beget" fresh images. The "complexities" are broken, purged out in a dancing process we have seen alluded to before and will see again. In "The Double Vision of Michael Robartes," the dancer was a figure representing antithetical purity. In "Upon a Dying Lady," there was proposed a "predestined dancing place" in death, which from the point of view of "Byzantium" seems to be a place of purgation. In later poems, certain dancers will be recognized as having, under great pressure, effected in life a momentary contrary to complexities. We see that the usage of dancing in "Upon a Dying Lady" expressed a willful desire to imagine the lady in an antithetical condition even in death.

"Byzantium" poses art as an antithetical form of the miraculous, which means that it is humanly made and opposed to the rule of negation. This is quite the opposite of the miracle experienced by the Virgin Mary in the contrasting next poem, "The Mother of God" (261, 249; 269, 499); that miracle is primary and of inhuman external origin. As in the case of the rape of Leda, the medium of external force is a bird, but here it is the traditional dove of Annunciation paintings. It is worth noting that the realm of birds in the *Book* is itself full of contrariety and that context and attitude rule them primary or antithetical. The recipient, who speaks the poem, is terrified. This is no image of miraculous human artifice; it is uncontrollable power from elsewhere. The poet treats the whole matter with the utmost seriousness. His own antithetical nature does not try to triumph and negate primary force; the poem brings in the opposite.

"Vacillation" (262, 249; 270, 499) properly follows with a meditation on man's existence between two extremes:

Between extremities
Man runs his course;
A brand, or flaming breath,
Comes to destroy
All those antinomies
Of day and night.

(262, 249–50; 270, 499–500)

This first part of the meditation by no means completes the thought.
Flame, which has played a role in the two previous poems, appearing first
on the dancing floor and then as a fallen flare, is here the messenger of
death. Though the poet declares that the antinomies of day and night are
destroyed by the flame, this is only to extend the opposition beyond those
familiar in life (day/night) to death/life, which requires its contrary, something that belongs to neither or to both and may be opposed to both. The
poet also declares that the body dies and that the heart thinks of this flame
as the beginning, before rebirth, of a mithridatic process named "remorse," which would include the dreaming back and return. The remaining something is "joy," apparently the antithetical form of the miraculous,
which is usually identified with the primary. The poem moves in its later
sections between the poles of joy and remorse and finally to a willed, joyful reassertion of antithetical life. It must remain in its opposition respectful of the primary. Otherwise, it would commit negation.

Part 2 appropriates for its own purpose a cryptic image from *The Mabinogion* of a tree half-flames and half-green, representing here the imagery
previously associated with life and death. This tree the poet turns into a
strange synecdoche, declaring each half to be the whole, one consuming
the other. It is a figure related to the two opposing bobbins or gyres—life
in death and death in life—and related also to the golden bird. It has close
connections to previous trees in the *Book* that the poet has employed with
wonder and respect—the "sooty finger" of "The Tower," the great-rooted
blossomer of "Among School Children." This tree is more clearly an emblem, the dying god Attis hung at its center. The poet imagines a mysterious ritual that involves identical opposites and thereby experiences a
strange, previously unknown emotion, which is not grief for the dying
god. This is an early suggestion of the joy—still later, the tragic joy—that
subsequent poems emphasize. It apparently stands opposed to the sentimental emotions usually connected with death and birth. Other parts of
"Vacillation" will not so name it but will describe the experience of it to
the extent that the experience can be captured by memory.

This idea having been established, though with much mystery, part 3 offers antithetical maxims on life and concludes with some advice about meeting death that squares with what the *Book* has been gradually establishing as a specifically antithetical virtue:

> No longer in Lethean foliage caught
> Begin the preparation for your death
> And from the fortieth winter by that thought
> Test every work of intellect or faith
> And everything that your own hands have wrought,
> And call those works extravagance of breath
> That are not suited for such men as come
> Proud, open-eyed and laughing to the tomb.
>
> (262, 250; 270, 500–501)

This stanza begins as if Soul were again advising Self, but there is a switch. A voice of antitheticality utters what Blake would have called a "Proverb of Hell." The previous stanza has also performed a reversal, the first three lines advocating primary external purpose, the last four bringing in the opposite.

Part 4 offers a moment of joy, unnamed as such, for the experiencer "knows not what he knows." The experience is in the form of a remembrance, perhaps from as much as a decade before. It involves not just the soul but also the body, which "blazed" in a happiness so great that the poet "was blessèd and could bless." This poem (262, 251; 270, 501) describes a moment that produces the same condition we saw dramatized in the movement from "A Dialogue of Self and Soul" to "Blood and the Moon"; the poet recognizes being blessed and proceeds to bless.

But such moments pass and have in memory a mysterious quality. They also have their opposites, which carry forward the oscillation that governs the whole of "The Winding Stair." The opposite in part 5 is the renewed moment of conscience and responsibility:

> Things said or done long years ago,
> Or things I did not do or say
> But thought that I might say or do.
>
> (262, 251; 270, 501)

The poem stirs our memory of those moments of conscience or questionable action that were the subjects of earlier poems. A capacity for self-criticism remains. Sometimes, the poet acknowledges, it is not his conscience but his vanity that is appalled.

This moment is followed by an attempt through a strange persona to reestablish gaiety In part 6, the poet attributes the phrase "Let all things pass away" to a conquering Chinese warlord, who utters what seems to be the ultimate antithetical heroic decree. It implies that achievement of the object of desire is the death of desire, that desire itself is the value, and that heroic gaiety is the acceptance, indeed the insistence, that all objects of desire, even the world itself perhaps, pass away. In the last stanza, man's heart becomes the root or tree trunk recalling the Mabinogion tree, from which the branches that contain the opposites actually spring. Man is thus identified with Attis, a dying god, an antithetical creator of his world. It is he who is responsible for the very same desire that requires the created other, which, were he to achieve it, would no longer provide desire. "Let all things pass away" acknowledges with gaiety the necessity of such distance. The poem extends further the assertions made in "The Wheel" and establishes a more complicated stance toward the situation of desire.

In part 7, there is a further twist to internal argument. Soul remains; Self is replaced by the familiar Heart, creating a more spare opposition. The Self is gradually being reduced, and further dialogue can occur only between the remaining rudimentary elements. It is for this reason, I think, that the heart plays an increased role in the remaining poems of "The Winding Stair," as if it were the last refuge of antithetical utterance. Heart has had a history of troublesome behavior reaching as far back as "The Folly of being Comforted." On the other hand, in "A Dialogue of Self and Soul" it was the place where, upon being blessed, sweetness flowed. It was also the place of anguish for Swift. His heart was responsible for his being "dragged . . . down into mankind," an experience of tormenting ambiguity, for we later learned that "he served human liberty." The heart has insisted on renewed life by calling death "remorse," implying the dreaming back and the cycle back to life. The heart has just been declared the trunk of a human tree, and later the poet will violently and scornfully lament that Cosgrave and De Valera might better have eaten Parnell's heart. Finally, the poet, near death, will say that he must "lie down . . . in the foul rag and bone shop of the heart," having to be satisfied with what heart he still possesses and with that alone.

In part 7, Soul is a Platonist: "Seek out reality, leave things that seem." Heart is stirred to respond in astonishment: "What, be a singer born and lack a theme?" Heart has the last word, a rhetorical question that sets the tone for part 8, where the poet sympathizes with the theologian Von Hügel but chooses to take his stand with Homer, whose theme he has already declared to be "original sin" and whose heart is "unchristened." It is difficult to see Homer's theme as "original sin" until one realizes that Heart speaks in Soul's language and assumes that from Soul's point of view anything secular is sinful, pre-Christian or not. The poem's last voice, in part

8, sides with Heart. The poet sees himself as predestined to play his anti-thetical role even as he accepts Von Hügel's attitude toward religious miracles.

This is an important moment in the *Book*. By acknowledging that his antitheticality is "predestined," the poet accepts the necessity of the conflict between primary and antithetical types. Further, by expressing his sympathy with Von Hügel, he recognizes the need to embrace the primary as a contrary and not a negation. This is a position that the primary, with its emphasis on external law and difference from all others, cannot take. The primary is the condition of univocal belief. The antithetical is the condition of what Richard Ellmann aptly called "affirmative capability,"[1] where nothing is dismissed, or, as Blake put it, "Everything to be imagined is an image of truth." "Vacillation" ends by taking a stand embracing vacillation itself as contrary to primary fixity.

The five poems that complete "The Winding Stair" therefore continue to gyre. "Quarrel in Old Age" (263, 253; 271, 503) recalls an earlier stage of the poet's story where his poems documented events of the heart. The old ways of the poet seem to have surged up to dominate for a moment a now different life. The subject is a quarrel with the old beloved, beginning with an exclamatory question of irritated surprise—"Where had her sweetness gone?"—and proceeding to describe her rage at some malicious public attack on her. The implied contrast is with her chastising remark to him years before in "The People": "Never have I, now nor any time / Complained of the people" (164, 151; 171, 352). The question for the poet is how to cope with this change of attitude in her. The final comment of the first stanza—"I had forgiven enough / That had forgiven old age" (263, 253; 271, 504)—is ambiguous and can be read as complete or only partial forgiveness.

The second stanza seeks to recover her lost sweetness by recourse to a Platonism that would preserve not just the idea of her sweetness and former existence in an eternal realm but the image as well—a sort of antithetical Platonism, which may be as much antitheticality as old age can muster. In "The Results of Thought" (264, 253; 272, 504), however, there is a contrary to this process, which would seem to rescue everything from passing away after all; this turns out to be the poet's antithetical work. It is the poet who summons back past images *as images*, not primary ideas. However, if this is so and the poet has developed this ability in years of toil, he must ask what the present, troubling images before him are. He is

---

1. Richard Ellmann, *The Identity of Yeats* (New York: Oxford University Press, 1954), pp. 216ff.

troubled by the question of whether or not the "wholesome strength" of
friends of the past whom he can summon up poetically is their reality:

> What images are these
> That turn dull-eyed away,
> Or shift Time's filthy load,
> Straighten aged knees,
> Hesitate or stay?
> What heads shake or nod?

(264, 254; 272, 505)

The question haunted him before in "Among School Children." It appears
here in an equally intense personal context, when the primary threatens
poetic power.

Yet he does claim to have that power, fostered by having attained "so
deep a thought." In the next poem, "Gratitude to the Unknown Instructors" (265, 254; 273, 505), the instructors cryptically alluded to in "The
Gift of Harun Al-Rashid" are recalled. He remarks on their capacity to
carry out their aim, as he carried out his. They brought that deep thought
to him. Just what was the nature of that thought?

> What they undertook to do
> They brought to pass;
> All things hang like a drop of dew
> Upon a blade of grass.

(265, 254; 273, 505)

The figure is a slightly disguised synecdoche. The instructors' message
seems to have been of the figure of synecdoche as fundamental to poetic
art, that is, to the antithetical vision of life. It indicates also a certain limit.
The instructors, he observed, acted within the limit of their own purpose.
In the later stages of his life, the poet seems particularly to appreciate and
understand limitation. The winding stair and the oscillation of climbing
suggest a limiting circumferential order.

The next poem treats of chafing against that limit, invoking the heart
once more; and the last poem of the section reintroduces the theme of mysterious antithetical freedom just as the sense of limit seems to have closed
in. In "Remorse for Intemperate Speech" (266, 254; 274, 506), the poet
characterizes his "heart" as fanatic and in stirring, bitter lines accepts fanaticism as inevitable to his Irish background:

> Out of Ireland have we come.
> Great hatred, little room,
> Maimed us at the start.

> I carry from my mother's womb
> A fanatic heart.
>
> (266, 255; 274, 566)

But in "Stream and Sun at Glendalough" (267, 255; 275, 506), dated June 1932, the latest date of any of the poems in *The Winding Stair*, the poet recalls a moment in the sun, with its suggestion of primary force, when his "heart seemed gay." The moment is interrupted by distracting remorse over some past event. It is this tendency toward "repentance" or conscience, always so troubling to the poet, that he feels corrupts him, for under the dominion of the sun he imagines that conscience itself implies the arrogant attitude leading him to believe that he can be and really is superior to others. So he must ask what the moment of gaiety was. Was it a motion of sun or stream or a motion of his own eyelid that brought about the moment? Through "The Winding Stair" we notice some waning of antithetical confidence and growth of primary humility, even as allegiance to antithetical values is vigorously reasserted. The sequences that follow are written out of this reordering of oppositions and apprehension of its tragic implications.

"Words for Music Perhaps"

Quite a lot has been written in recent years about Yeats's sequences. The thesis of this study is, of course, that Yeats's poems form one large, deliberately shaped, dramatic-narrative sequence. Virtually all discussions of Yeats's sequences have either explicitly or implicitly dismissed chronology and narrative. Some, like that of M. L. Rosenthal and Sally M. Gall, have seen the absence of temporal structures as characteristic of modern poetry:

> It has devolved more and more upon private sensibility to carry the impossible yet necessary heroic burden. In the process, classical and narrative dramatic structures have given way to the subjective primacy of lyrical structure. The concepts of "protagonist" and "plot" and "argument" and even "voice" are still convenient for critical discourse, but these terms are not, finally, accurate. Instead, the succession and interaction of the larger units of affective language and the related streams of tonality running through a work have emerged as the key to the intrinsic movement and quality of poems, and to poetic art itself. They alone

create whatever resemblance of consciousness may be said to inhere to a charged structure of verbally evoked awareness.[2]

This impresses me as a quite inaccurate dismissal of narration and drama
in Yeats's work and possibly in modern poetry generally. In the first place,
several of Yeats's sequences (Rosenthal and Gall regard "Meditations in
Time of Civil War," "Nineteen Hundred and Nineteen," and "Vacillation"
as sequences) have, as I hope that I have shown, a definite dramatic-
narrative, temporal development. In the second place, all of the sequences
belong to a larger autobiographical fiction in which the poet's consciousness is dramatized and developed over a substantial temporal span from
young manhood to old age. Even the obviously distanced late sequences—
"A Man Young and Old," "Words for Music Perhaps," "A Woman Young
and Old," "Supernatural Songs," and the poems beginning with "The
Three Bushes"—all have some internal temporal ordering or an inferred
time in which events take place. It is true, of course, that in all of these
sequences there is much interweaving of "units of affective language," a
density of interrelated dictional elements; but even that is only a local intensification of qualities present in the *Book* as a whole.

One importance of these later sequences (many earlier groups can be
treated as sequences in Rosenthal and Gall's manner) is that they involve
newly invented protagonists, plots, arguments, and voices. These inventions display the poet's new energy, a certain distance, and a capacity to
sum up experience in a sort of microcosm with the implication of universality. The strictly autobiographical does not quite allow this to characterize the typically personal meditations we have been reading. More than
anything else, these sequences represent the results of experience that the
poet is willing to form apart from the record of the most intense moments
of his own life. Of course, they are also part of that record, but indirectly
so. They are not to be read as telling about events. They are fictions within
the larger fiction of the *Book*. This larger fiction has by now begun to display the poet's desire to sum up, to work out the implications of his experience rather than to add to the sum of it. This, of course, is not *entirely*
true; events continue to take place, but through the rest of the *Book* there
is as much of a recessional quality as can properly be allowed in a life that
to the end struggles antithetically against primary force.

"The Winding Stair" has constantly brought in the opposite. It is entirely appropriate that somewhere in the *Book* the female countertruth of

2. M. L. Rosenthal and Sally M. Gall, *The Modern Poetic Sequence: The Genius of Modern Poetry* (New York: Oxford University Press, 1983), pp. 101–2.

"A Man Young and Old" should appear. We recall that the old man in that sequence declared that he possessed "old women's secrets." We learn now that there are secrets he did not have. *The Winding Stair and Other Poems* provides two sequences dominated by women. The first, which has Crazy Jane as a major character, generates her parallel-opposite in Ribh of "Supernatural Songs"; the second, "A Woman Young and Old," contrasts with "A Man Young and Old" of *The Tower.*

"Words for Music Perhaps" begins with the voice of a character at least as intemperate of speech as the poet, who has only recently expressed "remorse." "Remorse" is the heart's word for death, we recall from "Vacillation," the word being connected with an antithetical vision of the afterlife, where remorse is worked out. The poems about or spoken by Crazy Jane have a loose chronology from middle to old age, and they express a movement from antithetical hatred of primary authority to stirrings of what I shall call, in connection with "Supernatural Songs," antithetical religiosity. This is evident particularly in Crazy Jane's dialogue with the bishop, in which she proposes a violent antithetical metaphysics.

Crazy Jane has a heart the gaiety of which has turned to fierce anger and which expresses itself combatively. Under the pagan oak tree (268, 255; 276, 507) she is to commune with the ghost of her first lover, banished by the man who has now become bishop. One of the two refrains, *"All find safety in the tomb,"* is fiercely ironic in that it implies the safety, found in death, from ecclesiastical meddling, while the second violently and unfavorably compares the "coxcomb" bishop to her lover. In the second poem (269, 256; 277, 509), however, Crazy Jane is obliquely reproved for her commitment to an earthly love.

The third (270, 257; 278, 510) begins to offer an antithetical metaphysics. Whether the title, "Crazy Jane on the Day of Judgment," refers to her comment about that day or about an event that takes place on that day is uncertain. I read it here as a comment. Contrary to some readings that claim a synthesis of her attitude with that of the bishop, I hold that she insists on unity of body and soul against the bishop's requirement that they be separate. Only a love involving both is a satisfaction. She does not privilege the body but insists on its involvement with soul. She thinks of her lover (271, 258; 279, 511) and imagines love unwinding like a bobbin "between the dark and dawn." She predicts cyclical return, but in the end she asserts for good measure that her ghost would walk the night to join her lover if it could. For her, ghosts are sensuous and passionate. She goes on to insist that in spite of mutability, the lovers of the world remain, if only in passionate memory, haunting the places of their most intense moments of life (272, 258; 280, 512). Finally, in old age, she meets the bishop by chance "on the road" (273, 259; 281, 513), that area identified with wise beggars, fools, and poets. Earlier she had declared she would spit at him, but now she argues her antithetical metaphysics:

". . . Love has pitched his mansion in
The place of excrement;
For nothing can be sole or whole
That has not been rent."

(273, 259–60; 281, 513)

We do not hear the bishop's answer, which one might imagine as an exasperated snorting.

In the last Crazy Jane poem, Jane observes a man and woman dancing and recognizes violence and hatred in sexual attraction. Sexual love is therefore seen as an expression of recklessness. She asks God to bless (and, I think, in some way to preserve) the times when she herself had so danced:

God be with the times when I
Cared not a thraneen for what chanced
So that I had the limbs to try
Such a dance as there was danced—
Love is like the lion's tooth.

("Crazy Jane Grown Old Looks at the Dancers," 274, 260; 282, 514)

The conflict that to her seems fundamental to life is invoked as part of a repeated ritual of courtship.

Conflict becomes the shaper of the remaining poems in the sequence and leads eventually to the antithetical theology of the eccentric monk Ribh. There is an alternation between the voices of a woman and a man in two pairs of poems. Then the two speak together, then again separately. The voices of various men dominate the poems that follow these, except for one, which is spoken by the bone of the dead woman. A variety of passionate moments is explored. The organizing principle is no longer mainly temporal, though as the poems proceed the speakers become older and finally, with Old Tom, aged.

"Girl's Song" (275, 260; 283, 515) expresses a theme introduced in "Among School Children" and never thereafter completely relinquished, for it shows up as late as "A Bronze Head": "Saw I an old man young / Or young man old?" (275, 261; 283, 515). The man's song is on the same theme. He is gallant, or rather his heart is. The poem is yet another dialogue between Self and Heart, but now there appears the idea of a sensuous ghost: "No withered crone I saw / Before the world was made" ("Young Man's Song," 276, 261; 284, 516). The heart's vision still insists on being heard here, though now with recourse to a sensuous, antithetical Platonism.

The developed opposition is that of her anxiety and his early confident gallantry and continued faithfulness, even as "dread follows longing." The voices age after "Lullaby" (283, 264; 291, 522), which is a poem not to a child by a man but to a beloved woman. Then an old man speaks to his beloved and declares it fitting for them to "descant upon" what he declares is the "supreme theme of Art and Song": "Bodily decrepitude is wisdom; young / We loved each other and were ignorant" ("After Long Silence," 284, 265; 292, 523). This is a view that Crazy Jane would respect, for she has said that she had "learned in bodily lowness / And in the heart's pride."

The old man addressing a male friend in "Mad as the Mist and Snow" (285, 265; 293, 523) invokes one of the *Book's* repeated images, the "foul wind" against which the shutter must be bolted. He begins in a way that suggests the possibility of the kind of ecstatic statement with which "All Souls' Night" ended. But the poem turns instead toward expression of the suspicion that "everything," even the great Cicero and Homer, is "mad as the mist and snow." From this point on, the sequence's voices express what might be called an aged wise madness, which is well exemplified by lines from "Those Dancing Days are Gone":

A man may put pretence away
Who leans upon a stick,
May sing, and sing until he drop,
Whether to maid or hag:
I carry the sun in a golden cup,
The moon in a silver bag.

(286, 267; 294, 525)

If he does not actually control what sun and moon represent, he has mastered their meaning.

But though those dancing days are gone, as they were for the poet of "Sailing to Byzantium," who settled for Soul's song, there are still dancers. One of these, in "'I am of Ireland'" (287, 267; 295, 526), calls on a man to come dance with her. She seems to be Cathleen ni Houlihan, but only one man in a crowd even listens to her and refuses the invitation to dance, declaring that Ireland is "a long way off," the "time runs on," and the musicians and instruments no longer function anyway. His statement about time running on echoes hers, but the two seem to mean opposite things by it. She seems to be calling for the renewal of a commitment, the need for renewal because time has passed (in a later poem, the poet will recall that Pearse said that in every generation Ireland's blood must be shed). The man, on the other hand, seems to mean that there isn't time any longer to do what she asks, that it is too late, that things have changed. He seems to speak of more than his own sense of time; he seems to imply the end of an era.

In the next poem (288, 268; 296, 528), a dancer, probably female, does report having danced in Ireland and having reached a state of ecstasy in which it seemed that all living creatures praised God. This form of divine madness ushers in the lunatic old man, Tom, who is perhaps connected to the earlier Tom O'Roughley. He speaks in even more gnomic poems a faith that imagines all creatures standing in "God's unchanging eye" (289, 269; 297, 529), the sexual coupling of time and eternity, and the flowing of everything from some central source like marvelous sailing ships. He praises the "self-begotten," who are declared not to fail despite impediments that human beings have created throughout history to the moment of self-begetting (dancing, etc.) (291, 269; 299, 530).

The sequence ends with the voice of the Delphic oracle (292, 269; 300, 530), who describes Plotinus, suffering the impediment of blinding "salt blood," swimming strenuously toward Elysium, where Rhadamanthus beckons and the immortals stroll about. The oracle emphasizes the difficulty of the journey and of seeing the goal. The poet is doing more than simply alluding to a passage in Porphyry's *Life of Plotinus:* Almost all of the details are taken from it. The vision of Plotinus that the oracle commends to us shows him still en route, still swimming boldly, buffeted by seas of salt blood that all things sailing "out of perfection" must cross. The sequence ends emphasizing that movement but emphasizing, too, the Elysium imagined by poets, the primary world viewed through an image-making, antithetical lens. As Porphyry has the oracle of Apollo describe it:

> You enter at once the heavenly consort:
> where fragrant breezes play, where all is unison and winning tenderness and guileless joy, and the place is lavish of the nectar-streams the unfailing Gods bestow, with the blandishments of the Loves, and delicious airs, and tranquil sky:
> where Minos and Rhadamanthus dwell, great brethren of the golden race of mighty Zeus; where dwell the just Aeacus, and Plato, consecrated power, and stately Pythagoras and all else that form the Choir of Immortal Love, that share their parentage with the most blessed spirits, there where the heart is ever lifted in joyous festival.[3]

3. Porphyry, "Life of Plotinus," in *The Enneads,* trans. Stephen MacKenna (London: Faber and Faber, 1956), pp. 16–17.

The poem is dated August 19, 1931, and thus indicates that "Words for Music Perhaps" is temporally entwined with the last poems of "The Winding Stair." It carries out the idea, offered in "Sailing to Byzantium," of the soul's singing in behalf of the body. The "perhaps" of the title expresses some reticence about claiming that the poems can actually be put to music, there being for the poet no singing school other than the studying of monuments of the soul's magnificence. One of these monuments for the poet was *The Enneads*.

But does not the turn to Plotinus mark a rejection of the earlier dismissal of him and Plato in "The Tower"? Several observations must be made about this. The statement in "The Tower" was made under pressure of the early experience of aging. The perspective has now changed. The voice has become less personal (the speaker is neither quite the poet nor Old Tom but, rather, the sequence summing itself up). The situation has become gradually primary, a soul singing, or something nearly a pure soul trying to sing (the music is only hopefully anticipated) for "every tatter in its mortal dress." The Elysium to which the heroic, blood-blinded Plotinus swims has nothing of the annihilation of self or image that has been the otherworld of the primary. Blake said that there was "war and hunting" in heaven: for Plato and Pythagoras there must at least be dialogue, which for Blake was war and hunting's unfallen heavenly form.

"A Woman Young and Old"

The final notes of "Words for Music Perhaps" may have been too decisively identifiable with ascension to death. "A Woman Young and Old" will, at its conclusion, bring in descent as the opposite. Parallels to the earlier male sequence and some echoes of "Words for Music Perhaps" are developed. The speaker of the first poem (293, 270; 301, 531) slightly recalls Crazy Jane's bishop. It is a father reporting his ranting against his daughter's love for a man with a bad reputation. The female counterpart of the young man of "A Man Young and Old," transformed by a smile, refuses the father's logic. Her behavior is not quite appropriately described as defiance. She is simply beyond reasoning with. Indeed, through the whole sequence the woman is not much touched by abstract argument, invocation of law, theological guilt, or, for that matter, concern for the soul or the afterlife. We observe her reflections of her sexual life from youth into old age. Both young womanhood and old age are marked by dialogues with a lover. The sequence ends with a translation of a chorus from *Antigone* (303, 276; 311, 540), thus paralleling "A Man Young and Old," which ended with a chorus from *Oedipus at Colonus*. The parallel is present for the sake of contrast. The Oedipus chorus advised endurance, forgetfulness, and "a gay goodnight," claiming that "never to have lived is best." This sequence concludes with rage at Antigone's death, a rage that asks for the destruction of all order. Only resentfully the chorus recognizes its role, much as the poet did in "Easter 1916":

> Pray I will and sing I must,
> And yet I weep—Oedipus' child
> Descends into the loveless dust.

(303, 276; 311, 540)

The chorus takes the woman's part; she has been, by contrast to the man of the earlier sequence, earthier, less deluded, more practical, and (perhaps it is fair to say) more inclined to recognize herself in a certain role, more willing to face her lot as a lover and to declare that role "chosen."

When very young she expresses some of this in "Before the World was Made":

> If I make the lashes dark
> And the eyes more bright
> And the lips more scarlet,
> Or ask if all be right
> From mirror after mirror,
> No vanity's displayed:
> I'm looking for the face I had
> Before the world was made.

(294, 270; 302, 531–32)

This antithetical Platonism identifies the image made by artifice, recalled from "Adam's Curse," with the idea of the mask. Other poems are also recalled: "For Anne Gregory" is on a similar theme, and the "Young Man's Song" in "Words for Music Perhaps" declared that his love's eternal image was not that of a "withered crone." In the second stanza, another matter is taken up, as if to offer from another perspective the view of the young woman who was accused of aloof coldness in "A Man Young and Old." It turns out, if this is the same young woman now speaking, that she had not loved him, that she had another beloved all the time, and that she had offered the appearance that she did, flaunting her beauty, to attract him to the eternal image.

> What if I look upon a man
> As though on my beloved,
> And my blood be cold the while
> And my heart unmoved?

> Why should he think me cruel
> Or that he is betrayed?
> I'd have him love the thing that was
> Before the world was made.
>
> (294, 270–71; 302, 532)

The poem turns into a piece of casuistic self-justification that makes her seem no less cold than the young man had thought her.

"A First Confession," however, is more straightforward. She accuses herself of "dissembling" and "coquetry," confessing to a desire to attract men. She would try to make the night, with which she identifies herself, stay. The last stanza is cryptic:

> Brightness that I pull back
> From the Zodiac,
> Why those questioning eyes
> That are fixed upon me?
> What can they do but shun me
> If empty night replies?
>
> (295, 271; 303, 533)

Are those questioning eyes the confessor, daylight, and reason, or are they everyone? Is she right that they will shun her if she does not play her appropriate moon role and instead replies but as "empty night"?

"Her Triumph" (296, 271; 304, 533) seems at first an odd title, for in the poem she recalls her lover's triumph over the dragon that had enslaved her. In an earlier poem, Michael Robartes had called a similar dragon the lady's thought. Here she calls it her coquetry, to which she now imagines herself having been enslaved. Her triumph is having put away that behavior, but she treats the triumph passively, seeing in it something miraculous and beyond control: "And now we stare astonished at the sea, / And a miraculous strange bird shrieks at us" (296, 272; 304, 534). The shriek of this bird echoes back through the *Book* to those peacock screams and even earlier birdcalls that seemed to signal some momentary heightening of experience or a miraculous incursion into what had been mundane and ordered.

There was little consolation in "A Man Young and Old": Not to have lived would have been better, the chorus concluded. Here the woman seems to answer that chorus with a defense of life for its sexual pleasure. She thinks on original sin, attributes the depth of her sexual excitement to knowledge of it, and concludes, "But where the crime's committed / The crime can be forgot" ("Consolation," 297, 272; 305, 534). This might mean that in the sexual act itself all is momentarily (at least) forgotten, and this is enough for her to justify transgression. It is more likely though that she refers to the slow purging of memory in death. It is not a matter of external forgiveness or self-absolution, as it was for the poet in "A Dialogue of Self and Soul." She is not finally concerned with matters of guilt or morality, and she mentions them only as heightening excitement in the transgression. She is *naturally* reckless and, once freed of coquetry, lives the moment. In "Chosen" (298, 272; 306, 534), she goes further to accept her lot as chosen (fated) and to describe the moment in zodiacal imagery. In "Parting" (299, 273; 307, 535), a dialogue with her lover, she would prolong the moment, despite a bird's morning cry, to which her lover is alert. Throughout these poems she provides a contrast to the more self-tormented, nostalgic, and bitter young man of "A Man Young and Old."

In the poems in which she is an old woman, the contrast continues. The old man, as the lover Paris, takes pleasure in the memory of his Helen's passion. He lives in memory, sharing stories with old women. The old woman ("Her Vision in the Wood," 300, 273; 308, 536), in a rage, imagines men and, thinking that she could "a greater with a lesser pang assuage," tears at all of the most erotic places on her body and makes herself bleed. Contemplation of her own blood generates the image of her past lover as the dying Adonis, himself bloodied and borne on a litter by "stately women." She comments:

> It seemed a Quattrocento painter's throng,
> A thoughtless image of Mantegna's thought—
> Why should they think that are for ever young?
>
> (300, 274; 308, 537)

This last line is uttered after the fact and at some distance, but the sense of the eternal youth of the women (because they belong to art) must at the time have contributed to her being caught up in grief. Yet this grief for lost youth is muted by comparison to the grief generated by her recognition that the scene contains not merely a symbol out of some mythology but her own past lover, who is both the victim and the torturer of her heart. Suddenly we recognize in this figure the young man of the earlier sequence, who played that victim. But now she declares herself a victim, too. The parallel contrasting poem, especially its last stanza, is "His Memories" (232, 223; 239, 454).

"A Last Confession" (301, 275; 309, 538) indicates the extent of the old woman's religiosity. She acknowledges that she loved in misery when she gave her soul but took pleasure when she loved bodily and in the knowledge that her lover thought she had given her soul. Her pleasure was in part the knowledge that "beast gave beast as much." Yet she imagines a lovemaking of souls in death that would be complete. In this she anticipates the antithetical theology of Ribh in "Supernatural Songs." The emphasis on the sexuality of souls anticipates for her a situation in which no crying bird would dare to put an end to the passionate moment. Unlike the old man, she looks antithetically to the future. She goes beyond Crazy Jane, who, full of resentment at the bishop, declares that her ghost would walk to find her lover but does not speculate about the condition of souls. The fact that this is an antithetical confession indicates her own defiance, resentment replaced by self-assurance.

In "Meeting" (302, 275; 310, 539), the conversation of the old lovers anticipates the concept of hatred developed by Ribh. Observing each other, they hate what they see. By contrast to the man, who is now clearly connected with the man of "A Man Young and Old," the woman rejects the nostalgic boasting of "His Memories." In reciprocal hatred, they look at each other in their present states. Her view, here finally accepted by him in anger, is that their essence is only what they now are and that the present moment, whatever its awfulness, takes precedence over the past. She will not indulge in the idea that they *once* loved, but she does admit she could even now have "found a sweeter word" "Could we both discard / This beggarly habiliment" (302, 276; 310, 539).

The voices that hurried the old man on his way in "A Man Young and Old" counseled a "gay goodnight." The voices that lament the woman's passing sing, weep, and rage. Out of these conflicting emotions is generated the fierce, antithetical theology of Ribh.

["Parnell's Funeral and Other Poems"] (1935)

The pivotal poem of "Parnell's Funeral and Other Poems"[4] is "Church and State." The poems before it have to do with politics, the "Supernatural Songs" after it with religion. "Church and State" (308, 283; 317, 553) begins by implying that the poet has been searching for a subject matter appropriate to old age. (This search continues to be in the poet's mind even as late as "The Circus Animals' Desertion.") In the first stanza, the appropriate subject matter is declared to be "might of the Church and the State," as if the poet would play a laureate role. But the second stanza responds to this by declaring it a "cowardly song" and asking whether church and state may not be "the mob that howls at the door." Critique of the church con-

---

4. As Richard J. Finneran points out, in his *The Poems of W. B. Yeats: A New Edition* (New York: Macmillan, 1983), p. 660, these poems appeared in *A Full Moon in March*. The heading "Parnell's Funeral and Other Poems" appears on the page preceding the poems in that volume. I follow Finneran in adopting that title for the group.

tinues in "Supernatural Songs," where the monk Ribh criticizes Saint Patrick and certain orthodoxies.

In "Parnell's Funeral," the poet has attacked the politicians who came to
power in Ireland after 1916. Parnell is seen as a sacrificial figure in a cruel
ritual; his fall is associated with previous historical events that play major
roles in the poet's view of history—those alluded to in "Two Songs from a
Play," for example. The poet asserts that eras stand in opposition to each
other. He contrasts the deaths of Emmet, Fitzgerald, and Tone at the
hands of the foreign English to the death of Parnell, of which he declares
the Irish themselves guilty. The first part of the poem ends in the poet's
identification of himself with communal guilt, the desire for accusation,
the expression of a need to declare that "all that was said in Ireland is a
lie," and the implication that it is the mob that rules. One recalls that in
"Meditations in Time of Civil War" the poet, for a moment caught up in
his vision of mob thirst for vengeance, nearly cried out with that mob.
Here he identifies himself with the mob and calls the identification "contagion." All that he excepts from this contagion is "the rhyme rats hear
before they die." The line apparently refers to the alleged power of the old
Irish satirists to kill rats with their words. It is implied that only savage
satire would be able to utter the truth in this situation. The poem itself
seeks to be savage enough.

In part 2, the poet declares he has said enough despite there being more
to say. He must, however, unsay one sentence in the poem, where he has
stated that the Irish, himself included, had savagely eaten Parnell's heart.
Changing the metaphor from that of hounds dragging down a quarry, he
imagines a primitive ritual in which Parnell's successors eat his heart. Both
metaphors enhance the violent scorn. Unfortunately, De Valera and Cosgrave did not eat Parnell's heart, and demagoguery won the day. The poet
offers the thought that if even O'Duffy had eaten there might have been a
worthy statesman in Ireland. However, the name of O'Duffy halts the
poet in midsentence. O'Duffy was for a while the leader of the Blueshirt
movement, which merged with the Cumann naGaedheal party to form
Fine Gael, of which O'Duffy became the leader for a short time before
abruptly resigning. Mention of O'Duffy has been an irritant to many readers because of O'Duffy's fascist connections. The poet's "Had even
O'Duffy—but I name no more" shows that he has offered the name with
some reservation and evades further discussion. Actually, to name
O'Duffy was merely to complete the list of recent leaders of the major
political factions of the time. The point is that the poet dismisses them all
as schooled in commonality, O'Duffy apparently being the least acceptable. Parnell's master, he declares, was that same antithetical solitude we
have seen treated before, though not so often with respect to men of ac-

tion. Parnell is identified with Jonathan Swift and thus with the Anglo-Irish tradition of great men.

Following "Parnell's Funeral" comes "Alternative Song for the Severed Head in 'The King of the Great Clock Tower'" (305, 280; 314, 549). In that play, it is sung by the severed head of an executed itinerant poet while a queen dances preparatory to kissing its lips, as the poet when alive had insolently predicted she would do. The superiority of the reckless strolling poet to the king, representing, of course, the state, is implied here. The stroller's act is identified with the "heroic wantonness" of the great mythological figures who have been appropriated or reinvented by the poet. Also invoked from one of the poet's own stories is a fabulous king who had feathers for hair, hardly the usual sort of king.

The two songs that follow (the text indicates that they also are from plays, the second song being expanded and revised) are love laments sung recklessly by old men. The first (36, 281; 315, 550) is a traveling man who expresses desire for his *Paistin Finn* (Fair Maid) but is old and alone, whistling in vain. The second is a poet, also alone, who wishes he were a blind beggar who would not be able to see his lady "go gallivanting by." "A Prayer for Old Age" (307, 282; 316, 553) opposes both of these voices with an expression of desire to remain always a "foolish, passionate man," for it is only in this way that one will "sing a lasting song."

"Church and State," then, begins with a suggestion of "fresh matter" for the poet, but it is the wrong matter: "Might of the Church and the State / Their mobs put under their feet" (308, 283; 317, 554). These words are quickly rejected as presenting a subject expressing cowardice. There then follows "Supernatural Songs," which expresses an antithetical form of religion, truly a "matter for old age meet."

"Supernatural Songs"

What would antithetical religiosity be? Until very recently in the *Book* it has seemed to be an impossible oxymoron. However, in the aged characters Crazy Jane and Old Tom we began to see emerging something we might so name. These characters were invented in the poet's own old age as vehicles for exploration of antithetical passion and its relation to last things. "Supernatural Songs" is the sequence most explicitly concerned with religion. Like Oisin, Ribh could almost be a contemporary of Saint Patrick. His era is not specifically indicated, but he replies to Patrick as if Patrick were alive. Ribh does not, however, represent a heroic pagan Ireland, as did Oisin in his quarrel with Patrick. We can place him in Patrick's time or in our own. There is no nostalgia in his utterances. That he is old, irascible, and visionary is more important than his era.

Ribh is a monk with tonsured head and holy book, but he reads his book antithetically in the supernatural light of the heavenly copulation of two dead lovers. In a series of short poems he lays out the main tenets of an antithetical theology in a spirit mixing elderly irascibility with ecstatic vision. These pieces of wisdom are delivered with a certain contempt for the listener, as if he were concerned less with communication than with making the utterances and getting on toward death. On occasion, the utterances seem coexistent with the vision itself. The poems are frequently and defiantly cryptic, crabbed, and angry, as befits antithetical thought under the most extreme pressure of impending primary victory. The poems still celebrate life and especially sexuality.

The main tenets of this antithetical theology are as follows: Spiritual love is sexual; Baile and Aillinn "hurry into each other's arms" on the anniversary of their deaths, forming a light by which Ribh can read his holy book. (Angels are said also to engage in sexual intercourse.) Ribh's book is either the Bible read in that light to produce an antithetical theology or some heretical book. The Christian trinity is false because it is entirely masculine; the true trinity is formed by father, mother, and child, allowing for procreation. Ribh takes up the Platonic notion of a hierarchy of imitations, but he rejects the Platonic idea and insists on the image. The difference is not between a bodiless purity of idea and a mortal body that is an inadequate copy of it but between a supernatural, self-begetting sexuality and one that begets multiplicity in an imitative effort to beget self. Ribh describes earthly couples as copying God, but he very nearly implies that God's procreation copies the earthly: "As man, as beast, as an ephemeral fly begets, Godhead begets Godhead" ("Ribh denounces Patrick," 310, 284; 319, 556).

This argument is generated by or generates a complicated figure:

> When the conflagration of their passion sinks, damped by the
>   body or the mind,
> That juggling nature mounts, her coil in their embraces
>   twined.
>
> The mirror-scalèd serpent is multiplicity,
> But all that run in couples, on earth, in flood or air, share God
>   that is but three,
> And could beget or bear themselves could they but love as He.
>
> (310, 285; 319, 556)

"Conflagration" recalls the light of the lovemaking of Baile and Aillinn. The damping of earthly passion is caused not necessarily by the mind, not necessarily by the body, but always by one or the other. That prevents their being able to love fully. God can. As their passion "damps," nature "mounts." Nature is "juggling" because it presides over this cyclicity and opposition. Nature "mounts" (with the sexual implication, though nature is nevertheless treated as feminine—a complication Ribh does not pursue), with the implication of its rising up into control, entwining earthly lovers as their passion wanes and they realize they cannot "love as He." Nature is a coiled snake wrapped around the earthly lovers, preventing them from mounting to the condition of God. The snake is familiar to readers of Blake's work and perhaps has Gnostic sources. All of this identifies Ribh with heretical thought, though this snake, unlike the snake of Gnostic lore, does not bring knowledge except that of difference and limitation. As nature, this snake presents a multiplicity of mirrors in its scales, and the world is described as a descent from the original sexual family into the reflecting many.

Ribh makes clear in the next poem, "Ribh in Ecstasy" (311, 285; 320, 557), that he does not care if this utterance has been too cryptic for a listener, nor does he clearly remember what he has said. All that is important is his remembrance of his soul's having found for a moment "all happiness in its own cause or ground." Ribh's utterance would seem to be an endorsement, by an antithetical (and heretical) ecclesiastic, of the poet's own moments of momentary self-begetting in "Vacillation" and the visions of self-composed dancers here and there in the *Book*.

In "There" (312, 285; 321, 557), Ribh goes on to imagine the primary Sun (capitalized) as the place where unity is fully existent. This affirms one's impression that the poet's later characters acknowledge ultimate primary victory while still affirming antithetical values. Yet these values are now characterized differently, with considerably more willingness to declare them terrible in their own way—a willingness that has its seeds in the perception of violence and its relation to the moon in "Blood and the Moon." All of this has been generated by the natural drift toward the primary in old age. Thus, in "Ribh considers Christian Love insufficient" (313, 286; 322, 558), Ribh rejects the idea that love is really knowable to human beings. Hatred is, or should be, the supreme human emotion because it is possibly free of self-deception. The ultimate self-deception is the human effort to think God. One must hate every idea of God, every thought of this kind that is a garment for the soul, because the soul must go as a bride naked to God (the notion first appeared in "A Woman Young and Old"). The idea of hatred, which first appears in the *Book* with the young man's perception of the indifference of his beloved in "A Man Young and Old" and is further developed by Crazy Jane with respect to human sexual attraction as she observes the dancers, is carried into antithetical theology by Ribh, as if it were the antithetical counterpart of the

Word. Ribh is not Crazy Jane, much less either Hic or Ille. He would surrender himself to God:

> At stroke of midnight soul cannot endure
> A bodily or mental furniture.
> What can she take until her Master give!
> Where can she look until He make the show!
> What can she know until He bid her know!
> How can she live till in her blood He live!
>
> (313, 286; 322, 558)

These are in form rhetorical questions, not the questions typical of the poet at critical moments of earlier works. Each ends not with a question mark but with a sign of exclamation.

This poem concludes the presentation of Ribh's theology; the rest of "Supernatural Songs" is not explicitly attributed to him. However, the voice is very like his; it is as if the poet's voice has become Ribh's or vice versa. The voice continues to express attitudes consistent with Ribh's. In "He and She" (314, 286; 323, 559), fear of the possible loss of self in the sexual relation (of soul to sun, among other things) is dramatized, the female figure being identified with the moon's coy dance in which she fears the sun's blinding light and declares her light the greater the farther she flees from him: "All creation shivers / With that sweet cry" (314, 287; 323, 559). This dance of attraction and repulsion affects the whole of life, which responds passionately to it.

"What Magic Drum?" (315, 287; 324, 559) and "Whence had they Come?" (316, 287; 325, 360) both offer questions that come to be answered (in a way) in the last poems of the sequence. Yet the questions are posed so ecstatically that they virtually force the impression that they contain their answers. The first of these poems is perhaps the most cryptic. It is a vision of a male forest creature (we are unsure whether it is man or beast) that plays the role of "Primordial Motherhood" with a child. A mysterious magic drum beats out a rhythm of life. Though the beast and drum remain unknown, the vision, for the moment, seems enough. "Whence had they Come?" questions other mysteries, including what was just witnessed, in which "a passion-driven exultant man sings out / Sentences that he has never thought" (316, 287; 325, 560). The words recall the ecstatic Ribh. Such moments are attributed in the poem to "Dramatis Personae," as if at such times the ultimate role or mask had been achieved and only the dramatic part was real and exercised full control. Such personal moments are regarded as moments of eternity, the poem declaring that "eternity is passion." On the larger stage of history, they raise questions about the origin, growth, and decline of cultures and the appearance of world-transforming historical figures.

After these questionings come gnomic moments of antithetical knowledge wherein the visionary power of language is stretched to the breaking point. The result is the taut couplets of three poems, "The Four Ages of Man" (317, 288; 326, 561), "Conjunctions" (318, 288; 327, 562), and "A Needle's Eye" (319, 288; 328, 562). There are no questions here. All ages of the individual are presented as full of conflict, each with different antagonists: self/body, self/heart, self/mind, self/God. The *Book* began with the second of these, treated the third in equal detail, and now has reached the fourth: "Now his wars on God begin; / At stroke of midnight God shall win" (317, 288; 326, 561). The couplet suggests the theme of hatred enunciated earlier by Ribh.

"Conjunctions" (318, 288; 327, 562) brings back the "mummy wheat" of "On a Picture of a Black Centaur by Edmund Dulac," mentioning an astrological conjunction that the poet apparently identifies with the antithetical. "Mummy wheat" seems to refer to the belief that certain wheat growing today came from grain discovered in ancient Egyptian tombs.[5] This is related to the tautly wound "mummy truths" of "All Souls' Night" and seems to imply the possible rebirth of ancient creativity at the time of the conjunction. By contrast, the second couplet emphasizes a mixture of death, love, and conflict. Together, the two couplets express, respectively, the growth of life from death and death from life.

All through these poems, cyclicity and conflict are central, cyclicity being conflict stretched out into temporal alternation, conflict being cyclicity compressed like a spring into the moment. Such thought produces the figure of the gyre, and "A Needle's Eye" (319, 288; 328, 562) provides a variation: a stream bursting from a vortex. The stream is driven by both things past and things future. The answer to the question "Whence had they Come?" is partly: from both past and future. In history, the needle's eye is the passionate moment: the rape of Leda by Zeus, the Annunciation, and, on the same scale, perhaps, the engendering of the great rough beast. On a lesser scale there is the engendering of Charlemagne and the tearing of the spinning jenny from the side of Locke.

At this point, the ecstatic vision fades away and is replaced by a poem that continues to offer antithetical knowledge but does so with perhaps the principal aim of enacting an attitude it is necessary to take toward the violent history that the vision has offered. "Meru" (320, 289; 329, 363) invokes an image of the human being in conflict with a cyclicity now declared to be the reality:

5. See Finneran, *The Poems of W. B. Yeats: A New Edition*, p. 653, n. 221.7.

> Civilisation is hooped together, brought
> Under a rule, under the semblance of peace
> By manifold illusion; but man's life is thought,
> And he, despite his terror, cannot cease
> Ravening through century after century,
> Ravening, raging, and uprooting that he may come
> Into the desolation of reality.
>
> (320, 289; 329, 563)

Cyclicity itself is an ordering principle of nature or of its "manifold illusion." We have been returned to the "mirror-scalèd serpent." Man's nature is to think, and apparently this means to think away the illusion, but the result, if he were successful, would be what the poet in "Lapis Lazuli" will call "black out." According to the final poem of this sequence, which begins in a forthright, prosy, self-confident style, the result of Ribh's theology ought to be willingness to accept complete destruction, not because things will return (they will) but because they disappear. One must not make a refuge of cyclicity. That would be merely to shift antithetical nostalgia into future hope for rebirth and to sentimentalize nature. Hermits on Mount Meru know this. Ribh has declared that we must hate every thought of God, but we should not in old age embrace the "manifold illusion."

7

Tragic Joy and Its Discontents

New Poems (1938)

"The Gyres" and "Lapis Lazuli," which begin *New Poems*, set a tone of tragic yet joyful acceptance of the sweep of history and of current events. In the first of these poems (321, 293; 330, 564), address is made to a mysterious figure called "Old Rocky Face." Critics have usually identified it with the "rocky voice" of a later poem, "Man and the Echo"; there is some reason to connect the two, though there is also a difference between them, which I shall discuss later. Here it appears that the poet has invented a new name for the antiself, which he then proceeds to treat in a new way. The antiself now seems to be identified with some enduring, living aspect of nature, perhaps human nature, some spirit that can be imagined to have observed all of history. In the past, the antiself had been hopefully sought or awaited. Here the poet calls it forth, speaks to it, and seems to speak for it as well. It is as if the poet has for a moment managed to identify self and antiself and speaks out of their identity. Indeed, he seems to give voice to something that has been slumbering or in retirement, as if his discovered role were now actually that which gives voice to the total body of historical conflict. This may account for the boldness of the poem's gestures and the sweep of its vision. In conflating the cycles of history and recognizing that the present too will pass, the poet accepts what he so feared in "Meditations in Time of Civil War"; with almost a frenzy of satisfaction he calls forth Old Rocky Face to survey the whole panorama of cyclicity. He asserts that together the two of them "but laugh in tragic joy," the "but" expressing a casual, reckless attitude earlier identified with the mask. It becomes clearer in the following poem that "tragic joy" is involved specifically with the mask of drama. At this point, the poet describes himself and Old Rocky Face as onlookers, thus emphasizing their detachment and disinterest.

But for their part it is an interested disinterest, precariously built and held. The poet indirectly recalls previous passionate fears. The "ancient lineaments" blotted out recall his earlier concern about his own family. The "irrational streams of blood" return us to "Blood and the Moon." "Numb nightmare" suggests the poet's horrible vision of Robert Artisson in "Nineteen Hundred and Nineteen." The "blood and mire" of "Byzantium" reappears. These fears are all dismissed with the reckless gesture, "What matter?" repeated from "A Dialogue of Self and Soul" but now referring not just to his own life and its possible repetition but also to universal destruction.

In the face of the passing away of all that has been lamented, even the proper "conduct" of life presented earlier in such poems as "In Memory of Eva Gore-Booth and Con Markievicz," Old Rocky Face finally speaks the one word, "Rejoice." At the critical moment, we learn that the rejoicing is in anticipation of the creative repetition of the new cycle and that it is this that makes possible the poet's willingness to say farewell to the past. This is not to make a refuge of cyclicity but rather to reject the sentimental great modern myth of progress; the gyre, as a principle of history, is therefore "unfashionable," but the poet embraces it fully. He implies that it makes no difference from where the rebirth comes. Those who bring it about will always be "lovers of horses and women," the next manifestations of the reckless, heroic type, and they will "disinter" the traditional figures of "workman, noble and saint." It is interesting that the saint is included in this group. The poet apparently now sees the movement of creativity as actually producing those primary figures who earlier seemed to oppose it. The vision has become larger, more inclusive, and more deliberately inclusive of conflict.

The attitude is extended in "Lapis Lazuli" (322, 294; 331, 565), but not in the form of the prophetic ecstasy of "The Gyres." It is now more reflective, and in the end the gaiety is modulated and the role of wise observer emphasized. But this occurs only after a beginning that expresses dismissive irritation at those who lose their nerve in the face of events and frantically criticize those poets and artists able to maintain gaiety in the same situation. The nervous accuse the poets, as the poet obliquely accused himself in "Meditations in Time of Civil War," of failure to act, though the accusers do not know what action should be taken.

In the poem's second stanza, the mask of tragedy is invoked to illustrate, by contrast to the "hysterical women" of the first stanza, the stance of "gaiety transfiguring all that dread." Hysteria is judged wrong because it means abandonment of the mask, which is what makes one capable of any action at all. It is here that the stage, drama, and acting quite specifically become figures for heroic behavior. Life, it is implied, should be seen as a role in a dramatic performance. The mask of tragedy is the heroic *playing* of the role. This play is always an expression of gaiety. Even in "tragedy wrought to its uttermost," which is the universal destruction accepted in "The Gyres," there remains the gaiety of playing the role:

> . . . they, should the last scene be there,
> The great stage curtain about to drop,
> If worthy their prominent part in the play,
> Do not break up their lines to weep.
>
> (322, 294; 331, 565)

Not only ought there to be gaiety in the playing of the role, whether in life or on the stage, but the great dramas end not in tears but in ecstatic dramatic utterance. It is in both senses that "Hamlet and Lear are gay," and this gaiety is not merely a cover for dread but a true mask, a made reality "transfiguring dread." Furthermore, this is the case (for the whole stanza is an encouragement to such behavior) with respect to even the worst possible dread:

> All men have aimed at, found and lost;
> Black out; Heaven blazing into the head:
> Tragedy wrought to its uttermost.
>
> (322, 294; 331, 566)

Birth, life, death, God's triumph—this pattern is the shape of the ultimate tragedy, which is both destruction and repetition. The poet has earlier had to come to terms with loss and then with cyclicity. Here the two are seen as one, and the pattern of both history and the individual life is synecdochically established and accepted.

The piece of lapis that the poet contemplates shows two old Chinese men climbing a mountain. The poet delights in the way the artist has made use of his material and dwells lovingly on the object. His imagination carries him to think of their climb paused at a "little half-way house." He imagines them there listening to the music played by their servant and surveying the scene of tragedy below. They are their masks, their attitude one of disinterest in wise old age: "Their eyes mid many wrinkles, their eyes, / Their ancient, glittering eyes, are gay " (322, 295; 331, 567).

This poem is immediately followed by "Imitated from the Japanese" (323, 295; 332, 567). That it is labeled an imitation suggests either that the poet may not quite want to acknowledge its sentiments as entirely his or that as poet he is adopting a mask of the East in emulation of the sages of the previous poem. It may be both, the mask being on the level of the poetic technique and the disguise being on the level of self-expression. At the age of seventy, the speaker welcomes with pleasure the spring and wonders at his never having "danced for joy." In the end, one feels that the poet is taking stock behind a formal disguise and is wistfully criticizing the way he has lived. He has not, perhaps, ever achieved the gaiety he has been describing and advocating.

"Sweet Dancer" (324, 296; 333, 568), which follows, observes a dancing girl apparently released from the cares the poet imagines for her. In the light of the preceding poem, her release seems a contrast to his own bondage:

> The girl goes dancing there
> On the leaf-sown, new mown, smooth
> Grass plot of the garden;
> Escaped from her bitter youth,
> Escaped out of her crowd,
> Or out of her black cloud.
> Ah dancer, ah sweet dancer!
>
>   (324, 296; 333, 568)

He would have her be allowed to finish her dance; he would not have observers justify her being led away on the ground that she was happy because she was crazy. The charge of madness is, in any case, an affront to the poet's symbolism, which has frequently identified the dance with the perfect antithetical condition. The happiness is the dance itself; just as gaiety is the mask.

There is a curious masking in the authorial attribution of "The Three Bushes" (325, 296; 334, 569), the first poem of a sequence of seven. The poet playfully adopts a vulgar and slightly pornographic pseudonym, "The Three Bushes" being described as "An incident from the 'Historia mei Temporis' of the Abbé Michel de Bourdeille." Richard Finneran points out some possible puns here on "bourde" or fib and "bordel" or brothel.[1] Thus we have Michel of the Tall Tale conflated with Michel of the Bordello. Edward B. Partridge has gone further and suggested "Mike the Pimp," as if the author were in some way the arranger of the poem's events.[2] This clothing of the story with an obviously false medieval attribution and the return of the ballad form to the *Book* suggest considerable emphasis on the necessity in old age of a mask of simplicity and of a deliberate gaiety sought in earthiness. One senses the poet's effort to exploit the sexual as inspiration. He will later tell us that he has remaining to him only lust and rage to "spur [him] into song."

---

1. *The Poems of W. B. Yeats: A New Edition*, ed. Richard J. Finneran (New York: Macmillan, 1983), p. 669.

2. Edward B. Partridge, "Yeats's 'The Three Bushes': Genesis and Structure," *Accent* 17, no. 2 (Spring 1957): 80.

Dealing explicitly with the relation of body to soul, the sequence is more "metaphysical," in the Donnean sense, than anything else the poet has written. As a sequence, it is unique in two ways. The six poems that follow the first are made to be the poet's response to the alleged work of the fictive Michel de Bourdeille. Also, the first poem presents the whole story, and the rest are particularizations of some part of it imagined by the poet as spoken by the various participants. The subsequent poems, therefore, are really a modern imagining of an allegedly medieval story.

The story is of a gallant, active lover, a singer and horseman (he possesses two abilities that the poet always likes to see in one person), and a lady, who, although in love with him, cannot bring herself to give her body to sexual passion. She sends her chambermaid in the disguise of darkness to lie with her lover. He is subsequently killed in a horse race, and the lady dies of shock. The chambermaid confesses in old age, dies, and is buried beside the lovers by a sympathetic priest, who

> . . . set a rose-tree on her grave.
> And now none living can
> When they have plucked a rose there
> Know where its roots began.
>
> (325, 298; 334, 571)

The ballad has an unsettling refrain, "*O my dear, O my dear,*" which seems a disembodied comment lamenting the story and/or finding it poignant. What is the source of that poignancy? Is it the tragic end to which the lady's insistence on the separation of soul and body, even in love, takes things? Not exactly, for this causes neither the lover's death nor hers. It is the missed experience and its manipulation of reality by the lady's casuistry that is emphasized in the poems that follow. The refrain of the first poem views this with sadness. In the *Book*'s terms, the lady takes the primary view that soul and body are separate, that soul is pure, and that body's behavior can tarnish it. This is a familiar negation characteristic of the primary attitude. The lover, as antithetical hero, knows no such distinction. Therefore, he can sing the song his friends ask of him, in which the sacred and profane are not separate:

> "A laughing, crying, sacred song,
> A leching song," they said.
> Did ever men hear such a song?
> No, but that day they did.
>
> (325, 297–98; 334, 570)

The refrain is a comment of sad regret for the lady's point of view and for experience missed. Only symbolically in death is the negation made to seem to disappear in the rose tree, familiar from "Baile and Aillinn," which grows from the chambermaid's and the lover's graves. But the refrain has the last words: "*O my dear, O my dear.*"

Not only is body/soul opposed; so also is the class difference between lady and maid, lover and maid. The refrain comments again with sadness, yet the refrain may also be directed at the refrain's auditor, suggesting that she may be caught up in similar oppositions, as the poet had earlier cautioned Anne Gregory.

The poems that follow in the sequence explore, in the arranger's imagination, various perspectives on the situation. It has been pointed out that they are separate songs and yet at the same time part of a larger contrapuntal arrangement.[3] In "The Lady's First Song" (326, 299; 335, 572), her passion nearly overcomes her, but she resists it by insisting on the soul/body division that she covertly denies, masochistically attributing sexual passion to her soul. In "The Lady's Second Song" (327, 299; 336, 572), the chambermaid's question about the lover is deflected, first, by the lady's declaration that his nature does not matter, they are "but women,"[4] and the chambermaid should prepare her own body for the lover's pleasure, and second, by the lady's imagining that the lover will love only the maid's body and at the same time the lady's soul.

In the process, however, two things occur that betray the lady's argument. The lady begins to play the role of the chambermaid's servant—"I have cupboards of dried fragrance / I can strew the sheet" (327, 299; 336, 572)—and she foresees the lover making love to the chambermaid's body "untroubled by the soul." She asserts, against her own argument, that it is the soul that troubles the body. The body, therefore, cannot be the culprit. Further, the lady pays no attention to the possibility that the chambermaid may have a soul that could be seriously involved in all this. The chambermaid is but a servant and apparently soulless, though the lady begins to serve her body as if that were the aristocratic part. Through the whole second song the lady continues to try to convince by casuistry. The result is cyclicity, with body or soul getting the upper hand by turns.

"The Lady's Third Song" (328, 300; 337, 573) marks the climax and completion in irresolution and ambiguity of the lady's persuasion. Decorously displacing her description of the sexual act to "tunes" played "between [the] feet, " the lady admonishes the chambermaid to "speak no evil of the soul." It is a curious statement. "Soul" refers first to the lady herself:

3. Partridge, "Yeats's 'The Three Bushes,'" p. 75.

4. Richard J. Finneran has adopted the punctuation of *New Poems* and therefore does not show a comma after "what matter": "What matter we are but women." I can make sense of the line only if the comma is at least implied.

"Speak no evil of me," but it would not occur to the chambermaid to speak evil of the soul in such circumstances. The lady worries, at the same time, that the chambermaid will "think that body is the whole," in other words, that she has given and taken completely. The lady expresses jealousy here, and the statement is both a warning to the chambermaid to keep to her place and a declaration of ownership of the lover. It is a denigration of the body (and of the chambermaid), even as it is an expression of fear of the body's (and of the chambermaid's) power. So the lady invokes the idea of a code of honor that keeps each to each in a situation of negation. But the phrase describing this betrays her with its ambiguity:

> But in honour split his love
> Till either neither have enough,
> That I may hear if we should kiss
> A contrapuntal serpent hiss,
> You, should hand explore a thigh,
> All the labouring heavens sigh.
>
> (328, 300; 337, 573)

The phrase "either neither" marks the lady's ultimate crisis. It is a phrase echoing, as several critics have noticed, Shakespeare's "The Phoenix and Turtle":

> Reason, in itself confounded,
> Saw division grow together
> To themselves yet either neither
> Simple were so well compounded.
>
> (41–44)

In Shakespeare's poem, the description is a synecdoche in which each is itself yet inseparable from the whole. The lady's syntax, though perhaps intending to appropriate the Shakespearean idea, seems actually to have said the opposite. Neither of them will have enough of either his love of her soul or his love of her body, or either of them will have enough of neither. Either way, the result would be the opposite of the confounding of reason in Shakespeare's poem. Thus, when the lady hears the serpent hiss or the chambermaid the heavens sigh, it will be both a reminder of what is not present in the act and the sustainer of desire, as if the sustaining of desire were the actual end. This is a notion we have seen offered by the poet before, but never by exploring negation and the separation of body and soul.

"The Lover's Song" (329, 300; 338, 574) is not the song that the lover's friends called for in the ballad. It is a later, now more thoughtful song about desire—the ubiquity of desire even where desire seems to have a knowable object. It also identifies achieved desire with rest and inaction. There is even an unspoken implication, taking us back to "The Wheel," that achievement of desire is equivalent to death. The chambermaid's two songs, the lover in her arms, allude to achieved desire as repose, also with suggestions of death: "What's left to sigh for, / Strange night has come" (330, 301; 339, 574), and, in her second song, "His spirit that has fled / Blind as a worm" (331, 301; 340, 575), where, incidentally, the chambermaid claims that his soul, or at least his spirit, *has* been present.

The theme of rest and the idea of the momentary repose of achieved desire as a sort of death are immediately picked up in the poet's own personal meditation, "An Acre of Grass" (332, 301; 341, 575), which follows the sequence. He is uncomfortable with his own state of retirement. The poem presents another midnight scene. In "All Souls' Night," midnight was the moment to call up ghosts; but now, especially since "The Four Ages of Man" (a Ribhian prophetic utterance), midnight is identified with death or, more specifically, with an analogy that generates thoughts of death. The contrast is between a visionary antithetical moment and an ecstatic primary one. No ghosts are called; no images come. In a sort of repose, the poet recognizes that his own desire is quiescent:

> Neither loose imagination,
> Nor the mill of the mind
> Consuming its rag and bone,
> Can make the truth known.
>
>   (332, 301; 341, 575)

The characterization of imagination as now "loose" reveals some suspicion of its powers, as is proper to man in the primary phases; but this is still an antithetical man, and reason is declared equally unproductive. Employing a phrase in Blake's debt ("the mill of the mind") to describe reason, the poet imagines himself chewing over old material. Nothing can come of it, he thinks. At this late stage there is yet, however, a glimmer of desire; there is the desire to desire, the desire to achieve yet another mask: "Grant me an old man's frenzy. / Myself must I remake" (332, 301; 341, 576). The statement is a secular prayer (no God is mentioned) that he may play a new and "frenzied" role. (The bird symbolic of this mental condition is the eagle.) A secular prayer is an assertion of the will to act. (The wild old wicked man of a later poem is one face of this new, deliberately and strenuously chosen mask.) Alone, "forgotten else by mankind," the poet will recreate desire when the usually recognized forms of natural desire are dissipated. One more form is always imaginable, it seems, for in "What Then?" (333, 302; 342, 576) the voice of Plato's ghost keeps driving the character presented in the poem (certainly the poet) onward to ever-new objects of desire, implying an unattainable ideal or, to put it antithetically, the endless desire for desire.

Here the poet seems at first to have embraced the very same Plato who had been rejected in "The Tower," but in fact he has antithetically turned the primary, ultimate, timeless Platonic form, by a deliberate misinterpretation and appropriation, into what may fairly be called an antithetical temporal impulse. It is not an end, for the whole point is the endlessness of desire. The whispering ghost is desire itself; the whole matter is radically temporalized.

The search for new activity begins in "Beautiful Lofty Things" (334, 303; 343, 577), even though the poet is but consuming "rag and bone." The poem exemplifies what I have already named antithetical nostalgia, even as it memorializes high dramatic moments in which those remembered have acted magnificent parts. The poet seems to be searching through his memory for inspiration, but all that he discovers is a heroic recent past that now, he imagines, is gone forever. He seems to be between acceptance of personal loss and embrace of the concept of a cyclicity that will not bring back many loved things soon enough for him to see them again. Among them is Maud Gonne, the beloved who is named for the first time but treated only in the far memory, as if the naming were safe only at this emotional distance. From this point forward, the turn to personal concerns threatens to drown the poet in nostalgia, while the vision of the larger cycles of history generates an opposing gaiety.

"A Crazed Girl" (335, 303; 344, 578) is a deliberate effort to discover something marvelous in the present. Alluding to a quite recent event, it offers once again a dancer. This time, by the poet's own admission, the dancer is indeed mad, "her soul in division from itself"; yet the poet does not declare that she is happy being crazy, leaving it at that. He would willfully make out of this pathos a new "beautiful lofty thing" to take its place with the others he has long kept in his memory and has just recalled in the previous poem:

> . . . that girl I declare
> A beautiful lofty thing, or a thing
> Heroically lost, heroically found.

(335, 303; 344, 578)

Yet something causes him to qualify his memorialization. This dancer, this singer, this crazed girl is remembered as wound in "desperate" music. She is described also as "in her triumph." The word, we must remind ourselves, is one that the poet previously used to describe the end to desire, which is not desirable. For the poet to achieve "triumph," he said in "The Tower," would be to drive others mad. Here the crazed dancer's being "wound" in "desperate music" results in the poet's invoking "triumph" in connection with madness. Her dancing madness is not the tautly wound self-containment of the dancer Michael Robartes saw, even though the poet attempts to make his heroical declaration stick. The poet's determination to create has caused him to seize on what turns out to be an inadequate subject, the main virtue of which is that it is near to hand. The inadequacy requires the willfully insistent assertion "declare."

It may be the poet's awareness of this failure (I do not mean that the poem is a failure; it is quite the opposite in the *Book*) that leads him to write a poem of encouragement to a younger poet, as if he were passing on the torch. He encourages Dorothy Wellesley to follow the path of antithetical tradition. He places her in a situation that recalls the poet of "The Phases of the Moon" in his study at midnight or the poet of "All Souls' Night" calling on ghosts at midnight. It is nighttime in his imagination: "Climb to your chamber full of books and wait, / No books upon the knee and no one there" ("To Dorothy Wellesley," 336, 304; 345, 579). What will come if she is worthy of the poet's hope? The ancient Furies, whom he declares to be misrepresented as revengeful tormentors by the classical authors. The poet considers that these authors had misunderstood as an expression of pure, unrelieved enmity the message of antitheticality. "Do be my enemy for friendship's sake" was Blake's message (never actually sent) to his friendly tormentor William Hayley. Dorothy Wellesley should greet the Furies as antithetical inspiration, for inspiration comes from conflict.

The contemplation of this visitation is apparently enough to generate the "old man's frenzy" that had been hoped for but that up to now had remained absent. The poet creates five ballads glorifying figures of recent Irish history and then produces "The Wild Old Wicked Man" as an oblique expression of a new mask. There follows on this, in the same way that the mask of Ribh produced gnomic prophecies, a series of short, aphoristic poems. After two more ballads, which are not political but which submit modern material to the folktale, the poet writes "A Model for the Laureate." I shall take up this poem first because I believe that it comments obliquely on the writing of those I have just mentioned and leads to "The Old Stone Cross," which follows it.

"A Model for the Laureate" (350, 316; 359, 597) is an ironic poem with political overtones written by an Irishman, and has some connection in this regard with "On being asked for a War Poem." That poem, years before, was an Irish poet's response, barbed with politeness, to a request to write about England's war. This poem is an Irish poet's response to the whole idea of being the poet laureate of England. In short, it asks rhetorically how a poet could keep a lover waiting in order to execute the duties and enjoy the prerogatives of that office. The poet scorns "those cheers that can be bought or sold." What is particularly interesting about this poem's placement is that it follows a series of ballads celebrating heroism and a group of aphorisms asserting a stance as nearly antithetical to that of the ideal, decorous laureate as it can possibly be. Yet one senses that *antithetical* laureateship is exactly what the poet is aiming at. He is now famous and revered. If there is a poet laureate of Ireland, it is he. Yet he is not and has never been willing to play the laureate to political authority or to one whose cheers can be bought and sold. He has "applauded" no "modern throne." Even as an Irish laureate he has been eccentric. He has criticized power. He has attacked Paudeen's lack of culture. His major poem on 1916 dramatized an initial unwillingness to memorialize some whom he disliked. Recently, in "Parnell's Funeral," he has attacked one by one all the possible leaders of the Irish Free State. His vision of antithetical heroism does not square with modern politics, and in the next poem, "The Old Stone Cross," he is not loath to say why. An antithetical laureate, then, he is in no one's pay to write celebrative poems or to impart official wisdom. He imparts what he wishes and in his own time. His celebrations of Roger Casement and the O'Rahilly are composed well after the events that made their deaths famous. Furthermore, some of his poems do not put modern Ireland in a very good light.

This is true of the first of the balladic group, "The Curse of Cromwell" (337, 304; 346, 580). Here, in the role of traveling poet, he finds nothing good to report. Cromwellianism is usually identified with the plantation of Ulster and vicious suppression of the Celtic Irish. But the poet overplays the term provocatively by identifying Cromwell with bourgeois materialism and commercial competition. For the poet, it is not, as most Irishmen would think of it, identifiable only with Protestantism and Unionism. It has invaded the whole fabric of a declining society, both Protestant and Catholic. Even schooling is detestable. (The refrain is particularly an expression of disgust.) The poem ends with a visionary dream of a great house all lit up at midnight and occupied by the poet's dead old friends. (We shall meet them again in "The Municipal Gallery Revisited.") It is they, he avers, for whom he continues to write; or at least he writes for the ideal types they represent. They—swordsmen and ladies, gallants all—"can pay the poet for a verse," and he remains their servant in an ideal world that understands the poet's role of antithetical laureate and rewards it. Roger Casement, subject of the next two ballads (338, 305; 347, 581, and 339, 306; 348, 583), was a "gallant gentleman," whom the poet thus classes with the swordsmen. His name is subjected to lies ("The Old Stone Cross" tells us who the liars are—statesmen and journalists), and the culprit is England, which put him to death and then, in the poet's opinion, slandered him. In a refrain, Casement's ghost is *beating on the door*," presumably demanding justice.

The O'Rahilly (340, 307; 349, 584) is memorialized for his gallant, reckless giving of his life and particularly for his final antithetical gesture, the writing of his name—the name and title that he claimed—in blood as he died. In this act, the poet observes, "he christened himself with blood" in the same kind of personal ritual that the poet had antithetically employed in forgiving himself and blessing the tower. The O'Rahilly's bitterness at Pearse and Connolly is not overlooked, the poet here avoiding the conventional hallowing of those two leaders.

Nor in the next poem, "Come Gather Round Me Parnellites" (341, 309; 350, 586), is there any conventional praise or unwillingness to criticize Irish politics. Not many Parnellites remain alive by this time; the poem is again written longer after the fact than one might expect. But that is part of the point. Those who remained true to Parnell *are* now few. The rest are the ghosts called up in the writing of this poem. All the more reason to sing out and to sing particularly the antithetical values that are rapidly disappearing. The bishops, the party, and Captain O'Shea are bitterly accused. Parnell is praised because he "saved the Irish poor," helped the farmers, and loved his lass. This final point is emphasized because it illustrates Parnell's recklessness. Unlike the ungallant politicians of "A Model for the Laureate," Parnell did not "keep his lover waiting" (the reference is, of course, to Kitty O'Shea). The importance of this story is its model of behavior, its vision of the gallant, antithetical politician, who, the poet fears, is perhaps now an anachronism, even a contradiction in terms.

With all these poems, the ballad form is adopted to enter them into a folklore that will be antithetical to the official histories. As balladeer, the self-created laureate declares his freedom from laureateship as it is usually (primarily) understood, and at the same time he defines an antithetical political role for the poet.

Such a stance in old age is next boldly and outrageously characterized. In "The Wild Old Wicked Man" (342, 310; 351, 587), the poet offers a disreputable, randy old traveling man, who sings to the commenting refrain, "*day-break and a candle end,*" of his desire to die on the roads; who brags that he has words no young lover, too full of love, could possess; who is rebuffed by pious women who have given themselves to God; and who goes on to seek other women not so pious. Like the poet of "Vacillation," this old man chooses against absolution and annihilation. But he goes even further toward embrace of the antithetical, as in old age he feels he must:

> "That some stream of lightning
> From the old man in the skies
> Can burn out that suffering
> No right taught man denies.

> But a coarse old man am I,
> I choose the second-best,
> I forget it all awhile
> Upon a woman's breast."
>
> (342, 311; 351, 589–90)

The cold, violent, aphoristic poems that follow attempt to disabuse the auditor of some of the illusions that politics and cant create. The theme of the first three is the illusion of progress, the return of the same. In one of these, Parnell is memorialized as refusing to hold out false hope in order to gain support. The fourth, "The Spur" (346, 312; 355, 591), indicates that the mask of lust and rage is not a perfect fit. Masks are more imperfect in old age, for the antithetical is by then substantially invaded by primary power. There is the need, one might say, for a willed excess of will to compensate for a lack of natural recklessness. The poet is well aware of this:

> You think it horrible that lust and rage
> Should dance attendance upon my old age;
> They were not such a plague when I was young;
> What else have I to spur me into song?
>
> (346, 312; 355, 591)

He persists in wildness and wickedness in order to rescue his antitheticality. So the drunk man in "A Drunken Man's Praise of Sobriety" (347, 312; 356, 591) asks to be kept dancing and turns dancing into a desirable drunken form of sobriety. In "The Pilgrim" (348, 313; 357, 592), another drunkard, who claims to have returned from a fantastic penitential pilgrimage in which he heard the dead speak and saw a black bird with a twenty-foot wingspread, is back in the pub telling the tale of his pilgrimage and punctuating it with the refrain "fol de rol de rolly O," which is what the dead spoke to him and, as far as he can see, is the only comment worth making on anything. This drunken recklessness is added to lust and rage as incitements to song—part of the necessarily coarse mask of active old age. The words advocated are pure reckless gesture.

In "Colonel Martin" (349, 314; 358, 594), the last of the ballads, we seem to have moved to the opposite of the metaphysical ballads of love offered early in *New Poems* that deliberately recalled (with a certain irony) a tradition of romance. Here nothing of romance or metaphysics remains. The colonel, betrayed by his wife with a rich young man, is awarded damages in court. It is the bourgeois world with a vengeance. But the colonel is different. A man of the great world who knows many languages, he has disguised himself as a beggar to trap the lovers and later scatters among the townspeople the gold won for damages. The refrain *"The Colonel went out sailing"* expresses his difference from the others and returns to one of the themes of these ballads, which memorialize antithetical recklessness in the face of a modern world where it seems to be absent.

"A Model for the Laureate," already discussed, and "The Old Stone Cross" (351, 317; 360, 598) follow. In the latter, the poet speaks for an ancient Irish warrior buried under a cross. He observes the modern world, attacks the statesman and journalist of democracy, advises withholding one's vote, observes "Folly link with Elegance," yet is finally most irritated by "actors lacking music." This is, of course, no ancient Irish warrior but the poet himself in disguise, who hates the style of acting that has won the contemporary stage even more than the leveling process of which it is apparently a part. (There will be more to say about the poet's view of democracy and of political ideologies generally in the next chapter.)

But then it seems that the mask of the wild old wicked man is dropped. Perhaps in old age there has been something too contrived about it, or perhaps the poet has said all that he cares to say with it. *New Poems* ends on more personal and elegiac notes, which indicate that the mask has been worn out, that in old age a mask is indeed difficult to sustain.

"The Spirit Medium" (352, 318; 361, 599) marks a moment when the poet, burdened by recent deaths, takes to the simplicity of gardening in order to deflect thought and, perhaps, the search for the mask itself. Even poetry and music are banished in favor of "root, shoot, blossom, or clay." But the moment turns out to be a personal renewal after all, for in the very next poem ("Those Images," 353, 319; 362, 600) the poet, in a new burst of energy, instructs his reader-poets to "leave / The cavern of the mind," for "There's better exercise / In the sunlight and wind" (353, 319; 362, 600). The sunlight and wind refer, of course, to the garden where he has been at work, and this garden retreat has turned out to engender a new engagement. In the rest of the poem, the poet counsels against adoption of either Catholic or Marxist ideologies and advises seeking out a deeper, more fundamental imagery: "Seek those images / That constitute the wild" (353, 319; 362, 601). In advocating return to primordial images, the poet seems to align himself again with Ribh.

The images that surround the poet during a visit to the Dublin Municipal Gallery (354, 319; 363, 601) draw him out of the cavern of his own mind and into his own history and the history of modern Ireland externalized before him. Everyone is there: Roger Casement, Arthur Griffith, Kevin O'Higgins, Robert Gregory, Hugh Lane, Hazel Lavery, Augusta Gregory, John Synge. There are others unnamed in his meditation, and there are pictured events. In a moment of deep feeling, he regards much of this as "my permanent or impermanent images." He dwells especially on Augusta Gregory and John Synge. He anxiously expresses the fear that such as she will not be seen again; he laments once more the anticipated end of the house at Coole, and, quoting appropriately from Spenser's "Ruins of Time," he recognizes that at least "no fox can foul the lair the badger swept."

His brief period of thoughtless gardening reported in "The Spirit Medium" seems to stand as a symbol of regenerated remembrance, for here he states that he, Lady Gregory, and Synge felt that "all that we did, all that we said or sang / Must come from contact with the soil" (354, 321; 363, 603). He identifies his work with theirs. Readers should not judge his book, this *Book*, alone but should visit the gallery to understand how their work is intertwined with Irish history. We have read the lines he has uttered in a shock of recognition:

> . . . "This is not" I say
> "The dead Ireland of my youth, but an Ireland
> The poets have imagined, terrible and gay."
>
> (354, 320; 363, 601–2)

The *Book* in which this statement occurs is one in which the poet has himself frequently attempted to goad Ireland into gaiety. The Dublin Municipal Gallery, as the history composed by artists, has for this moment completed the task, and it would seem that he is content. The vision is different from those sudden, earlier moments where conflict seemed unaccountably to cease. Here the force is not from beyond or wherever but from the realization that an artistic history to which he belongs and which he helped to create has been made.

But the poet is not content. If he belongs to Irish history, he also claims a more personal genealogy. In "Are You Content?" (355, 321; 364, 604), he calls on his ancestors for judgment on his life. We remember that he addressed them many years before with apologies that he had produced no children, only a book. As usual, no ancestral ghosts come to speak a judgment, nor can he himself speak in judgment on his own work. This is different from the assertions of "What Then?" where the old man of the poem is for a moment satisfied, as in these lines:

> "The work is done," grown old he thought,
> "According to my boyish plan;
> Let the fools rage, I swerved in nought,
> Something to perfection brought."
>
> (333, 302; 342, 577)

This seems to have been meant as a description of the ideal or perhaps acceptable career. Plato's ghost goaded that speaker on, of course. Here there is not even that moment of satisfaction before the ghost whispers. Indeed, no ghost needs to whisper. In "The Municipal Gallery Re-visited," the poet made a grand, magnanimous public statement, the statement of an Irish laureate made with the appropriate gesture of strong emotion and self-effacement while still calling attention to his historic role. The poet seemed to have virtually enshrined himself, closed his career: "Think where man's glory most begins and ends / And say my glory was I had such friends" (354, 321; 363, 604). But such a closing gesture would be uncharacteristic of the attitudes toward search and laureateship developed through the *Book*. Indeed, the formal gesture of "The Municipal Gallery Re-visited" may in retrospect have been something of an embarrassment. Had the wild old wicked man and the bitter gaiety disappeared so completely that he could now only be "heart smitten"?

Facing his ancestors, who, presented as "half legendary" reckless men, stand as the goad of conscience, he finds himself not contented after all. He cannot allow himself to cease from work, though he admits to hating it. At least in old age, antithetical pride is not any longer an inherent quality; it must be deliberately cultivated. We have already observed his calling upon "lust and rage" in this endeavor, as if they were last resorts. In the last of *New Poems*, their presence has diminished, yet it is clear that the work of this *Book* can end only with the poet's death. There still remains enough pride to force continued labor and the large cyclical view of history to make the work bearable.

8

The Spiritual Intellect's Great Work

[Last Poems] (1938–1939)

Scholars now generally recognize that Yeats's epitaph poem, "Under Ben Bulben" (356, 325; 386, 636), belongs, by his own intention, at the beginning of the so-called *Last Poems*, which may or may not have been given a title by Yeats. Curtis Bradford was the first to argue that "Under Ben Bulben" is properly placed as an introduction to the last poems; he thought that the poems following it were designed to be imagined as spoken from the grave.[1] In my opinion, it is part of the drama of "Under Ben Bulben" that the poet deliberately imagines himself speaking as his ghost to younger poets; he must be alive to do this. The poet utters what he imagines at the time to be a final and summary statement, but it turns out also to be introductory to further statements of great variety. Some of these can be called elaborations and others extensions of the poet's life into still new attitudes. Indeed, in the final poem, "Politics" (374, 348; 382, 631), the poet goes out singing a song not of summary finality at all. In the light of this, it is possible to say that the poet has his ending and yet eschews it, which is the way of antitheticality. This situation is characteristic not just of the *Book* but also of *A Vision* and of that other incredible cyclical performance of modern Irish literature, James Joyce's *Finnegans Wake*.[2]

"Under Ben Bulben" should be regarded as a summary that is also an introduction. The poem is the culmination of a tendency toward bold assertion apparent since *The Winding Stair and Other Poems*. This would be consistent with a gradual intensification of the primary condition that inevitably occurs from middle age onward. But the assertions themselves are

1. Curtis Bradford, "On Yeats's Last Poems," in *Yeats's Last Poems*, ed. J. Stallworthy (New York: Macmillan, 1968), pp. 75–97.

2. For other connections with Joyce, see my "Yeats, Joyce, and Criticism Today," in *The Uses of the Past: Essays on Irish Culture*, ed. Audrey S. Eyler and R. Garratt (Newark: University of Delaware Press, 1987), pp. 64–78.

antithetical in that they constantly treat of oppositions. These oppositions were early at the core of the poet's consciousness, even when he did not have a full grasp of their positive creative relation to each other. "Under Ben Bulben" takes them up in all four of its middle sections.

That the poet imagines himself as a ghost is indicated by the suggestion, in the repeated word "swear," of the ghost of Hamlet's father. That ghost desired revenge, the usurper removed from power, and the proper succession restored. "Under Ben Bulben" is an address to a younger generation of artists who are admonished to bring about the supplanting of unworthy usurpers in Ireland. In calling for an oath, the poet raises surreptitiously the idea of the *geis*-bound ancient Irish warrior, of whom Cuchulain is the poet's favorite example, and implies that his auditors should live up to that ideal. Engaging in a sort of syncretism, he identifies his message with the thought of early Christian sages, the pagan Witch of Atlas of Shelley's poem, and the ancient Irish Sidhe. He imagines the Sidhe as having lived out their passions in death and returned now as spirits of earth. The communal message is one of oppositions (in part 2, the oppositions are those of race and soul, life and death) and the message is cyclicity: The individual comes back; a brief parting is "the worst man has to fear." Part 3 emphasizes completeness in opposition. In hatred and anger generated by opposition or desire comes the completion of the "partial mind" in war or sexuality. Again the idea suggests the figure of Cuchulain, who in the *Tain* enters into a frenzied madness in preparation for battle. This is the moment that the poet has earlier treated as mysterious, irrational, and fleeting. The ghost gives it substance by identifying it with the violent confrontation of opposites.

In part 4, the young artists are finally addressed as such and are reminded of what the ghost regards as their traditional task: "Bring the soul of man to God, / Make him fill the cradles right" (356, 326; 386, 638). The second task apparently brings about the first. How are artists to accomplish their eugenic role? By providing the ideal of sexual desire. This notion will be further developed in "The Statues." Here this capacity is identified with the invention of mathematics in Egypt and Phidias's application of mathematical proportion to sculpture. The impulse flowered in the Quattrocento, Michelangelo, and the great romantic artists but died out in the nineteenth century. Michelangelo's work was "proof that there's a purpose set / Before the secret working mind" (356, 326; 386, 639), an idea exploited in the later "Long-legged Fly," where the fate of civilization is in the hands of those who seem to act instinctually, as does here the "globe-trotting madam" who responds sexually to Michelangelo's Adam. The end sought is expressed in an oxymoron, "profane perfection of mankind," which refers both to an art that has combined mathematical abstraction

and minute particularity and to the perfection of mankind by a sexual desire fueled by artistic forms such as Michelangelo's creations. In both
cases, the ideal emerges from oppositions: abstraction and concrete representation, male and female.[3]

There is a further opposition: antithetical and primary. Michelangelo's
work is earthy and antithetical while still embodying the beauty of the
mathematical abstract, appealing to sexual desire. The Quattrocento
painted "on backgrounds for a God or Saint, / Gardens where a soul's at
ease" (356, 326; 386, 639), as if all were a momentary opening of the heavens. Here desire for the primary is emphasized, but eventually in history
there is confusion.

At this point in the poem, the young poets are addressed as those who
must restore the proper succession by scorning "the sort now growing up"
and singing the heroic song, in other words, by carrying on what the poet
assesses his task to have been. This will keep alive the proper heroic models and fuel sexual desire for a certain beauty and heroic greatness. The
models are all examples of those who express the gaiety early defined and
later (in *New Poems*) insisted on as the means to deal with tragedy.

A definite connection is made with the seven centuries following the
Norman invasion; the poet does not speak directly of Ancient Ireland, so
long his ideal; now he glorifies everything that preceded the recent domination of the hated middle class, "all out of shape from toe to top" and
with no memory of history and tradition. It is the poet's last shot at Paudeen in his shop and the new rich who would not support the efforts to
establish the Lane gallery, who have dominated Irish politics on all sides,
and who have married folly to elegance. They are "base-born products of
base beds," the eugenic theme returning; but the poet's eugenics, frequently attacked as fascistic, has nothing to do with any concept of selective breeding controlled by the state. Indeed, in one poem we saw that
both state and church are identified with the very same mob that the poet
now characterizes as usurpers. The poet has proposed a cultural role for
art that has never, to my knowledge, been uttered before. It is the artists
who must offer the sexual ideal to the culture and thereby encourage the
seeking out of proper mates, and these artists are antithetical to state plan-
ning, which belongs to external primary power. The emphasis is on a tradition based on romantic principles of feeling and empathy. As he did in
"Are You Content?" which follows "The Municipal Gallery Re-visited,"
the poet identifies himself not just with Irish tradition but with his family
tradition as well. But he does not press this notion or glorify family so

3. See my *Philosophy of the Literary Symbolic* (Tallahassee: Florida State University Press,
1983), pp. 300–312.

much as try to solidify his own relation with the past: He is buried at Drumcliff, the ghost casually mentioning that "an ancestor was rector there / Long years ago." He emphasizes the conventionality of what is carved on his tombstone. The words speak to the viewer and encourage, in a last willful act, that viewer to be a certain kind of person. Already he has included in the Irish ideal the memory of "hard-riding country gentle- men," holy monks, porter-drinkers, and "lords and ladies gay." In the epi- taph he chooses to address the first group, who form a link to the hard- riding Sidhe of part 1. They are to read the admonition to "cast a cold eye on life, on death," and continue their ride.

The poet's ride also continues, but almost all the poems are summariz- ing ones. The writing of the epitaph generates in the poet a new burst of activity, but this activity is influenced by realization of impending death and the limited resources of energy remaining to him. The poems are now harsher and more spare in tone. They are sometimes more cryptic, with the poet employing a sort of shorthand that requires knowledge of what has come before in the *Book*.

The horsemen of "Under Ben Bulben" now appear in the refrain of three ballads under the title "Three Songs to the One Burden" (357, 328; 365, 605). In the background is the suggestion of their ghostly presence as an admonition to the reader. The first speaker, Mannion, who claims de- scent from the Celtic sea god Mannanan Mac Lir, is a roaring, fighting, hard-drinking tinker who scorns common breeding and would "throw likely couples into bed / And knock the others down" (357, 329; 365, 606). In the second ballad, Henry Middleton, apparently the last of his line, has retired from modern life and pities the young. In the third, the poet's voice is heard to invite "players" to praise the Easter Rising. "Players" refers particularly to the Abbey Theatre actors, one of whom, Connolly, was the first person to be killed in the Rising. But the players also stand ideally for those who transfigure dread (as in "Lapis Lazuli") and help to perform the artistry advocated in "Under Ben Bulben." Thus the poem expands its concern to include actors as objects of the advice already given to young poets and sculptors. Presumably included for advice are those actors, scornfully mentioned in "The Old Stone Cross," who lack music. A final implication is that there may have to be yet another revolution, which will this time overthrow commonness; the idea is not surprising if we consider the sentiments of "Parnell's Funeral," and the poet quotes Patrick Pearse to support it. The three ballads continue the attack of "Under Ben Bul- ben" on the state of culture in Ireland and move toward what can be read as a politically subversive conclusion. The phrase "And no one knows what's yet to come" seems innocent but may also be slyly ominous.

Though a ghost might truthfully say that, because of cyclicity, the worst one has to fear is a "brief parting," this does not mean that one can conveniently abandon old loyalties and commitments or act in other ways on such belief. "The Black Tower" (358, 331; 385, 635) seems to begin as the ghost's admonition not to depend on cyclicity. Its example is a heroism that holds to its loyalties even after loss of all hope that the absent object of loyalty will return. The poem is again directed toward younger poets. It dictates a subject for their poetry:

> Say that the men of the old black tower
> Though they but feed as the goatherd feeds,
> Their money spent, their wine gone sour,
> Lack nothing that a soldier needs,
> That all are oath-bound men;
> Those banners come not in.
>
> (358, 331; 385, 635)

These are men who remain oath-bound though isolated and subjected to bribery, threat, and the irritating optimism of the foolish cook, who thinks he hears their leader returning. It is their refusal of belief combined with their continued faithfulness that makes them the poet's most extreme example of the heroic. The threats and bribes suggest that the speaker is very suspicious of foreign influences. The refrain indicates a relation between ancient Irish heroes, said to be buried upright, still on guard, and these embattled men:

> *There in the tomb stand the dead upright,*
> *But winds come up from the shore;*
> *They shake when the winds roar*
> *Old bones upon the mountain shake.*
>
> (358, 331; 385, 635)

There is something ominous in the rustling of these old bones, as if the ancient warriors are very nearly moved to rebirth and action by sympathetic identification. Some suggestion of the poet keeping his own commitments in his isolated tower is present.

The ghostly speaker merges, as the poem proceeds, with the men in the tower; and at midpoem we hear the voices of the men speak of those who would "bribe or threaten." The stanza is oddly ambiguous and contributes to a weird, almost surreal effect:

> Those banners come to bribe or threaten
> Or whisper that a man's a fool
> Who when his own right king's forgotten
> Cares what king sets up his rule.
>
> (358, 331; 385, 635)

All that is clear enough, but the next lines can be regarded as spoken either by the bribers or by the men in the tower:

> If he died long ago
> Why do you dread us so?

> (358, 331; 385, 635)

From this point onward the voice is no longer just that of the original speaker but is also that of the men in the tower themselves, the ghost (if it is a ghost originally speaking) being strongly identified with these men. With all of these poems, the effect, despite the emphasis on impending death, is of something ominous, some revolutionary possibility: "And no one knows what's yet to come."

This powerful work is followed by one that reminds us again of impending death. It is the poet's treatment of the death of the heroic figure Cuchulain ("Cuchulain Comforted," 359, 332; 384, 634). An accomplished example of terza rima, the poet's first effort at the form, it is dated January 13, 1939, apparently to mark a time near his own anticipated death. Yet, characteristically, it is a new departure in technique. The poem describes Cuchulain as striding among the shrouded dead and in a world of shades, meeting his opposites—"convicted cowards all by kindred slain"—and learning from them the most difficult of all things, to sew his own shroud and to sing, taking the voice of birds.

Cuchulain's death leaves us listening to a modern man who, in the first of "Three Marching Songs" (360, 333; 369, 613), rejects his father's song glorifying earlier heroic Irish generations, including, presumably, the Cuchulain legend. "All that is finished," his refrain says, "let it fade." The poem itself offers the refrain as an irony. It is not as angry as the refrain of "September 1913" ("Romantic Ireland's dead and gone, / It's with O'Leary in the grave"), yet it expresses a disdain for the notion that all that has gone before is irrelevant or that "time amends old wrongs."

In the second poem, there is a dialogue between a father and son. The father speaks cryptically and perhaps a little madly in bold assertions and questions that mention cyclicity, the growth of greatness, and the collapse of order. The treatment of the state or nation as a tree, adopted earlier from the writings of Edmund Burke, returns here. Great nations blossom, but, the father asks, "What if there's nothing up there at the top?" What if there are no leaders? Such leaders as there have recently been were found wanting in "Parnell's Funeral." What must now occur? Another revolution? This is implied, but when the son thinks he hears something "marching through the mountain pass," the father replies, "No, no, my son, not yet." He fears what might come and cautions against it, perhaps out of distrust of revolutionary fervor, preferring a deliberate time working its destiny. There is something impatient and perhaps too optimistic (like the hope of the cook in "The Black Tower") in the son's thinking he hears the marchers coming.

The third poem consequently goes back another generation to find recklessness in the grandfather, who sings a tune on the scaffold (recalling the values of the tinker Mannion) in the face of his own execution. Robbed of his tambourine, the refrain tells us, he takes down the moon to accompany himself. The antithetical connection is apparent, but so also is reckless destruction.

The next poem, "In Tara's Halls" (361, 336; 366, 609), goes back even farther in time. An old king of Tara wills his own death at age one hundred and one, after declaring, "God I have loved, but should I ask return / Of God or women the time were come to die" (361, 336; 366, 609). He wills to die before he commits an act of unheroical self-interest. It is implied that this decision is the right act of leadership; the example has had to be found in the heroic past, not the present.

The decision now is to elaborate a statement made in "Under Ben Bulben." In "The Statues" (362, 336; 367, 610), the poet expands on the line "Measurement began our might"; he sees in ancient Greek statuary, inspired by the Pythagorean numbers, the marriage of passion and character. It was this, and not the victory over Persia at Salamis, that turned back the East and gave to European culture its particular nature. The poet, speaking with all the authority of the ghost of "Under Ben Bulben," makes a parallel to Ireland and imagines that the inspiration Pearse summoned up in Cuchulain was similar to that of the Greeks. He identifies the Irish originally with the Greeks and sees them wrecked, as Greece was, by the tide of modernism, not by the Asiatic tide.

The last lines are cryptic. The Irish, in spite of all this, will "climb to our proper dark, that we may trace / The lineaments of a plummet-measured face" (362, 337; 367, 611). The lines suggest that at the end of European civilization, identified with the darkness and specifically the moon's darkness, the Irish will convert this darkness into a new life cycle. Rather than descending, which is normally associated with darkness and death, the Irish ("We Irish," for the poet identifies himself with them) will "climb to our proper dark," that is, the place of death from which a new cycle begins, and perform once more the act of the Greek boys and girls who recognized the sexual ideal that set in motion a new civilization.

"News for the Delphic Oracle" (363, 337; 368, 611), a deliberately arrogant title, recalls "The Delphic Oracle upon Plotinus." The poet, acting the ghost, has shown himself to be the Irish oracle and now informs the predecessor oracle at Delphi of the results of Plotinus's swim across his "many-headed sea," picking up the story where the previous oracle left it and bringing it up to date. The Delphic oracle had imagined Plotinus struggling blindly to conquer the vague, immense salt seas in order to approach Elysium and his great predecessors. This Irish oracle sees him to his destination and, furthermore, populates Elysium with Niamh and Oisin. Plotinus joins them, sighing of love like the rest.

In this vision not only Plotinus arrives; all those who relive their deaths in dreaming back and return, like the spirits of "Byzantium," also arrive. (The vision seems to be generated by contemplation of a Byzantine mosaic.) The shore onto which they come is also the shore of rebirth. Contemplating a painting that has been identified by T. R. Henn as "The Marriage of Peleus and Thetis" in the Dublin National Gallery, the Irish oracle is inspired to see it as an expression of desire for the sexual ideal that has been so closely associated in these poems with the notion of cyclical rebirth.[4] On the shore, life returns in Peleus's lust for Thetis and her listening belly. The music they hear is not the music of the choir of love that greeted Plotinus. It is the sensual music of Pan appealing to sexual instinct. These pieces of news seem to be based on either literary or pictorial art, as is appropriate to the antithetical mode of oracularity. In each case, the realm of death is declared to have a sensual dimension, as is characteristic of antithetical thought.

"Long-legged Fly" (364, 339; 370, 617) extends the treatment of instinctual behavior in the preservation or rebirth of culture. Caesar, Helen of Troy, Michelangelo—their minds "move upon silence" like the long-legged fly on the stream. If we allow the stream to have its traditional (and Yeatsian) associations with time, we see that these minds play on the stream of time, not quite of it, not quite against it. They represent not ephemerality or dogged resistance to the flow of time but the persistence of human genius, desire, and beauty, whether conscious, like Caesar's, unconscious, like Helen's, or neither or both, like Michelangelo's.

This powerful poem, in which a suggestion of the ballad in the refrain merely emphasizes by opposition the meditative tone, brings to a close one phase of these last poems, emphasizing the fortunate mystery of instinct and especially sexual instinct. It is something beyond the control of human engineering, but not of inspiration and unconscious human power. It must be *let be* to do its work. It is this that makes possible the ghost's confident prediction of return, his hints at revolution, and the expectation (with some urging directed at poetic heirs) of antithetical survival and eventual renewed power.

All that having been said, it would seem that the poems have at last achieved summary. However, the poet is still alive, and as long as he lives,

4. T. R. Henn, *The Lonely Tower* (London: Methuen, 1950), p. 228.

he is subject to conflict. We are once again reminded that conflict is a principle of life, to say nothing of the relation of life and death. Life floods back in just as we have thought that the ghost has uttered a last word. The conflict of heart and self, heart and reason, persists, though changed somewhat by old age into wondering reminiscence. I refer, of course, to "A Bronze Head" (365, 340; 371, 618). It is noteworthy that in composing "The Municipal Gallery Re-visited" the poet did not make reference to the bust of the aged Maud Gonne standing to the right of the entrance. It seems that the omission must have been deliberate in a poem devoted so proudly to memorialization. Was it the old reticence suppressing comment, or was it the poet's unwillingness to confront *that* part of his and Ireland's history? Was the omission because she still remained special and therefore must be separately memorialized, as befits her role in the story? Was it because a trace of the old pain remained and he must concentrate on her alone in order to speak of her at all?

Now, later, the poet confronts what he had then passed by silently. Perhaps he has returned to the gallery to do this, or perhaps now he recalls that earlier moment of confrontation and writes about it. In either case, "A Bronze Head" marks an incursion of personal life returning us to the living poet, not the imagined urgent ghost of "Under Ben Bulben." This is the poet in the familiar role of questioner, though some of the poem (indeed, its conclusion) is a remembrance of questions. Even these, however, remain unanswered in the present.

The poem strongly echoes lines from "Among School Children":

No dark tomb-haunter once; her form all full
As though with magnanimity of light
Yet a most gentle woman's; who can tell
Which of her forms has shown her substance right.

(365, 340; 371, 618)

It is the old question once more, and all the poet can say in answer (he has never been able to rid himself of the question of Maud) is to refer hopefully to "profound McTaggart." (The characterization of McTaggart suggests a strain of the autodidactic in the poet. He is perhaps a little too impressed by McTaggart or by himself for having read him, but how carefully and with what comprehension is uncertain. One senses throughout the poet's later years his fragmentary learning and, for that reason perhaps, his curious intellectual attachments and excitements based on partial knowledge. His tendency is to make *use* of the material, in a selective way, as he seems to have done with Swift, Burke, Goldsmith, and Berkeley.) The idea of the compositeness of substance that the poet draws from McTaggart is, in his hands, a somewhat distorting synecdoche and becomes but a hopeful

gesture toward an answer. He now imagines his own early foreknowledge
of his life, which was surely in fact anxiety about his own relation to Maud
but which is treated here as only one aspect of a conflict within himself
about her, for he also imagined her as "supernatural,"

> As though a sterner eye looked through her eye
> On this foul world in its decline and fall,
> On gangling stocks grown great, great stocks run dry,
> Ancestral pearls all pitched into a sty.
>
> (365, 340; 371, 619)

This is not the beloved we have seen, but a new projection. The identification is with aristocratic disdain. The eye is cold, like that recom-
mended to the horseman figure. In the final couplet, the poem expresses
the poet's sense of an impending catastrophe that is supposed to bring all
things around again. But will it? "Heroic reverie mocked by clown and
knave / And wondered what was left for massacre to save" (365, 340; 371,
619). Thus Maud Gonne passes from the scene, already having been enveloped in these lines by the poet's more general concerns about destruction. She is remembered again, but briefly and only in connection with
the poet's personal distaste for his early work.

Yet in the next short poem, "A Stick of Incense" (366, 341; 372, 619),
we seem invited to connect its opening question with the previous discussion of Maud: "Whence did all that fury come?" Then, with the question
that follows—"From empty tomb or Virgin womb?"—we realize that a
new subject is being introduced. It has to do with the meaning of the
whole cycle of Western history since Christ. The questions move to a
larger arena. We notice a continuing effort to sum up, a movement that
goes back and forth between personal and more general historical concerns, between abstraction and concretion, and always a conflict between
the desire to welcome cyclicity and the tendency to lament loss. "Hound
Voice" (367, 341; 374, 621) welcomes cyclicity, but with nostalgia. At the
same time, it praises a certain stance, considers the women he has loved,
and locates what they have had in common. He and they, he imagines, had
chosen each other as if by instinct and understood "those images that
waken in the blood." The poet continues to identify imagination and poetic power with the heart and blood. This leads him to imply that something instinctual and deeply genetic is the source of strength. Thus the
emphasis of the poem, with its chilling rhetorical climax, is on the tradition of the hunt, the return of ancient hounds, and blood wounds.

This has been high talk, and the contrast with the next poem is marked;
the move is consistent with the poet's glorification of extremes: of aristocrats on the one hand and beggars, traveling men, and the so-called folk on

the other. In "John Kinsella's Lament for Mrs. Mary Moore" (368, 342; 373, 620), Kinsella laments his "old bawd" and eulogizes her for the stories she told and her ability to "put a skin / On everything she said." By implication he rejects the church and its tales of perfection. He would have Mary Moore back: "What shall I do for pretty girls / Now my old bawd is dead?" (368, 342; 373, 620). This poem brings down to earth the high talk about women in "A Bronze Head" and "Hound Voice" and begins the last movement of these last poems, which opposes both the oratorical ghost and the reminiscing aged lover. The poet now tries to come to terms with his final condition at the door of death.

This last movement begins with "High Talk" (369, 343; 375, 622), where the subject is performance, and is thus related to the whole development of the mask. But now that development is subtly, coldly mocked. The poet sees his performance now as a circus act with a pair of stilts. The stilts are substantially shorter than those of his great-grandfather, who would be of the same generation as a previous figure who tore down the moon and sang on the scaffold; but no matter, they are as tall as anyone's today. There are explanations of why he wears them: the animals alone are insufficient "shows," children demand stilts, women want the excitement of a face at an upper-story window. The turn of the poem in its last lines is obscure. His learning has "run wild." He is "all metaphor"—his name, his stilts, everything; he is his mask. But this achievement is no longer ecstatic. We find him at daybreak stalking on relentlessly. Daybreak is "the terrible novelty of light," as if it were an environment for which he is not prepared and in which the mask—now his reality—is totally revealed in devastating primary light in all of its elaborate fashioning. The "great seahorses" of the poem's last line complete its nightmarish quality. These creatures are not of his circus. They belong to the seas, identified with life; and, unlike him, they can "bare their teeth and laugh at the dawn." In a poem about a circus performer, theirs is the only laughter.

The weird quality of this poem is extended into the refrain of "The Apparitions": *"Fifteen apparitions have I seen; / The worst a coat upon a coat-hanger"* (370, 344; 376, 624). But on the whole the poem is not surreal. Instead, it is low talk in which the poet explains that his talk of an apparition, under which term we must presumably classify his "instructors" (though they did not actually *appear* to him), was designed as protection against the "popular eye." He declares that he had long planned his present "half solitude" and that his joy "grows more deep day after day." But at this point the poem turns and admits the need for the strength of joy because of "increasing Night."

The refrain calling up his strange vision is, then, deliberately ambiguous. It is a statement subject to derision and thus protective of the half solitude he enjoys. It is also a terrifying vision identified with death. In its strangeness it has some relation to the image of the stilt-walker and emphasizes the walker's direction toward death.

The aphoristic couplets of question and answer that compose "A Nativity" (371, 344; 377, 625) may be a residue of the unintelligible talk to which "The Apparitions" refers:

> . . . I can sit up half the night
> With some friend that has the wit
> Not to allow his looks to tell
> When I am unintelligible.
>
> (370, 344; 376, 624)

"A Nativity" shows the poet in his Delphic role for the last time. The first couplet and the last, which frame questions and answers about art, apparently refer to a painting of a nativity. The answerer of the first question indicates that the nativity implies cyclicity, having followed upon an earlier annunciation and birth. But the last couplet forms two questions: "Why is the woman terror-struck? / Can there be mercy in that look?" (371, 345; 377, 625). Neither question is answered. The oracle is oracle no longer.

That this is so is demonstrated by "Man and the Echo" (372, 345; 383, 632), a poem of questions. If in "Under Ben Bulben" the poet plays the role of knowledgeable ghost, a suggestion of Hamlet's father, here the living poet's words for a moment reflect Hamlet the son: "There is no release / In a bodkin or disease" (372, 345; 383, 632). The poet questions his life in a scene that at first appears to be a dialogue with an oracle but is in fact a dialogue with himself. The half solitude of the old man lecturing a diplomatically silent friend has now become full solitude, and the friend has been replaced by a wall that echoes only his own voice: "Lie down and die." But he cannot do this, for his intellect is not yet sure that he has ordered things and therefore has not yet stood "in judgment on his soul." The thought is antithetical: The judgment will be self-judgment, like the self-forgiveness of a previous internal dialogue, but now the situation is perceived more harshly. The earlier self-forgiveness does not now seem sufficient to antithetical man in the late primary phases. He must arrange his life and call himself to *judgment*.

In this process, the certainty of "The Gyres" is shaken. In that poem, out of the cavern, like the word of a true oracle, came the word "Rejoice," even though one might have suspected it was merely an echo. Now, old, ill, and alone, the speaker is not so sure that the rocky voice of "The Gyres" was not merely echoing his own desire:

> O rocky voice
> Shall we in that great night rejoice?
> What do we know but that we face
> One another in this place?
>
> (372, 346; 383, 633)

In "The Gyres," Old Rocky Face had said nothing about rejoicing in "that great night"; he had said only, "Rejoice," which presumably meant then and there. Here and now the speaker imagines a situation of utter solitude, a man and only an echo. He can no longer remember to decide whether the experience has been "joy or night"; the primary closes in. But suddenly he hears the cry of a "hawk or owl" and the stricken cry of a rabbit. He is returned from solitude to life, but also to the vicarious experience of death.

The poet does, in fact, go on to stand in judgment on his work in "The Circus Animals' Desertion" (373, 346; 381, 629). What he sees he does not like, for all of his poetic accomplishments reveal to him the hidden purposes that impelled them. In this perspective the "high talk" of circus performance seems artificial in the derogatory sense that "artifice" had not carried in "Sailing to Byzantium." The "stilted boys" of the poem convey not just the notion of the grand performance of stilt-walking but also the less admirable side of artificiality. The tone is one of slightly disgusted dismissal. His "Wanderings of Oisin" had been a cover for sexual frustration. *The Countess Cathleen* expressed his anxiety about Maud, which generated a "dream," now treated as an unfortunate illusion: "It was the dream itself enchanted me." He now considers, in this moment of self-judgment (he being now very nearly only his past work), that he had come to love only the emblems he had made of things, not their reality.

Yet he still has some respect for those images. They were "masterful," but so masterful that they mastered him by taking all his love. From where did they come? This is a question asked before about other things:

> Where got I that truth?
>
> (219, 214; 226, 439)

> . . . Whence had they come,
> The hand and lash that beat down frigid Rome?
> What sacred drama through her body heaved
> When world-transforming Charlemagne was conceived?
>
> (316, 287; 325, 560)

> Whence did all that fury come,
> From empty tomb or Virgin womb?
>
> (366, 341; 372, 619)

The answers to these questions have not been clear; the questions have invoked mystery. The answer to the one that plagues him now is not easy to utter, but in completing self-judgment he attempts to do so:

> Those masterful images because complete
> Grew in pure mind but out of what began?
> A mound of refuse or the sweepings of a street,
> Old kettles, old bottles, and a broken can,
> Old iron, old bones, old rags, that raving slut
> Who keeps the till. Now that my ladder's gone
> I must lie down where all the ladders start
> In the foul rag and bone shop of the heart.
>
> (373, 347–48; 381, 630)

He spoke earlier with a certain pride of his "fanatic heart." Now the heart is a "raving slut," who is all the muse he has left. This one "keeps the till" in a junk shop comprising all his old, worn creations: characters, themes, everything. He had earlier described his life becoming quiet as the mill of the mind consumed its "rag and bone," and his secular prayer had been for the gift of an "old man's frenzy." That frenzy seemed to take him nearly through *New Poems*. Now he must lie down ("Lie down and die," his own voice has earlier echoed) in this shop, surrounded by his creations. But now he imagines that "all the ladders start" in such a place, presided over by a mad muse selling used and wrecked material. Is this because what is there has been tossed up by a "filthy modern tide" and he has had to make his poetry out of its refuse? Or had it been a more personal, free choice? Has the heart, seen in this moment, caught in the "terrible light" of the primary, always been that "raving slut"?

Yet before the dark is complete, the antithetical voice regains the stage and asks a question, clearly rhetorical, that blends so completely into the assertions following it that a question mark cannot punctuate it:

Politics

> "In our time the destiny of man presents its meanings in political
>   terms."
>
> Thomas Mann

> How can I, that girl standing there,
> My attention fix
> On Roman or on Russian
> Or on Spanish politics,
> Yet here's a travelled man that knows

What he talks about,
And there's a politician
That has both read and thought,
And maybe what they say is true
Of war and war's alarms,
But O that I were young again
And held her in my arms.

                                                                    (374, 348; 382, 631)

It is an answer, in a manner of speaking, but the answer is really in the
form of an antithetical gesture. The poet declares at the end that if "in our
time the destiny of man presents its meanings in political terms" it is up to
the poet, even an old one who can only vainly wish to hold a young woman
in his arms, to declare the antithesis of Thomas Mann's proposition. The
declaration is slightly meandering and garrulous, but it summons up a
disdainful impertinence as it both acknowledges the expertise of both traveled man and politician and dismisses them in a single gesture. Almost a
gay goodnight after all.

Concluding Remarks

With the *Book* ending in a poem entitled "Politics" and that poem opposing
the political, and with so much recent criticism wishing to interpret poetic
meaning in political terms, the question is raised as to what we are to do
with a book that seems to speak against this desire, yet seems nevertheless
to have political implications. A full answer to this problem would require
another study, which, I would hope, would have to build upon my reading
of the *Book*. Let me, in closing, suggest the lines it would have to follow,
given the case of Yeats.

Yeats has been attacked principally for his elitist attitudes, for his alleged fascism, for his deluded glorification of the Anglo-Irish Ascendancy,
for his view of women, for his attitudes toward history, and, more recently, specifically for his vision of Irish history. Soon, no doubt, he will
be criticized for his commitment to his idea of the individual, which recent
dominant critical theory has conflated with the hated epistemological
"subject." Each of these attacks is an attack on what would have to be
described as Yeats's politics.

Yeats treats "politics" as a word implying the activity of people quite
opposite to his own nature. "Politics" deals with abstractions and masses
and quickly loses attachment to concrete realities. As a result, Yeats saw
himself as antithetical to this primary activity. He saw all artists and all art

in this way: Art always expresses what ideology tends to suppress or cover over. His view does not imply aloofness, however; rather, it implies commitment to all that "politics" threatens to disregard or, more accurately, negate (as Blake would say). Yeats himself said foolish things from time to time. Some were said recklessly in the spirit of antitheticality and are best understood in the light of the object of hatred, disgust, or impatience at the time.

Elizabeth Cullingford's conclusions about Yeats's relation to the political categories of his age, though not always arrived at without squeezing a perhaps too simple result from pieces of evidence, seem nevertheless generally correct about how to characterize Yeats in Irish political terms:

> The nature of his convictions makes it wrong to place him in any political category save that of a nationalist of the school of John O'Leary. . . . He was not a socialist, though he was sympathetic to some socialist ideals, because socialism seemed to him contrary to the Irish spirit of individualism and inappropriate to a peasant-based economy. He was not in theory a democrat, though in practice he conformed meticulously to democratic principles, because democracy in Ireland, in his eyes the tyranny of the lower-middle class, was destructive, mean-minded, and conformist. He was not a Tory, though he approved the predominance of the landed gentry, because the vision of Church and State in Ireland threatened liberty of conscience. He was not even a conservative, though he loved tradition, because his commitment to the Irish cause made him a revolutionary against the *status quo.* Of all political stances he was probably closest to that of Burke's Old Whigs: an aristocratic liberalism that combined love of individual freedom with respect for the ties of the organic social group. But modern liberals, identified as they were with *laissez-faire* capitalism, had little appeal.[5]

We might expect the *Book* to be more antithetically disposed than the Yeats who wrote letters, reviews, and tracts. The fictive poet who is the *Book*'s main character is not even as categorizable as Yeats. He is a political gadfly who utters things that should not be uttered. He is against those who attribute every problem to the social environment; his emphasis on instinct and genetics is an outrage to them. He is against the totalitarian's denigration of the individual, yet for him individuality is the mask. He is

5. Elizabeth Cullingford, *Yeats, Ireland, and Fascism* (New York: New York University Press, 1981), pp. 234–35.

against the liberal's view of progress, and he opposes the churchy statism of the Tories. He hates narrow nationalism, but he is a nationalist patriot.

The poet of the *Book* is less Cullingford's old-fashioned Whig than a lover and actor on the stage of himself, that is, a seeker of antiself and mask, a self-deluder, a critic of his self-delusions, a vacillator, and a searcher. This is to say that he is a lover of life who is in many ways exceptional but is also like many of us in that he reaches for, adopts, and then lets go of many enthusiasms, hatreds, and ideas of the moment. If a study of the *Book* reveals anything, it reveals that the *Book*'s main character carries on an incessant dialogue, self to self, poem to poem, in which almost every abstractable view is opposed by some later qualification or simple refutation. He is, however, always a poet who inevitably returns to query the particular experience, whose abstractions are deliberately antithetical to those of politics, who castigates expression of self-interest in himself and others, whose antithetical stance suspects that both church and state are the mob at the door, who opts for love but suspects that it is wed to violence, who may imagine a utopia but sweeps it away by the device of an irony that does not spare himself, who celebrates life as an individual journey with the purpose being the journey itself, and who is driven or drives himself to those moments of impolitic excess for which political critics will attack him.

The poet of the *Book* comes closer than Yeats to the antitheticality that quite appropriately makes the political world nervous. We would be more than nervous—we would be properly terrified—if either politician or poet were completely and finally in control. The poet knows this and eschews "triumph"; the politicians and the political critics may or may not.

Epilogue

I have called the *Book* an autobiographical fiction. It is well here at the end to dwell on the implications of that term. When we think somewhat idly of an autobiography, we generally imagine a work of writing that we suppose to represent someone's real life. As such, we regard it as a special kind of history because it is written by a participant who is privileged not only to have *been there then* but also to have experienced his or her feelings about the events at the time they occurred. These are naive views, as many treatments of autobiography have shown. Autobiographies take shapes familiar to us from our reading of other works of literature. Indeed, even historical works less specialized and subjective than autobiography take such shapes and become imaginable as in some way fictive. We have learned that histories are written under the domination of presiding tropes that take them in the direction of the fictive even prior to selection of materials, thematic emphases, and so forth.

When I refer to Yeats's *Book* as an autobiographical fiction, I mean something more radically fictive than either autobiography or history. I mean something even more radical than the popular notion that writing viewed as referring to the external world by way of correspondence is false, or, whether false or not, is at least not productively viewed in that way because to do so leads to tired old philosophical questions. Yeats's autobiographical fiction (or fiction of autobiography, if you wish) is about a Yeats who never *was*, a "Yeats" constantly constructed textually.

Two things are involved here, and they parallel each other on what I shall call two levels. First, throughout the *Book* and Yeats's writings in general, the lurking idea of the mask of drama implies that selves are not to be regarded as something existing to be revealed by some form of description. Selves are to be made, to be fashioned (to employ a term recently made popular in this connection). The *Book* dramatizes a story of a process of such fashioning. Yeats seems to have believed that the fashioned self is a process and is never fixed, though perhaps the process itself has a certain fixity (or so he speculated) by virtue of cyclicity. This is the reason that Yeats could continue to hold to the idea of search ("Je me cherche" was inscribed on his bookplate), even though the search was not to find or recover something prior and external but to make something, and even though that making was to conclude only with death. That making would involve a certain way of acting.

Second, for a poet the self is fashioned not only by action, as it is regarded in "Ego Dominus Tuus," but also (and principally) by writing regarded as an ethical act. History tries to constitute selves by recovery. Poetry would do so by making a verbal construct not judgeable by correspondence to some presumed external truth. If Yeats does not recover his life in the *Book* but instead makes a verbal fiction of a life, of what value or use is it to others? It is a symbol for meditation, a potentiality for interpretation and intellectual devouring. The instructors of *A Vision* seem to have provided the Yeats of that book such a symbol. I offer again words from *A Vision*, quoted at greater length in chapter 1: "Now that the system stands out clearly in my imagination I regard them [his "circuits of sun and moon"] as stylistic arrangements of experience. . . . They have helped me to hold in a single thought reality and justice" (pp. 34–35). The fictive Yeats of *A Vision* struggles between commitments to recovery and to making. "Reality," it seems to me, represents the former here, and "justice" the latter. With the introduction of "justice" Yeats began to see the instructors' "metaphors for poetry" as opening up a field for ethical speculation.

The poet's makings, with their emphasis on the particular experience, open the mind to the possibility of an ethic free from a doctrine recovered from without. As historical figures, poets may be shown through recovery to have had not very admirable reasons. They may have been hiding something; they may have been hypocritical or offensive in some other way. Their motives may have been malicious, as some have said George Moore's were in *Hail and Farewell*. These will be important matters to decide on if our concern is to set the record straight. We may have good reasons to think less of Wordsworth for his failure to treat the episode with Annette Vallon in *The Prelude* or for his placing the Mount Snowden scene of the same poem at the wrong historical moment. Whether or not for these reasons we should think less of the poem as a fiction of autobiography is an entirely different question requiring us to free ourselves from one set of legitimate interests in order to embrace another that is perhaps more appropriate to the ethical space opened by poetry. Indeed, it is probably not possible to act intelligently on the former matters without a prior grasp of the latter: the made life that is constituted as a secular symbol for ethical speculation and not as a correspondence to another life external to it.

The verbally made life has a certain ideality about it, though not the ideality of either Platonic or empirical abstraction. It is particular in its ideality, like a Vichean imaginative universal. There are many, of course, who say that the self is an illusion of Enlightenment rationality, of bourgeois liberalism, or is simply the product of relations of power without any determinate integrity apart from these relations. Nevertheless, whether it is illusion or historically contingent, it is persistently desired by us, fictionalized either as a lost innocence or as something to be made— as history or poetry, as truth or ethical adequacy to the situation of contingency or of freedom, whichever fiction we adopt.

Yeats's *Book* is less than a true record of the making of a self if we seek to read it as a record. (Indeed, no book can perfectly live up to that demand.) It is more than or, more properly, *other* than a record if we constitute it, as it invites us to do, in the form of a dramatic-fictive verbal making. This means that the poet of the *Book* is always going to be different from— perhaps better than, perhaps worse than—the recovered Yeats of biography and history. For a poet to make a self is always also to make an *other*. Different kinds of criticism can be interested in different aspects of this situation: the historical poet's life, the relation of that life to the fictive created life of the poet, the psychological and/or moral implications of this relationship judged by some external standard; the constituting and interpretation of a fictive life seen as in itself a symbol.

This symbol is a space for the contemplation of ethical issues unencumbered by the anxiety of a prior determination of the truth-to-correspondence of a representation. This space is not the "golden" world of Sir Philip Sidney but is more, when it seems worth inhabiting, the "momentous depth of speculation" mentioned by John Keats in his remarks on *King Lear*. In this space it does not matter that in the *Book* Yeats's relationship with Maud Gonne has been distorted, that he has moved events about in time, that he knew Alfred Pollexfen better and Robert Gregory less than his elegies on these men imply. In the space of biography and history, in which the poems also can be constituted, we contemplate a different set of problems. There we shall never know everything for sure because some of the evidence is always theoretically out, so we may argue about truth (though we may still want to call such truth its own kind of fiction). In the space of the *Book*, once textually constituted, no new piece of evidence is going to appear. All is present but in that negative form of disaffirmation that is characteristic of a fiction aware of its own fictiveness and open to reading. Our contemplation will not be endable because there is no correspondence to an external truth. It will enter the space of the ethical without having had to pass through the question of fact and experience, the lower court (or perhaps higher, depending on your view) where the truth and falsehood of a dead man's statements and why he made them are debated.

This study has taken the view that we must read the text as a narrative-dramatic fiction as carefully as we can before it makes any sense to enter the debates that go on in the lower court. One reason for this is simply to construe as clearly as possible what the ethical implications of this fictive story are. But perhaps more important is to recognize that the poet's making is finally *other* than his historically recoverable self. The poet is always and inevitably, in this sense, two. Indeed, with a great poet like Yeats it is likely to prove less valuable that we recover what he did and the relationship between what he did and what he made than that we engage endlessly in the critical constitution of the fiction he made and the contemplation of its significance for our ethical life.

Index of Titles

General Index